A Different Way to Learn

A DIFFERENT WAY TO LEARN

Neurodiversity and Self-Directed Education

NAOMI FISHER

Illustrated by Eliza Fricker

Jessica Kingsley Publishers
London and Philadelphia

First published in Great Britain in 2023 by Jessica Kingsley Publishers
An imprint of John Murray Press

1

Copyright © Naomi Fisher 2023

The right of Naomi Fisher to be identified as the Author of the Work has been asserted by in accordance with the Copyright, Designs and Patents Act 1988.

Illustrations copyright © Eliza Fricker 2023
Front cover image source: Eliza Fricker.

A CIP catalogue record for this title is available from the British Library and the Library of Congress

ISBN 978 1 83997 3 635
eISBN 978 1 83997 3 642

Printed by Integrated Books International, United States of America

Jessica Kingsley Publishers' policy is to use papers that are natural, renewable and recyclable products and made from wood grown in sustainable forests. The logging and manufacturing processes are expected to conform to the environmental regulations of the country of origin.

Jessica Kingsley Publishers
Carmelite House
50 Victoria Embankment
London EC4Y 0DZ

www.jkp.com

To the children who show us they need something different, and to the adults who listen to them.

Contents

Contents

Acknowledgements

This book is based on the experiences of people who have generously told me their stories. Some of it uses direct quotes. For these, I interviewed parents and young people who were engaged in self-directed education, as well as autistic, dyslexic, PDA and attention deficit hyperactivity disorder (ADHD) adults who told me about their experiences of school.

All the families self-identified as having a neurodivergent child, and many parents told me that they saw similar characteristics in themselves. Families were living in either the UK or the USA and were all well established as self-directed educators. They came from a wide range of financial backgrounds, different ethnic backgrounds and a range of family constellations. Most are anonymous but some have chosen to use their first names. I also interviewed several academics and experts in the field, who have used their own names. All of the people I quote have given their permission for their stories to be shared and have checked the text.

I have also based this book on my clinical experience. I work as a clinical psychologist and have done so for over 16 years. In this time, I have had the privilege of hearing thousands of stories of people's lives. The case examples I use in this book are illustrative rather than case studies of real individuals. I have made them up to demonstrate a point. Any resemblance to a real child or family is accidental.

I thank all the people who contributed to this book. Without you and your wonderful stories, it would not have been possible.

Acknowledgements

Author's Preface

There have always been children who break the mould. Those who just don't like the things other children enjoy, or who protest about things which other children do without comment. Those who find unexpected things easy, and unanticipated things hard. Those who catch the adults around them by surprise with their reactions, and who experience the world in a different way. Those who learn things in an unpredictable order, and in unforeseen ways. Children whose emotions are particularly extreme and particularly sudden.

These children lead their parents to different ways of parenting. They refuse to comply with the norms laid down by society and they often have a strong sense of the way in which they themselves need to live. They are hard to squash and they do not bend easily.

One of the ways we currently think about these children in Western culture is through the lens of neurodiversity. This term was first used by Judy Singer in the 1990s. Neurodiversity is the idea that human brains differ on a wide range of dimensions and that this does not necessarily indicate disorder or disease; in fact, this diversity could be a strength of the human race. Some people are far more active than others, some have different ways of socially interacting, while others may learn to read and write later or earlier. Variation isn't the same as disorder.

Of course, these children grow up into adults, who will also have different and original ways of interacting with the world. Neurodiversity isn't just about children. Most of the parents I interviewed for this book (and many of the parents I work with) told me that they see their children's traits in themselves and their extended family. They told me that they recognised their children's struggles because they are the same struggles that they had themselves as children and continue to have today.

These children open up new ways of living. They challenge us to do better and they shine light on just how arbitrary and restrictive many of the practices of our society are. They are not new. They have always been there, and they have always led their parents to do things differently. For many families, this has led them to self-directed education.

Neurodiversity is a new word, but it isn't a new phenomenon; not in the world, and not in self-directed education. It's a new lens to apply to something which has always been there.

Appreciating and accommodating difference isn't an 'add-on' to self-directed education. It's not like school, where there is a system which has to be adapted or adjusted to try and make it 'fit'. Self-directed education puts the child's choices at the heart of their education, which means that children can carve very different educational pathways for themselves and learn very different things. The child and their families create the system which works for them.

Self-directed education (as we currently understand it in Western culture) has always been something which families found when they needed something different from the mainstream. Stories abound in the self-directed education literature of children for whom school just wasn't working. Professor Peter Gray (2013), research psychologist at Boston College, writes in his book *Free to Learn* about how his nine-year-old son Scott found school like a prison, and how he would consistently behave in ways which were directly contrary to the teacher's instructions, sometimes leaving the classroom altogether and walking home. Laura Grace Weldon, in her powerful article on her son's experiences in the education system, describes how she was pulled into school to discuss her six-year-old's 'messy work, lack of organisation and distractibility' and told that he needed medication (Weldon, 2012). Both of them sound very similar to the children I hear about today – some of the stories of whom are in this book.

Both Gray and Weldon discovered self-directed education, driven by the needs of their children, Gray in the form of Sudbury Valley School, and Weldon in the form of unschooling. Both of them found that their children could thrive when they were allowed to learn in the way which worked best for them, and they have written extensively about the process. Both these children went onto higher education and to lead fulfilling lives as adults. Their stories aren't unusual. Whenever you meet self-directed families, you'll hear similar tales.

Most people have never met anyone who has chosen self-directed education, and with this book I hope to fill that gap. I have sought out families and young people to tell me their stories. Many families choose self-directed education either because their children went to school and it's clear there wasn't a good fit, or because they anticipated from that start that their child was not going to conform well to school requirements, and so decided to skip it altogether. Self-directed education has always attracted those who felt they and their children didn't fit into the mainstream system and who felt strongly enough about it to act on those feelings.

Self-directed education allows those who are different to flourish, but it's more than that. It actively enables differences to flourish and develop. As a culture, we are often afraid of difference. School values conformity and standardisation, and many of us learn that we don't want to stand out. Parents sometimes think that their child's differences will become less visible when they take them out of school, only to find that in fact they become more visible when the child relaxes and is more able to express themselves freely. Self-directed education provides the space for children and young people to develop into people who may be very different from the way we are encouraged to be in the school system. They learn in the way which works best for them, often with their parents running behind, trying to keep up. As Laura Grace Weldon writes:

> I realised his 'problem' was my insistence that he learn as I had done – from a static page. ... The more I stepped back, the more I saw how much my son accomplished when fuelled by his own curiosity... Gradually I recognized that he learnt in a complex, deeply focused and, yes, apparently disorganized manner. It wasn't the way I'd learnt in school but it was the way he learnt best. His whole life taught him in ways magnificently and perfectly structured to suit him and him alone.

What I'm trying to say with all of this is that if you are a parent worrying whether self-directed education will work for your child, because you have been told that they have special needs which can only be met in the school system – think again. It is the children who do not thrive in the school system who are at the forefront of the self-directed education movement and they always have been. They provide the impetus for change, because they demand something different. They will not settle for anything less than the best. I hope that the stories in this book will give you the confidence to support them in that.

These children include those whose academic learning is far in advance of that which is expected by school, and those who are behind; those whose experience of school means that they cannot learn, or that they are constantly punished; those who are desperately unhappy or who refuse to go at all; those who consistently, through their behaviour and actions, say no. They are the canaries in the mine, who show up the inadequacies of the system for us all.

This book is for them.

A Note on Language

This book places at the centre the children and families who are usually on the margins. It talks about the experiences of those who are often invisible, those for whom the way in which society, and particularly school, is organised really doesn't work. They are marginalised, and they are often talked about in this way, being compared to an apparent 'norm', usually to their detriment.

People understand this experience in a range of different ways. Some of these people see their differences through a diagnostic lens, some of them do not. Some of them see a diagnostic term in pragmatic terms, as a means to get help and support, while others see it as a fundamental part of their identity. Some have identified themselves as autistic, ADHD, PDA or otherwise neurodivergent and don't feel the need for a professional assessment. Some have had several assessments by professionals. Some adults and children have tried to get diagnoses and have been told they don't meet the criteria for referral.

Those who are home educated from the start are less likely have a diagnosis than those who have been to school. Diagnoses can be helpful in the school system in order to access support, but are less important when you don't go to school. Some families told me they didn't think it was worth the effort to get a diagnosis as they didn't feel it would make any difference to their lives. Others were not able to access a diagnosis due to cost or other barriers, and some had cultural or personal reasons for not wanting one. Others did not want to define themselves by diagnostic categories.

For this book, I interviewed many people, including adults, young people and parents. They had different perspectives and this book is inclusive of all of their different ways of approaching neurodiversity. It's my belief that there is no one right way to understand difference and that this is something which families and young people should be able to choose for themselves.

In the interests of putting all these people centre stage and in order to avoid lengthy explanations, I will not always refer to the children and families in this book by their diagnosis or differences. Sometimes I may use these terms, particularly when the people I have interviewed them have used about themselves or when they are important, but in general I will simply refer to children and their families. I will not compare them to an apparent 'norm'. Read the examples and interviews, see if they resonate for you and/or your children, and take from this book what you need.

CHAPTER 1

NEURODIVERSITY AND SELF-DIRECTED EDUCATION

Leila got in touch over email. 'I'm worried', she said. 'My son seems so different to the other children. He's not happy in groups, he doesn't join in with other children's play in the playground and his main interest is roads and maps – we can't find any other six-year-olds who want to talk for hours about the best route to take from London to Oxford avoiding the M40. Sometimes he gets upset and I can't calm him down for hours. They say he's doing okay at school but his sleeves are drenched and chewed through when he comes home and every night he says that he doesn't want to go back. I've tried stricter boundaries and being firm. He just gets more distressed. I've tried going into school and they say he's fine there so the problem must be at home. I've read so many books on parenting and none of them help. Their approaches just don't work for us. What am I doing wrong? Is there something wrong with him?'

Parents contact me all the time with stories like this, and the first thing they want is usually an answer. They want to know why something is happening, why their child is behaving the way they do – and they would like me to help them fix it. They'd like to know how to help their child behave more like other children, or how to help them manage their emotions better (which is often really the same thing as behaving more like other children).

Why are things different for us, they ask? Why don't things seem to work in the same way as they do for other families? It's a very human need, this drive to know why something is happening. We hope that if we understand why, we might be able to work out how to change things.

Perhaps you also want answers. You've picked up this book for a reason. You're probably concerned about your child, and you want to know how to help. You might already have flicked through, looking for the chapter on autism or ADHD or dyslexia or PDA, hoping that I will have some specific answers to the difficulties that you are experiencing in your family.

You won't find lists of quick-fix solutions or strategies here, and you won't find descriptions of different diagnoses and what they mean. You won't find theories of autism and ADHD, not because they aren't important, but because they aren't the focus. There are many other excellent books which will tell you about those things (many of which are in the Further Reading section).

What you will find here is a different way of approaching education and thinking about your child's differences. I'll encourage you to widen your perspective from your child to the environment which surrounds them. I'll ask you to stop focusing on all the things which worry you about your child, and instead think about how they experience the world. I'll encourage you to take a deep breath and to see what you can do to help them develop into the unique people they are.

This book is about self-directed education, and why it is so well suited to many of the children and young people who are failed by the mainstream. And it's about children who are different, who for whatever reason don't fit the norms set out by society. For that reason, I'm going to start by thinking about differences – and the ways in which we think about difference in Western society.

Defining difference

When I was training to be a clinical psychologist, one of the first things we learnt to do were neuropsychological assessments. We had a heavy black suitcase full of tests, checked out from the Test Library. We would sit down with a child and work our way through lists of standardised questions and tasks. Some of the questions were things like, 'If you found a stamped addressed envelope in the street, what would you do?', while others involved things like repeating sets of numbers forwards and backwards, or copying complicated figures. There were right and wrong answers (that envelope should be posted in a nearby post box, not jumped on in a puddle). Sometimes I would test children's vocabulary, sometimes I would ask them to tell me what pattern came next in a sequence. I would keep going until the child started getting all the answers wrong, and then I'd move on to the next task. After a couple of hours of this, I'd score up all their answers, look through the test manual, and produce a set of results which compared the child to others of their age. I'd write reports which said which percentile a child was on – essentially, comparing each child with a very large group of others their age and rating them according to how their performance measured up.

Some children liked the tests and the individual attention. Some of the children were not very cooperative and didn't see the point in many of my questions, but I persevered if I could. I needed enough answers to calculate the scores and to compare them with the tables of 'norms' at the back of the manual. Persuasion was an important part of the skill set required. I would give children stickers and certificates when they finished their sessions with me, as rewards. Some liked that, others didn't.

Describing difference is one of things which psychologists have focused on over the last century. We use tests, standardised questionnaires and observational measures – and usually the question we are really asking is: 'How different (or similar) is this person to everyone else? Just how unusual are their experiences and behaviours?' We measure and quantify difference by using tests which compare the results of the whole population with the individual. Then we report back the results, and make recommendations. We say things like, this child has a vocabulary which is well above average for children their age, or, this child's separation anxiety is much more extreme than other children of their age. We compare children with others of their age because of the nature of child development. Behaviour which is very common for three-year-olds can be very unusual in ten-year-olds. Comparisons are at the heart of the process.

Psychiatrists (who are medically trained doctors who have specialised in mental health) are also focused on identifying and describing difference. They have developed manuals which divide up different experiences and behaviours by categories called diagnoses. In this case, they are looking for experiences and behaviours which they consider to be 'pathological' or 'disordered' because their approach is based on the medical model. For psychiatrists, difference is important when a person's life is significantly impaired by it. That means that some sort of intervention may be necessary. This is what psychiatric diagnoses in clinical practice are about, identifying who needs intervention, and what that might be. Adjustments at school, medication, psychological therapy, speech and language therapy or occupational therapy – all of these might be recommended as a result of a psychiatric diagnosis. Other professionals now use these psychiatric manuals and diagnostic criteria from outside psychiatry, but the fundamental principles remain the same.

Schools have their own ways to identify and quantify difference. Exams and tests are a way to identify those whose academic achievement is above or below the average. Schools, like psychologists and psychiatrists, divide people up by comparing them with others, but they do it differently again. They give children grades and put them in different classes according to who they think is doing well, and who isn't. Those whose reactions to the education system are very different from the norm are identified as having 'special educational needs' or perhaps being 'gifted', depending on which way their differences fall.

All of these approaches are based on comparisons. They compare an individual with others. Those who appear different in the classroom or at home are given tests and assessments which quantify their differences and compare them to the whole population. This culture of comparison starts very early, with the books which new parents are given with titles like *What to Expect*, detailing week by week what your new-born baby should be doing. Sometimes it seems as if children are compared to a fantasy, 'gold standard' child, who does everything on schedule and who never gets too angry or upset.

Comparisons

Difference is always about comparison with others around you. Quite simply, if you are surrounded by people like you, you won't be different. Let's say you're a nine-year-old child who hasn't learnt to read. In the school system, that will be enough to get you assessed or referred and you will be identified as different. You might be offered extra reading lessons or diagnosed with dyslexia. If you are living in a community where no one goes to school, however, it will be quite common for nine-year-olds not to be reading yet, and it won't mark you out as different in any way.

We are used to thinking about difference as something which reflects something about a person, but it is always defined by context and expectations. If you're of average height in your country, but then you move to another country where everyone else is very tall, you will suddenly feel different and statistically you will no longer be average. You may well be seen as deficient in some way, and could be offered interventions for your children in order that they might grow taller.

With children it's even more complicated. Comparisons have an extra dimension for them, because children are maturing and this happens at different rates. A child might be very short compared to their peers at age nine, but then one of the tallest by the age of 12. One of the things which we pick up when we compare children to one each other is maturity. Professor Sarah-Jayne Blakemore (2019), a cognitive neuroscientist and specialist in the adolescent brain, shows how, at any given age, young people's neurological maturity will vary greatly (and therefore, comparisons (like exams) which are used to determine the course of people's lives at age 16, could well be unfair).

When we compare all the children within a school year group, some of the difference will be down to maturity. This is something which adults typically underestimate or ignore, but the evidence of it is all around us. You can see this most clearly in the way in which the youngest children in a year group are diagnosed with special education needs at higher levels than the oldest children. A recent study by Dr Tammy Campbell (2021) at the London School of Economics looked at the six million children in state primary school in England between 2008 and 2018. She found that by the end of Reception (aged five), only 39% of summer-born boys (the youngest in their year group) were assessed as having reached a 'good level of development' while 80% of autumn-born girls (the oldest) were assessed at that level. By the end of Year 2 (aged seven), 27% of the summer-born boys had been identified as having some sort of special education need or disability (SEND) as compared to only 8% of the autumn-born girls.

Take a moment to think about that. This is a study of six million children. It's likely to be a robust finding, and it's telling us something that is happening to children right now. Being born male in the summer as opposed to female in the autumn means that your chances of being identified as having SEND by the age of seven have more than tripled. Dr Campbell suggests that inflexible and prescriptive expectations in primary schools (which are often couched in the language of 'high standards') are producing problems for children which school then fails to solve, instead identifying ever more children as having SEND. These differences don't disappear as children get older – a 2010 study by the Department for Education found that summer-born children were 6% less likely to achieve five good GCSE passes than their peers. This means that 10,000 young people failed to achieve five GCSE passes simply because they were born late in the school year. Those summer-born young people had other differences too. They were less likely to go to university, more likely to be bullied and more likely to be unhappy at school.

It really isn't plausible that being born in the summer causes thousands of children to have special educational needs. Something is going on in the interaction between immature children and a rigid school system. Immature children are being compared with their more mature peers, to their disadvantage, and this has implications which carry on through their lives.

You might be thinking that this doesn't really matter – after all, being identified with SEND can be a positive thing for children who get the support they need (although it often doesn't work that way). The problem is that we know that the way in which parents and children see themselves affects their development all the way through school and life. Children are sensitive to how they are perceived by others, and they are quick to pick up on whether they are seen as 'ahead' or 'behind'. They quickly learn to compare themselves to their year group. I've had (spontaneous) conversations with schooled children aged six or seven about how clever they and their friends are (or are not). They could usually tell me about all the other children in their class as well. They didn't include any nuances about birth month or relative level of maturity.

Of course, a child can be far from the average for their age in one thing, but right in the middle on other things. There's no reason to assume that just because a person has average levels of anxiety or sociability that they would also have average levels of reading or maths. Despite this, there is often the expectation at school that children should be at the same developmental level across the board, and school performance is valued above other strengths. Big differences in how a child performs in different areas – sometimes called a 'spiky cognitive profile' – are sometimes cited as cause for concern.

The children whose development is very different from the average stand out in the school system. They learn things very early, or very late. They can't sit still when everyone else can, or they find the playground overwhelming rather than fun. They may be bored because all the work is too easy, or totally confused because it is all too hard. The school system expects age-standardised development. Everyone starts at a similar age, and is compared to others in their year group. This is how we know if a child is 'doing well' or not, even if we try not to compare. We think about what others of their age are doing, and we judge it accordingly.

When standardised expectations meet unstandardised children

Evie's parents got in touch with me when she was seven. They were worried because she had been identified as 'behind' at school. She didn't like to sit and concentrate on her lessons, they described her as 'away with the fairies' and, most concerningly for the school, her reading and spelling was behind what they expected. She failed her phonics screening check in Year 1, and then had to retake it in Year 2 and had failed it again. Most concerningly for her parents, Evie had started to say that she was stupid and no good at anything, and had stopped wanting to read stories at home.

I asked what was happening at school. It turned out that Evie's school had what they described as 'high expectations'. This included all children from Year 3 (aged seven to eight) upwards writing in fountain pen, not pencil. Evie was left-handed and she constantly smudged her work and was told off for being messy. In Year 3, Evie's class, they were learning about subordinate clauses. Each child was expected to write down the aims and objectives for each lesson and to self-evaluate in writing at the end of each class. Evie found this extremely difficult – and of course, she also tended to smudge all her work. Even before the lesson had properly started, she had a smudged page of Aims and Objectives in her exercise book which frustrated her because she liked her book to look neat. When she got upset or refused to do something, the school saw this as bad behaviour. They said she had problems with emotion regulation.

Evie's school had decided what children in Year 3 should be doing, and they were judging Evie by whether she was able to comply with this or not. They had expectations and Evie wasn't meeting them. What wasn't being asked was whether these expectations were reasonable, and whether they took any account of child development and variability at all.

What was my role? Good question. I didn't think Evie had a problem, I thought it was the school expectations which were the issue. A lot of time and energy is spent trying to fit children into a system which was not designed for the full range of child development. Occupational therapists try to encourage four-year-olds to use the 'correct pencil grip' while behavioural systems are used to try to persuade active children to stop moving around and stay still. Parents tell me about referrals to an array of therapists, speech and language therapy for those whose language isn't sufficiently advanced, occupational therapy for those whose fine motor skills mean they can't yet write, and play therapy for those who are distressed by the whole thing and don't want to separate from their parent. Of course, the waiting lists for these therapists grows ever longer, and parents are deeply frustrated by the inadequacy of what is offered. But what if a lot of this therapy is only necessary because of the inflexibility of their environment rather than because there is anything 'wrong' with the child – and what if, if we gave more space for different developmental pathways, we might see more children developing these skills in their own time?

This puts therapists in a strange position, with referrals for children whose main problem may be that they are young humans in an environment which is inappropriate for them. They are asked to improve the child's skills in a range of different areas, but often that child's skills are entirely developmentally appropriate. There is no rule of child development which says that all seven-year-olds should be able to write with fountain pens or understand subordinate clauses. There is no natural law which says that those who can't do it at this age have anything wrong with them other than simply being immature (nor is there a law which says that people have to do these things at all).

I am left-handed myself and I smudged my writing throughout school. My nickname was 'Miss Messy' and the side of my hand was eternally blue with ink. My work was never beautiful. I still smudge my writing with a fountain pen and so I haven't used one for over 20 years. I use ballpoints instead. For an adult, that isn't a problem. I can adapt my environment.

Children in school rarely have these choices. When the environment is rigid, children and young people cannot make simple, practical choices which accommodate difference. This leaves them feeling that maybe there is something wrong with them.

Is it our fault?

Lisa was in tears when she talked to me. She was describing what had happened at school with her teenage son Ed. 'He started saying he didn't want to go to school every morning and one time he was so upset that I let him stay at home', she said. 'And they called me in and said that I wasn't being firm enough, and that they saw a lack of boundaries.' Her voice wavered. 'They said that I would ruin his life if I carried on like this.'

When a child isn't meeting expectations at school, often the first thing a school does is to call in their parents and discuss the problem. Parents tell me that they often feel that they are told at this stage that this situation is their fault and that it's up to them to change it.

This is highly stressful for parents and children. Parents tell me how humiliated they feel when everyone knows that their child isn't doing well at school or is refusing to go. One parent called it the 'walk of shame' back across the playground as her child refused to go into the classroom and she took her home. All the other parents were looking, and she felt judged as a bad parent in every way.

This doesn't just happen at school. Wider family members or friends, faced with a child whose behaviour is different, also often look for who or what to blame. They may make 'helpful suggestions' such as 'Have you tried Time Out?' or 'I wouldn't let a child of mine behave like that' or wonder out loud whether a child's behaviour may be because parents are not consistent enough in their approach to discipline.

Children are also blamed for their differences. Try harder, children are told if they aren't learning to read in the prescribed time frame. Or they're asked, 'Why can't you just behave like all the others?', a question for which there is no answer. They learn to feel bad about themselves, because they don't know why they can't be different, that is just how they are.

The medical model to the rescue

When a child and their parents have been immersed in blame for their differences and things have not changed, they will often be referred for assessments, all of which try to look at exactly what the problem is.

They'll usually see several different professionals, all of whom will write lengthy reports describing the difficulties. I have read many of these reports, because when I write a report, I read all the others that have been written first. Sometimes there are ten or more. They will all focus on the things that a child doesn't do as well as others their age. They can make demoralising reading.

For some of these children, these assessments will result in their being offered a psychiatric diagnosis of autism, ADHD, dyslexia, dyspraxia or many others. These diagnoses can come as a huge relief from the awfulness of the blame which has come before. Finally, it seems to say, we know what the problem is. You're not bad, or lazy, or stupid, or disruptive (or all the other negative labels which have been used) – instead, we'll give you a diagnosis. It offers an alternative explanation. For many parents and children, after years of blame it's like the lifting of a burden. They thought they were bad or not trying hard enough, and now instead they have a medical explanation for their problems. They hope that it will mean they can access better support, and for some, that is what happens.

More and more people are being given diagnoses such as ADHD and autism in adulthood, and many of them describe the process of getting a diagnosis as liberating and transformatory. Finally, they have a better explanation for their difficulties. Finally, they can stop blaming themselves. For many people, this is a way that they can find others who have had similar experiences and who share similar characteristics. If you're interested in the way that people experience diagnosis and what it means to them, there's more about this in the *Exploring Diagnosis* project at Exeter University, on their website. Some aspects are also explained in Ginny Russell's free-to-access and fascinating book *The Rise of Autism* (Russell, 2020).

Psychiatric diagnosis applies a medical lens to behaviour and emotional experiences. It takes behaviours and emotional reactions and defines them as symptoms. If you have enough of the symptoms, you can get a diagnosis. The medical model defines unusual behaviour and emotional reactions as a sign of pathology, of something wrong. Just like having headaches and a fever show that something is wrong with a person physically.

The medical model is the dominant way in which unusual behaviour and experiences are seen in Western society. For something so dominant, it's a surprisingly recent arrival. For most of human history, an unusually behaved child would not have been offered a diagnosis of anything, because those diagnoses did not exist. They are an invention of the 20th century, and our modern standardised understanding of diagnoses such as autism and ADHD only dates back to 1980 when the *Diagnostic and Statistical*

Manual of Mental Disorders (*DSM*) *Third Edition* came out. Even then, the criteria change each time a new manual comes out. We are now on the fifth edition which came out in 2013, and which significantly changed the diagnostic criteria for autism, meaning that many more people came under that diagnostic category. *DSM* is the American manual; there is an international one called the *International Classification of Diseases* (*ICD*), which is based on very similar principles.

These books are sometimes referred to as Bibles of psychiatry, but in fact they are more like dictionaries. They define many different 'mental disorders' with lists of 'symptoms'. The job of the professional is to work out if the person in front of them fits the diagnostic criteria. One of those criteria is usually that the person is clinically or significantly impaired by their symptoms. Looking for impairment isn't an optional part of the medical model. It's the reason why diagnoses are done and what they were designed for.

The medical model was not designed to appreciate or celebrate difference. It was designed so that doctors and health professionals can describe the problems a person has and the correct intervention can be identified, or they could carry out research. As Eiko Fried, Associate Professor in Clinical Psychology at Leiden University, puts it, psychiatric diagnoses are designed as 'clinically useful tools to facilitate treatment selection, planning, prognosis and communication' (Fried, 2021). Fried (and many others) argues that research has been seriously held back by the focus on diagnostic categories which are unreliable and don't reflect underlying biological processes.

Once a person has a diagnosis, this is often assumed to mean that an underlying disorder has been identified which is analogous to a physical health problem. Think of how this process works with COVID-19. Symptoms include a loss of smell and taste, a fever, fatigue and many others. You can have lots of symptoms, but the deciding factor of whether you have the virus is a laboratory test. If the laboratory test is positive you still have COVID-19 even if you have no symptoms at all, and you can have lots of the symptoms and still not have COVID-19. COVID-19 is the virus, not the symptoms.

Psychiatric diagnoses appear superficially to be the same as physical health diagnoses, but they are different. They define distress, unusual behaviour and emotional reactions as symptoms. They are defined in contrast to what is supposed to be 'normality' (or 'health'), in a way similar to physical illness. However, then the similarity stops, because there are no biological tests for a psychiatric diagnosis and no underlying mechanisms have been identified which account for the different diagnostic categories. If you have enough symptoms, you get the diagnosis. End of story. There's no biological test to confirm whether a person is autistic or has ADHD. We don't actually know what causes the symptoms. We don't know whether all the people who share a diagnosis have similar reasons for their differences. There may be many different pathways to a similar presentation.

This means that psychiatric diagnoses are descriptions rather than explanations. A diagnosis of COVID-19 explains what is causing a person's symptoms, a diagnosis of autism or ADHD brings a group of symptoms together and gives them a name. This means that what is meant by a diagnosis such as autism or ADHD literally changes over time. There are people who are diagnosed today who would not have met criteria before 2013, when the American Psychiatric Association last changed their diagnostic criteria.

This doesn't mean that these diagnoses aren't useful, nor that they aren't meaningful for people. What is does mean is that they should never be the end of the story. They don't mean that we've found the cause for why someone is behaving or experiencing life in the way that they are. And they aren't the only way to understand or describe difference. They are, however, often the only alternative that people see to blame.

Brain or blame

Professor Mary Boyle, Emeritus Professor of Clinical Psychology at the University of East London, suggests that society only offers two explanations for unusual behaviour and experiences. Either your differences are your fault, or it's because there is something wrong with your brain. She calls this the Brain or Blame dilemma. There's more about this in clinical psychologist Dr Lucy Johnstone's book, *A Straight-Talking Introduction to Psychiatric Diagnosis* (Johnstone, 2022), in which she outlines the way in which psychiatric diagnosis gives people relief from their struggles, and asks whether there are other ways to find validation and identity.

When the only two explanations offered are that you are to blame or you have a medical disorder, it is much better to go for the medical explanation. It holds the promise of help and support. Unfortunately, neither brain or blame are great ways to understand difference, partly because neither of them *is* really a way to think about difference. That is not what they were designed for. Blame is used to try and motivate people to meet expectations more efficiently, while the medical model is used to identify people who need intervention and treatment. Both locate the problem in the person who is assumed to either be at fault, or to have something wrong. Both of them apparently explain why a person is behaving in the way that they do.

When I talk about this topic, sometimes people will say to me, so are you saying that autism and ADHD don't exist? No. Differences between people clearly exist. As I said from the start, some children and adults find it much harder to manage in society as it is currently set up than others. These differences are real.

What I'm saying is that a psychiatric diagnosis is not the only way to understand these differences, and a diagnosis is a description rather than an explanation. We honestly don't know why some people have more difficulties in life than others, and giving someone a diagnosis doesn't change that. Psychiatric diagnosis has advantages and drawbacks, and no one should be obliged to understand themselves using this lens if they don't find it helpful.

Some people have tried to de-pathologise psychiatric diagnosis by using 'condition' rather than 'disorder' and writing new, less deficit-focused criteria. I think that rethinking a psychiatric diagnosis has to be more fundamental than writing a new list of criteria or avoiding the word 'disorder'. That's because it is the assumptions that are at the heart of the diagnostic system which are the problem, rather than it being about the specific criteria. The diagnostic system starts with the idea that people can be divided up into distinct categories by their behaviour and experiences (and that this reflects an underlying biological difference), and that some of these categories are 'disordered'. This is something which researchers are increasingly finding doesn't reflect reality, both on a behavioural and a biological level, and so they are moving away from this way of thinking (Insel, 2013; Plomin, Haworth & Davis, 2009).

Reclaiming difference

There is currently a movement from adults who identify as neurodivergent to reclaim words such as autistic and ADHD from the medical model. Many adults who have received a diagnosis or have self-identified will say that the psychiatric diagnostic criteria are limiting and do not define their experiences, while still identifying themselves as autistic or ADHD. They want to define the terms differently, through their lived experience. Some have developed new theories of autism which are non-pathologising and dimensional, such as monotropism, which encourage us to think about people's experiences in new ways (Murray, Lesser & Lawson, 2005). This means that when people use the term 'autism' or 'ADHD' they can mean very different things to each other, with some referring to something which is defined by the diagnostic criteria and others referring to a way of relating to the world which may have little to do with a psychiatric diagnosis.

Here we come to neurodiversity, as described by Judy Singer (2017). Neurodiversity was first suggested as a way to understand differences which run through the whole population. Neurodiversity, as Judy Singer describes it, sees differences between people as a matter of degree and dimension, rather than as something which falls into categories. She says in her original thesis that the autistic spectrum has 'fuzzy boundaries' and that she sees many people, including herself, as falling somewhere on a continuum between 'normality' and 'classical autism' (her words not mine). The concept of neurodiversity has spread far beyond autism, and now sometimes the term neurodivergent is used to describe anyone who diverges from the apparent societal norm, including those with post-traumatic stress disorder, obsessive compulsive disorder, depression and anxiety. This means that it's likely that the majority of people could be considered to be neurodivergent. A large-scale longitudinal study which followed all the people born in Dunedin, New Zealand in 1972–73 found that by the age of 45, 86% had met criteria for at least one diagnosable 'mental disorder' (Caspi et al., 2020). Of those who met criteria for one diagnosis, 85% had met criteria for at least one other at some point in their lives. The authors suggest that a reliance on diagnostic categories has held back research and clinical practice and that it is the norm for people to meet criteria for different diagnoses in turn during their lives.

There's more about the growth of the neurodiversity paradigm and movement in the free-to-access book, *Autistic Community and the Neurodiversity Movement*, edited by Steven Kapp (2020).

The difference environment makes

I worked as a psychologist before I had my own children. As part of this I would see children and young people. They would come into my clinic room, often timid and reluctant, and I would try to engage them with games or worksheets. Sometimes I was successful, sometimes not. Once or twice I bumped into these young people on the local streets, or in Sainsbury's. In that moment before they saw me, it was as if I'd seen a different person. Children who hardly said a word to me would be chatting away to their parents, those who seemed pinned to the spot in my room would be running up and down the aisle in the supermarket.

It wasn't until I had my own children that the importance of what I had seen really sunk in. My children were so different in different situations. When comfortable at home they could be articulate, loud and funny, but when we went to the doctor they were speechless and frightened. When in large groups of people, they would be overwhelmed and often unable to relax, in a small group of people they knew they would play and laugh and show their creativity. Environment made such a difference to how they functioned – and yet those who did not see them in those different settings might never have known – as I hadn't, with the young people I saw.

And here is one problem with the medical model. It focuses on biology and individuals, with very little account taken of the environment. It assumes that a person who behaves in a certain way does so because of something about them (or something in their brain), and rarely asks what in their environment is resulting in this behaviour.

In fact, when a child behaves in different ways in different environments then the emphasis is sometimes shifted to blame. 'You could do it fine yesterday' children are told, with the implication that you certainly should be able to do the same today, disregarding all the things which made yesterday different from today. Parents are told that the school knows a child is capable of more than they are doing, with the implication that they should be trying harder, rather than looking at what is not working for that child which means that they aren't able to 'do better'.

Differences between children become a problem when they come up against an environment where they can't be accommodated. A not-yet-reading six-year-old child will have a problem if they are at a school which expects five-year-olds to be able to read, but none at all if most children don't learn to read until they are eight. A very active child will have a problem if they are expected to sit still and listen for any length of time, but none if they spend most of the time in an adventure playground. The problem occurs in the interaction. This is where individual differences become a problem (Figure 1.1). This is the social model of disability. It sees disability as an interaction between the person and their environment, rather than something which is located solely in the person.

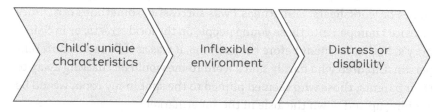

Figure 1.1: When a person's characteristics mean that they can't function in a particular environment, then this causes distress and disability

Much of the effort in school and parenting is focused on the child. The question asked is, how can we change this child so that they fit the environment better? How can we improve their reading, or persuade them to sit still or to stop hiding under the table? To this end, many reports are written and assessments done. Every aspect of them is scrutinised and compared to others. I've worked with children who have already had ten evaluations done before their fifth birthday – and still nothing is helping.

It's far more unusual to really look in detail at the environment, and ask why it isn't suiting the child. I have never seen an in-depth assessment of all the ways in which a school could change to better suit the child. Some tweaks might be made, but the fundamental principles of school can't be changed. Most schools are distinct environments with specific expectations and requirements, many of which make life more difficult and distressing for children.

The neurodiversity paradigm takes a different stance. It says, all humans are different, and some of them are not suited to particular environments but thrive in others. Rather than trying to change the people, let's look at what needs to change around them.

Self-directed education also starts with environment rather than the child – and that's why I think it's a perfect fit with neurodiversity.

Throughout this book I'm going to suggest that rather than asking how you can make the child fit an inflexible environment, you work on creating an environment which is malleable enough to fit the child. Every problem is a result of an interaction between the two (Figure 1.2) The less flexible the child is able to be, the more flexibility is required in their environment. A rigid environment is always going to cause problems for some – and the more rigid it gets, the more children it causes problems for.

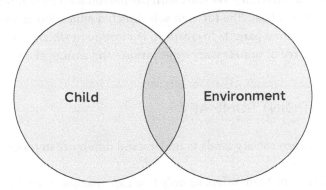

Figure 1.2: Another way to think of problems is as arising in the interaction between a child and their environment

Acceptance

You'll notice a common thread running through this book. Everything starts with acceptance of the child as they are right now. This is because, based on my work with children, families and adults, not feeling accepted for who they are comes up again and again.

Adults tell me that they spent their childhoods feeling that they should be different, and that a lot of the 'support' they were offered made them feel inferior or lacking in some way. Both the blame narrative and the medical model focus on what is wrong with someone. People carry the consequences of this with them for their whole lives.

Families sometimes tell me that they are afraid that if they accept how their child is right now, nothing will ever change. They see acceptance as giving up. This isn't how I see it. Through accepting where children are (and where we are ourselves), we start to free up the possibility of change, because we are no longer struggling against the current situation. We can put our energies into moving forward.

If we can see our children exactly how they are right now, then the task becomes how to work out how to change the environment so that they can best learn and thrive as the wonderful person they are. This does not mean giving up on change in the future, but instead creating the circumstances for growth. Change will happen, and it doesn't have to be forced. Too many children grow up feeling that they are wrong, or bad, or being constantly told that they are not meeting expectations. These are not good foundations from which to explore the world and learn about yourself.

Acceptance is at the heart of self-directed education, and also at the heart of neurodiversity. We start with the person with their interests and how they learn best. The focus in self-directed education is on enabling children and their parents to create an environment which works best for each child, free of unnecessary expectations and assumptions.

FIVE-POINT SUMMARY

1. Western society tends to understand difference in terms of blame or brain.
2. Blame or brain offers us only two explanations for difference: it's your fault, or there's something wrong with you.
3. There is significant evidence which suggests that differences between people are continuous rather than categorical but diagnostic categories do not yet reflect this.
4. Self-directed education focuses on changing the environment rather than changing the child, creating an environment which is flexible enough to accommodate difference and facilitate learning.
5. This is in line with a social model of disability and the idea of neurodiversity.

CHAPTER 2

NEURODIVERSITY
AT SCHOOL

Each year, a new crop of four-year-olds starts school in England. Some children will be just four, while others are nearly five. Some of them, due to a mixture of their developmental stage, their individual characteristics and their earlier experiences, will go into school and will find it easy. Their teachers will encourage them and will give them more to do, and they will learn. They will make friends. They will learn to feel good about themselves and their abilities.

Other children will be seen as 'behind' from the start, and for these children school will be quite different. Concerns will be quickly raised and they might be given extra help, which will often mark them out as different. They may be referred to educational psychologists or occupational therapists. If their behaviour is disruptive, they may have their names written up on the board, or they may be sent out of the classroom. They will learn that learning is hard, and perhaps that they themselves are 'bad'. The other children will know who they are.

These children are in the same class, but their experiences are very different. This will have an impact on their learning which will continue as they move up the school. The child who starts school and finds it hard will struggle to 'catch up', because the other children are moving faster than they are as well as starting out ahead, and no one is going to hold them back.

In Chapter 1, I introduced the idea that when a standardised school system meets a child who does not fit the standard expectations, problems arise, and that the response of most school and society is to locate those problems in the child. We either say that it's their fault (the blame narrative), or that there is something wrong with them (the medical model). It's rare to question the system and the fundamental assumptions on which it is based.

In this chapter, I'm going to focus on the experiences of people for whom this has happened. I've talked to parents of young people who struggled at school and adults who look back on their time at school.

Some of these experiences are hard to read, and many people, particularly teachers, will have an instinctively defensive reaction. The stories of those whose school experience is difficult are often hidden by shame and silence. These are all real stories of finding school hard, and of how difficult it is for schools to recognise this. Parents told me of feeling caught in the middle, between their obviously unhappy children, and schools which said that the only answer was to keep coming in, day after day. Of course this is not the experience of every family, but it is an experience which often goes unheard.

Parents

The parents you'll hear from now are all in different parts of the country and have children of different ages. All of them decided to take their children out of school and have pursued self-directed education for them.

John and Emma have two autistic daughters who are now unschooled. Their love for their daughters shone through as they told me about their elder daughter's experience at school.

> From the word go we were in school, talking to the head about issues and it remained that way. Throughout her school life we were always addressing something. Progressively that was more clearly to do with anxiety and she had art therapy through the school. They were a very small school with an outstanding Ofsted. Freya could learn, with her kind of brain, every name of every child, which felt really cosy. The families were a delight. They were lovely people, the teachers and the infrastructure of the school, everything.
>
> We were always paid the right lip service and all the right paperwork was done and we were listened to, but nothing was really seen through or solved.
>
> One thing they said was that she just won't get up from the carpet. Transitions were a problem, which I knew were a thing for me as well. If Freya is told to get up from a carpet, and she knows that she's been told, she's going to get up from that carpet. If she's not, there's something that's not making sense.
>
> She said, 'I used to sometimes hear the instruction, but I'd gone into sensory overload.' She couldn't get herself mobile. She literally couldn't mobilise herself and then she'd get told off. We started looking at the polyvagal theory and I think that she has complete shutdowns with anxiety.

By Years 2, 3 and 4, she was academically flying, they were so thrilled
with her. She was winning talent contests and things like that. We were
so confused by the fact that she was delivering what they needed, we kind
of rolled with it.

John and Emma were stuck between what school was telling them – that
their daughter was doing fine – and what they saw at home. What they
saw was extreme distress. They were encouraged to keep trying, because
they were told that apparently nothing was wrong at school.

She's pulling her eyelashes out and eyebrows out. She used to do it while
we were on holiday. The journey, any change of environment would always
trigger vomiting and sickness. With school, there was definitely a corre-
lation. She was just exceptionally anxious in Year 5. We were going in and
out all the time.

The school never gave us the impression that they weren't bothered or
weren't paying attention or any of that. They more or less did everything
they knew how to do. It just wasn't enough and it wasn't really properly
thought through.

One of the offers that they made for anxiety was to have a bit of time
towards the end of the day to talk with a particular person that she liked.
But then of course, in reality, what happens is you are singled out and
plucked out of your group at the end of the day. All of the focus is suddenly on you. Then there was one occasion where the person that she was
supposed to meet didn't show up to the place she was supposed to be, so
she was wandering around an empty school on her own. She had to go to
the classroom in front of all of her friends, it was just a disaster. If you're
going to promise something to help support, you've got to deliver on it.

She was having panic attacks every Sunday night. That was the zone
we were in when that was happening. They said, fine, we'll put her in with
the special educational needs coordinatior (SENCO) once a week and have
a chat. They gave her a form and asked her to tick boxes on a scale of 1 to
5, 'Do you feel this?'

Nicole and James also have two autistic children who are both unschooled. Nicole is a speech and language therapist and so was very aware
of the adaptations her son would need before he went into school. She
put an enormous amount of effort into getting things right for him. They
got a diagnosis of autism before their son started school. Nicole, with her
professional background, knew that her son was going to find mainstream

school challenging but couldn't find a specialist setting which seemed right either. Nicole and James told me about their son's experience.

> The reception class was quite nicely set up. It was quite a big room. It was a small group of 15 or 16 children. They had quite a bit of space and they had a visual timetable for the day.
>
> When we looked at the Year1/Year 2 classroom I remember walking in and thinking, 'Oh my goodness'. It was so busy. There was stuff hanging from the ceilings, the room was really small and there were 30 children. I just remember thinking, from a speech therapy point of view, this is massive overload. How are they going to pick out their visual timetable or whatever they need, when there's so much going on?
>
> We started Year 1, he struggled, but it wasn't too bad. He did half the day in the Year 1 class and half the day in Reception. We were still feeling that the basic things weren't happening: things like a visual timetable, giving him a now/next of the work that was expected of him, helping him with transitions, maybe letting him opt out of some things that he just wasn't coping with, giving lots of warning when there was lots of change.
>
> We ended up providing equipment to them. We provided symbols, sensory tools and equipment, we provided a board for him to write on. We ended up just giving them loads of things and we also paid for therapists to come in. It was so important that we had to make this work.

Nicole and James kept doing all they could to keep Sam in school, but things did not improve.

> By Year 2 he was still crying and screaming some days going in, 'Mummy don't leave me.' This was the third year of school and we were still having that, where he was screaming and hanging on to me. I'd been arguing for an education, health and care plan (EHCP). They felt he didn't need it because he just kept coping. I thought that 'coping' was not a good thing. I wanted him to be happy. I wanted him to feel comfortable and to thrive.
>
> Coping was where we were at. I didn't think he was coping anyway, but they felt he was and so he was not going to get the support. It all boils down to money, and it was a small school and they didn't have any extra finances. It's a complicated issue. Ultimately, they were not providing the basic things that he needed. The staff were not equipped to deal with children that are neurodiverse. They may have had some autism training or something for a day or so, but it was very minimal. It was often very generic. Things like sensory processing weren't even a part of that.

He was having speech and language therapy at school every week; we paid for that as well as Lego therapy and other things. We employed an educational psychologist to come and assess him at school. She said, 'He absolutely needs more support. Are you willing to go to court over this? Because they're not going to just give him the support.' Initially, she came in for a meeting at the school and it was one of the earliest moments of me thinking, 'We're going to have to think of something else here. I don't think we're going to carry on with this.'

We were talking about the same things that we were talking about in Reception. It still wasn't happening. I thought, even if I get additional help, I don't think it's going to really fundamentally change the problem. The problem is the environment, the problem is that he has to conform to what you're teaching him, which is not interesting.

We provided a sensory box which they used to let him have when he was struggling, but they began to restrict his access to that box. They felt he was just using it to get out of things. He got to the point where he used to go into the cupboard to use this box. We had alarm bells ringing. We thought, 'This is not working. This is not what inclusion is supposed to look like.'

Their daughter, Eva, was younger and very different. They told me just how different the two were, and how the school reacted differently.

Sam is more passive, hiding under the table crying, not coping, but then letting rip when he comes home, bottling up all day and then exploding. Eva has more challenging behaviour in the classroom. They were more on board that she was going to need an EHCP. They really dragged their feet because they said they'd got to build up evidence that she was not coping. We knew that Eva was going to be disruptive. They knew that she was going to be disruptive. They could see from the beginning that they were going to need to support her to make their lives easier.

We wanted to get that in place for her because I was concerned that she would be seen as a naughty child. She's extremely articulate and very verbal. Most people wouldn't understand that as autism, the 'girl type', and PDA. It was really difficult. She had problems at the first nursery, so we took her out because they were actually borderline unkind to her at times. We paid for the speech therapist to go in because we were worried about what was going on. The speech therapist said it was really hard for her to sit there and watch what was happening. Eva was really distressed at one point. So we moved her to a wonderful little nursery that was so supportive and understanding. At the time, Sam was really struggling and falling apart. We were still not even getting the bare bones of how to support him. Eva had started and was also struggling, but not to the extent of Sam because there was more free play. They were a bit more flexible in the Reception class. I just felt like we had to do something, I felt desperate, extremely concerned with what was happening.

Nicole told me about the impact on her.

There's a lot of regret and guilt that I have about putting them through school. I've got some images that are really upsetting when I think about them. Eva being pretty much held down and the teachers shouting 'go'. My gut was saying no, I always tried to ease them in. I was never wanting to be pushed out the door but in this one particular case, as I left I thought 'What on earth is going on?' You're almost bulldozed into it, and they say 'You're making this worse by staying', all of this kind of stuff.

One of the reasons that we continued with it for as long as we did is that their behaviour was so challenging at times. Sam was coming home from school and having really violent outbursts. He was quite violent to Eva as well, who was two years younger, and violent towards himself. I assumed that's what it was going to be like at home all the time, these outbursts. I thought, I've got to protect her from him, I've got to keep everything safe. But obviously school was fundamentally the problem, the social demands, the academic demands and the environment that from a sensory perspective he could not cope with.

Not all families had such a hard time early on. For some, it was the COVID-19 pandemic which led them to think more carefully about the experience their children were having at school and the impact on them. Ruth took her two secondary-school-aged boys out of school during the pandemic.

Really my children being home educated is more of a result of circumstances as well. My eldest boy was really quite excited about starting secondary school. I would have to engage with the teachers. I was having to explain that he was incredibly anxious. The teachers knew nothing about masking. Towards the end, before the pandemic hit, there was this moment where I was talking to my boy, I think we were walking to climbing. He will talk to me in certain contexts, and that's one of them. We had some lovely conversations. I said, 'Your teacher meets with you every few weeks, talk to her about the things that you're worried about.' He said, 'No, I don't tell her.'

I said, 'Why wouldn't you tell her what's difficult and then she'd do something about it?'

He replied, 'She'd do something about it and draw attention to me.'

He had already been taken out of a couple of things at lunchtime, and he just didn't want any emphasis on him. He doesn't want to be different. There's nothing quirky about him. There's nothing unusual. His autism diagnosis has come purely from us. School didn't have a clue. He's very anxious, very self-conscious. He wouldn't show anything to anyone.

The pandemic hit, and he was at home, and I realised he was happy. He was just a different child. My younger boy was the same. The school also provided next to no support, no resources, and what they provided was of such poor quality. I looked at it and I thought I could do better than this. My husband and I were mulling it over and we thought 'we're going to take them out'. The pandemic revealed to me the level of the masking. He was just lighter, happier, much more relaxed.

Some families spent years trying to make school work for their older children, and then decided to do something very different for their younger ones from the start. Emily is the mother of three boys, all of whom are very different. Her eldest son, who is now 21, went to school up to the age of 12.

Nathan was in school until comprehensive stage. The first year of comprehensive he had a statement of special educational needs. One of the things was he needed a safe place to go when he was overwhelmed, and it listed all his sensory difficulties. They never gave him a safe place to go. I'd have the phone call multiple times a week. 'He's up on the portacabin roof. Could you come and get him down?'

He had learnt that that was a safe place.

The school referred us four times to social services, saying that they thought there was neglect and abuse going on. I actually kept the final social services report. They said, 'This is a family that are doing wonderful things and coping incredibly well. But school are creating problems and not being supportive.'

It got to the stage where he was making his plans to take his own life. I remember it coming to a head. My husband found me in my bedroom having a full-on panic attack in the morning because I didn't want to go into his bedroom. Just in case.

Emily found that her life was dominated by trying to help her children manage school. She was constantly being called by the school and as a result had to give up her job. Her employer said to her that she would have to choose between answering the school's calls or her career – and as she said, there was no real choice.

Her second son has diagnoses of cerebral palsy and autism and it was clear from early on that mainstream school couldn't manage his needs.

> He got his diagnosis of autism at the age of five. At this point, the school couldn't cope with him. He was only going in for an hour a day in Reception. I usually would get home, walk through the door to a phone call saying, 'Can you please come, he's up on the roof of something in the playground? He won't come down. Can you come and get him?'
>
> Then he went to a learning support class attached to a mainstream school and it was wonderful. They got it right in the sense of inclusion, because even though it was the learning support class, they still integrated them whenever they could into the mainstream. Every kid in that playground knew who he was. If we were out in the supermarket, kids would come up and they knew him. It was wonderful.

This worked well for Mason, but when he was seven the learning support class ended and he had to go to a new school.

> Every day that we were picking him up from school, he was being sick in the car on the way home. Every day that we dropped him off at the school gates, I saw him physically shrinking. This is a boy who people describe as a ray of sunshine. He struggled with communication and in this new school, the kids were just a higher level of functioning and ability. I see that worry still lingers on now, he worries about new things, new situations.

After six weeks, they decided to take him out and he has been out of school ever since. He is now 15. Emily's youngest son is non-speaking autistic, and Emily felt under pressure to send him to a specialist school. She and her husband decided not to, and Liam has never been to school.

> When Liam came along, if I'm honest, we knew that he was autistic from about six months old, if not earlier. Liam is 11 now and he's still non-verbal. He's very classic autistic.
>
> Even as a baby, I'd lift him up above my head thinking, well, gravity should dictate he'll make eye contact with me and he wouldn't. He was diagnosed at two.
>
> They wanted him to go to a special needs school. At this point, school

was falling apart for the other two boys. We thought, why would we do this to our youngest, who is even more vulnerable and who doesn't have the ability to speak out for himself?

Looking back from adulthood

Parents can tell us how it was for them and what they saw their children going through, but what does it feel like from the inside? I asked several adults about their experiences of school, and they told me how challenging they had found it, even when they appeared to be coping. They talked of the mismatch between the environment they found themselves in, and what they needed in order to live and learn.

Alis Rowe runs the Curly Hair Project. She wasn't diagnosed with autism until she was 23 and told me how hard she had found school. Like many girls, she didn't express this through disruptive behaviour and so nothing was recognised.

School was emotionally damaging for me. I was very quiet and very anxious and school was completely overwhelming. People used to make fun of me because I did not speak. I did not fit in and did a lot of masking.

I didn't enjoy a single part of school.

Everything was challenging – interacting, socialising, coping with the busy, noisy environment, dealing with unfairness and people breaking the rules and getting away with it (e.g. a student did not submit their homework on time and the teacher gave them another week to complete it with no detriment), trying to manage having different hobbies from everyone else, not relating to what other students were talking about.

Autism wasn't really known when I was at school. It's so different nowadays. When I was at school, there were no accommodations or support for anyone with any kind of additional need.

No one suspected I might have autism. No one recognised how anxious I was. I think it was because I so quiet that I was invisible. I never caused any problems to anyone. I went through the whole of secondary school never getting even one detention. I was polite and well behaved and had no obvious difficulty with schoolwork so my difficulties were unnoticed.

I always say now, however, I might not have stood out for reasons such as 'challenging behaviour' or being naughty, but I must have stood out because I was always on my own and I did not speak. I wonder why those things didn't alert anyone to anything. I honestly think it is because autism (especially in girls) was practically unheard of in those days. As I said though, I went to a normal mainstream school. I have no recollection of anyone receiving any special support, so maybe that's just how school was back then. Even if someone had a diagnosis (I wouldn't have known), they still seemed to have to do the same as everyone else.

Natasha was academically capable, and got a bursary to go to a boarding school after primary school. She was mis-diagnosed with dyslexia when she was 18, the first time she was given any type of diagnosis. She has now been diagnosed with ADHD and has self-identified as autistic. She told me how she experienced school.

When I got to secondary school, I realised that I was actually quite out of my depth. I went from being top set in primary school for everything to bottom set everything in secondary. That in itself was a knock to my ego.

I was still playing with dolls at the age of 11. I would never dare tell anyone I went to school with that. I would get bullied. I think we're told it's not normal. I remember when I went to secondary school for the first day, I said, 'Where's the playground?' Everyone was like, there is no playground. I needed to have a designated playground. I used to play sardines with all the second formers. I think that's why they loved me because I was fun and willing to play like these childish games with them.

The age gap between me and my next sister is 11 years. My two older sisters went to the school there, and some of the teachers remembered them. When I came along, they put those kinds of ideas in my head: 'Your sisters could do this.'

There are certain things I just couldn't do the same as they could. If you don't get at least six A grades at GCSE they kick you out. I was lucky enough because I got five. I had other commitments like sports and music as well. They really want you to be a good all-rounder. I was doing the piano and netball and cross country for the school. It was intense, really high pressure, not just from the staff, but from the pupils. I was considered stupid. I cried on my GCSE results day when I got five As. I cried my eyes out. I didn't want to go back. I was distraught with my five As. It's crazy how the school can indoctrinate you to think that that's so bad. That was like failure. [...]

At my school, you were shamed for not being clever or not being smart. In normal schools, I could probably get away with it. At my school, you would be bullied if you were stupid. In my friend's school, she was very intelligent, and she got bullied for being intelligent. I was roasted or mocked for that and also for things like sensitivities in the classroom.

I used to hate it when the lights were really bright. I'd say every time

I walked into the classroom, 'Please can you turn them down?' I'd always get shouted at by the teacher. No, you need these for learning, you're going to fall asleep. I didn't know I had sensory difficulties. That's me expressing that. I don't like the lights. They didn't allow that. Boys would start laughing and poke fun at me. All these things fed into the self-loathing.

I didn't absorb anything. I'd leave the lesson and I may as well have not been there. I remember sitting down to write a timetable. The timetable itself took me about two hours. Then I actually sat down and thought maybe I can't fit all of these in because I'd put myself five subjects for one day. I'd sit down and start on science and go over the schedule by four hours. Then I'd spend half a day doing just one subject. I couldn't even time manage on my own. I just remember concentrating really hard on the subjects I knew I was bad at. It was like an obsession. I did every past paper going back to the 1990s. I went to the archives and found them.

Kieran Rose was diagnosed in his early twenties after a very difficult and unhappy adolescence. He now works as an advocate. He told me what he thought could have been different.

My school experience was that I was a people pleaser. I had middle grades. I was quiet. I struggled with relationships. I always had my nose in a book and all the narratives that we talk about around 'female autism'. The only thing that saved me was that I was a fast runner. I think that stopped me from probably getting pounded to a pulp. I went through my fair share of bullying and having friendships. I carried the same group of core friends from the age of five, when I started school, up until about the age of 19 or 20. Looking back now, they were not my friends. I was the one that was picked on and taken advantage of.

I was on antidepressants at the age of 13. I tried to take my own life for the first time the age of 14, and that was a regular kind of fixture in my teens. Suicide attempts and self-harm, but all hidden away from anybody else. Even my close family. I've always described it as not wanting to die and not wanting to end my life, but needing to step out because I didn't have a choice. It was like I'd been driven down a blind alley and had nowhere else to go. I didn't understand myself and nobody understood me, I thought my experience was the same as everybody else's. I didn't feel equipped to be able to deal with all this and literally just wanted to open the door, step through it and close it again.

I wish somebody had stepped in when I was little and said, 'Who you are is absolutely fine. Let's go off and explore this. Let's see what the world means to you and what you mean to the world. Let's figure this out. And you know, if things hurt you, then we're going to take a step back, we're going to think about why they're hurting you and what we can do to stop that from happening. If you want to tell me about the things you're passionate about, I'm listening.'

Those things weren't done for me for various different reasons. But if I had had that, I think I would be a completely different person now. I think I wouldn't have gone through all the negative experiences that I did go through.

Conclusion

School isn't the same for everyone. People experience things in different ways, and one person's ideal can be another person's torture. One person's bright happy environment is another's sensory overload.

This book isn't about 'bad schools' or 'bad teachers'. My intention is not to blame anyone. The schools that are written about here were often doing their very best, and were trying hard to be responsive. However, there are certain non-negotiable aspects to the way that schools are run which make them difficult environments for some children.

Large groups of people, a standardised curriculum with age-related expectations, busy playgrounds with no space to get away – all of these things are more difficult for some children than others. The lack of control which children have over their lives at school affects some more than others. Then there is the tendency of schools to use anxiety to motivate, which can be devastating for a child who already has a tendency towards anxiety. There is the culture of comparison, where some children are seen as high-achieving and others are behind, right from the start. All these things cause problems, and they aren't really things which can be easily tweaked. They are more fundamental than that.

No matter how good standardised schooling is, it won't work for everyone. There will always be those who don't fit. Human development is enormously variable, and the only way to create an education system which enables all children to thrive is to have an equivalent amount of flexibility. The more the child struggles, the greater the flexibility required.

FIVE-POINT SUMMARY

1. School can be hard in a way which is nothing to do with the academic work.
2. Neurodivergent adults described difficult experiences at school which they felt had affected their mental health.
3. Parents talked about their neurodivergent children literally becoming ill through their time at school, despite sometimes achieving academically and appearing to be 'fine' during school time.
4. Parents hoped that a diagnosis would lead to understanding and support but this was not always the case.
5. Even with very well-informed and resourced parents and with a diagnosis, school was still a struggle for some children.

CHAPTER 3

LEARNING AT SCHOOL

How do you learn? Do you prefer to sign up for classes, or do you learn better informally? Do you seek out a teacher and curriculum, or do you gather information more organically, though books, conversations and internet searches? Are you a fan of textbooks and online quizzes? How do you know when you've learnt something? Do you take a test?

Usually when I ask people these questions, they describe something they've learnt recently; perhaps how to change a tyre, or how to cook a sponge cake. Or maybe they describe a burning interest in the politics of Eastern Europe, sparked by the war in Ukraine, or the life cycle of polar bears. They talk about asking other people, looking up YouTube videos and podcasts and searching the internet. They sometimes read books (although they often say they don't finish them) and articles. They describe finding snippets of useful information in many different places, and bringing those together in order to learn something that is important to them.

They describe something quite different from what typically goes on at school – and sometimes they will ruefully refer to this. 'I was no good at school,' they say, 'it was only afterwards that I really starting learning.'

There's something odd about this. After all, schools are constructed as places for learning. That is their purpose. They surely should be places where we look back on some of the best learning experiences of our lives. Yet it's unusual for people to remember their school days as a time when they were learning particularly efficiently or joyfully. They rarely try to reproduce what they had at school when they need to learn something as adults. When they do talk about things they enjoyed at school, it's often relationships or break time rather than the content of lessons. It's friends, or a particular teacher or teaching assistant who they felt a connection with.

Following the curriculum

I visited several schools when my children were small. The London primary schools I saw weren't that different from the Bristol primary schools I attended myself. Echoey Victorian buildings with draughty assembly halls and huge windows. Classrooms full of tables and chairs, the children seated with the teacher at the front. On the walls were posters with times tables, or flags of the world, or pictures of Martin Luther King and Maya Angelou for Black History Month.

It's not just the buildings which haven't changed since Victorian times. The basic assumptions of school remain the same. Expert teacher at the front, children seated at tables. The teacher delivers the curriculum, the children's task is to learn it as efficiently as possible. The curriculum itself may have changed, but in many ways it's as if our understanding of learning and child development hasn't moved on since 1895.

The curriculum is important at school. In fact, a lot of the way we think about education and learning is defined by the curriculum. Children progress through a curriculum, they are tested on it and success is defined as being able to show you have understood and learnt the curriculum. Teachers are trained mostly in the curriculum, rather than in child development. In order to deliver the curriculum, schools generally prioritise one form of learning. Formal instruction. This is relatively easy to deliver in large groups, and means that the curriculum can be planned and delivered by a teacher. It's predictable and structured.

There's no inherent problem with this. Formal instruction is a useful and efficient way to deliver content to people who want to learn and remember that content. (There's less evidence that it's effective with those who aren't interested.) I frequently go on training days which are based on didactic instruction and I learn a lot.

However, there are some assumptions buried deep here which often go unchallenged. First, should an education be based mostly on learning a factual curriculum? What actually is learning? Might we also be interested in what children are learning about the process of learning and themselves? There's a lot of evidence that children are not small versions of adults and they learn in different ways. Their brains are different and less mature. Formal instruction works well for motivated adults, but is a struggle for many children. They learn differently, and this is both an advantage and a disadvantage. It's a disadvantage when it comes to sitting in rows and absorbing information; it's an advantage when it comes to experimenting, creativity, asking divergent questions and learning through play.

Unfortunately, schools often focus on the type of learning where children are disadvantaged, relative to adults. They devalue informal learning, play-based learning, social learning, practical learning and learning about things which children value in favour of learning the school curriculum, which is prioritised more and more as children grow up.

This doesn't happen right away. The best nurseries and Reception classes create a rich environment for children to play in, valuing play as the medium through which young children learn. Children's emotional and social needs are prioritised along with other forms of learning. Then, the early years of choice and play quickly give way to instruction and standardised assessment. The values of adults are consistently prioritised over the values of children.

As children move up the school, academic work is prioritised over play, and learning to comply is prioritised over learning to question. Intellectual skills are prioritised over emotional and social skills. By the age of seven or eight, children are spending most of their time seated at a desk, and play is kept for playtime. They are told that learning is about listening and remembering, and not about exploring and discovering. Many of them stop seeing themselves as active learners, they stop asking so many questions and instead they wait to be told what to do. Some of them start to say that learning is boring and they become less creative in their approach to the world. This is something Sir Ken Robinson, educationalist and international advisor on education in the arts, wrote and talked about extensively – I'd recommend finding his 2015 TED talk on YouTube.

The science of learning

In March 2021, Gavin Williamson (at the time the UK Education Secretary) spoke to the Foundation for Education Development.

> We know much more now about what works best: evidence-backed, traditional teacher-led lessons with children seated facing the expert at the front of the class are powerful tools for enabling a structured learning environment where everyone flourishes.

He sounded pretty confident that the science was in, and the puzzle of education was solved. Education policy followed suit.

Was he right? Does the evidence really show us that children learn best when they are seated in rows? Well, the first thing to acknowledge is that school wasn't set up as an evidence-based intervention. In the late 19th century, when universal education was rolled out in the UK, the USA and several other countries, they didn't start with research. No one did controlled studies looking at the different ways in which children learn, and concluded that rows of desks and textbooks were the best way to go.

Schooling is an intervention into childhood – a highly significant one, given that children often spend 12 or 13 years full time in school, but it generally hasn't been evaluated in the same way as other interventions. It hasn't been tested against a controlled condition. When a new intervention is developed in psychology or medicine, you have to show that it's better than the other interventions already on offer, and better than not doing anything at all. This hasn't been part of the research into school. There's no onus to show that school is a better way to learn than not going to school, because everyone assumes that of course it is. Most research studies assume that schooling is inevitable and learning a curriculum is the best way to become educated. I've read many research studies on education and child development, and the only studies I have found which discuss the impact of school (rather than the impact of different types of schooling) are those which are cross-cultural, looking at children who have not had the opportunity to go to school due to poverty or deprivation. Most researchers assume they know what happens if you don't go to school: you don't learn and you won't succeed. They equate no school with no education, and leaving school with 'dropping out'. As you'll see in the next chapter, this doesn't have to be the case.

However, back to school and how it defines learning. A focus on formal instruction has been around for a long time. The ancient Romans had schools where wealthy boys went to be taught reading, writing and mathematics. They sat facing the teacher and were caned if they didn't cooperate. This was based on the even older Greek tradition. Recently, formal instruction has had an extra boost, as you can see from Gavin Williamson's speech. This is because ideas from cognitive science have become popular among some educationalists, and these cognitive theories are used to argue that schools should be focusing on direct instruction.

Cognitive theories are about how we think, reason and remember. That's what 'cognition' means. Cognitive theories are about the mechanics of what is going on in someone's head when they acquire and retain knowledge. Like all psychological models, they are a way to help us understand things rather than a reflection of concrete reality. Cognitive models don't typically include emotional or social aspects of learning – those are usually studied separately in a different area of psychology.

The cognitive theories currently popular in education share a particular way of seeing learning. A good example is John Sweller's cognitive load theory (Sweller, 1988). Cognitive load theory defines learning as retaining information in our long-term memory store. Information passes through the short-term memory, which has a limited capacity, to the long-term memory, which does not. From this perspective, the aim of education is to make sure that young people process information from the curriculum, and then retain it in their memory stores, meaning that they can retrieve it at a later date. Taking account of the 'cognitive load' means not overtaxing the short-term memory so that learning is at its most efficient. Many books are devoted to how to apply this in the classroom, advising teachers on how to deliver information most effectively and to make sure young people retain and practise retrieving it. They aim to make children and young people 'think hard' about the topic so that they are more likely to remember what they are thinking about (Willingham, 2021). To this end, thinking must be kept on topic.

I have read many books and research papers about these cognitive theories. I wanted to understand the science, particularly because I have a PhD in developmental cognitive psychology, and there I learnt many things about children's learning, much of which didn't seem to relate well to these particular cognitive models.

As I read, I found that cognitive load theory is a scientific theory which sets out to explain a particular type of learning. It does that well. It is mostly based on laboratory studies, where people are required to learn things out of context – lists of random words, for example. It is not an applied educational model and there is not strong research evidence for its practical application in schools. The studies that do exist have not looked at all types of learning and all ages of children, focusing mostly on maths and science, and early secondary (ages 11–14). A recent review from the Education Endowment Foundation by Thomas Perry and colleagues (2021) looked at this in detail – it's worth a read if you're interested and it is available online.

These cognitive theories are essentially models of how information is processed. Information is the input, while the output is test results, or another way of measuring how much information has been retained by the learner. All well and good, you might think – except that processing information isn't the only thing we might think of as important in an education. Children are complex systems. Processing information delivered to them by an adult is only one part of what they do. Their learning can be affected by many things, including their emotional state, whether they are interested and whether they would rather be doing something else. None of these things appear in cognitive models.

I realised that one reason for my confusion is that we can define 'learning' and 'education' in different ways, and cognitive models don't account for this. That doesn't mean there's anything wrong with these models, it's simply that they weren't designed as theories of education. Any discussion about the purpose or philosophy of education just isn't part of the theory. The models are all about *how* we learn – to which their answer is information processing – and give no space at all to the question of *why* we learn. But when it comes to humans and learning, the 'why' is crucial. Learning is something we do best when it has meaning to us.

The other sciences of learning

When my daughter was about six, she went through an intense phase of experimentation. Wherever she was, she was testing things out. She mixed up little pots of wet tissue paper, and put them in the freezer, where they fell on my toes when I was looking for frozen peas. She mixed together jam, washing up liquid and flour, and then cooked it, with disgusting results. As we walked along the street, she'd be touching textures, putting twigs in holes and experimenting with hopping, twirling or jumping rather than walking. It was an unpredictable stage of life for her and me; she would find things to experiment with everywhere and I was always coming across the results.

It was a vivid example of one of the ways in which young children learn – through deliberate experimentation and hypothesis testing. Professor Alison Gopnik, psychologist and philosopher, describes this type of learning as 'child as scientist' (Gopnik, 2017). The idea is that the child is an active agent in their learning, bringing their own questions and thoughts to act on new situations. Gopnik discusses how children form hypotheses and test these out, interacting with their environment.

This is, of course, a form of learning through play. Learning through play is very different from direct instruction, but it also has an extensive evidence base showing that it works. It has other advantages – making connections though play is invigorating and fun, and young children are naturally driven to do this. In fact, it's hard to stop them. I remember the years when my children were very small and we had to play at having an adventure just to get out of the house or down the stairs.

Gopnik and her colleagues' studies found that direct instruction may sometimes inhibit learning – when they gave children a toy and told them how to play with it they explored less thoroughly and for less long than when they were given a toy without instructions. The group who were told what to do discovered fewer functions of the toy than the group who found things out for themselves.

This theory sees learning quite differently from cognitive load theory, where the learner features mostly as a series of boxes through which information flows. According to the 'child as scientist' theory, the child is always an active participant in their learning, and the questions they ask have real answers – unlike the questions they are often asked in school, which are tests of what they know. This is how young children learn naturally, when they are not seated in rows listening to an expert.

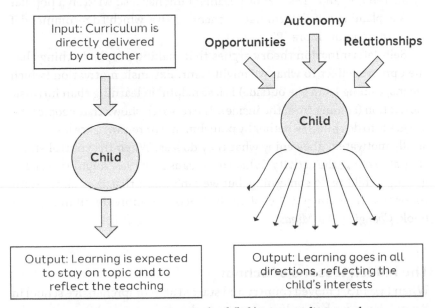

Figure 3.1: *Learning at school (left) is a more linear and predictable process than self-directed education (right)*

It doesn't take much research to see that there is a discrepancy between how children learn naturally (through discovery, inquiry and exploration, at least in early and middle childhood), and how schools try to teach them (by direct instruction, sitting and listening). All it takes is spending some time observing young children, and how hard they find it to comply with school requirements. As young people mature, the way they learn changes, but before this happens, it's a struggle to get children to comply with the non-academic requirements of school. Just sitting still is a challenge for many of them, not to mentioning attending to the task set by the teacher, holding their pencil correctly, and stopping themselves from blurting out whatever is in their minds. Schools spend a lot of time and effort trying to help children whose main problem is that they are young and not interested in what they are being taught.

Being not interested – or not motivated – is a recurrent problem in education, and there are reasons to think that the way school is organised may in fact be partly responsible for this problem. There is a lot of research which shows that being able to make choices about your life and learning affects whether you are internally motivated or not – and this motivation matters for the quality of your learning. This is self-determination theory, first formulated by psychologists Edward Deci and Richard Ryan (Deci & Ryan, 1985; Ryan & Deci, 2000). Daniel Pink has also written a popular book explaining self-determination theory, *Drive,* which I'd recommend if you want to know more (Pink, 2010).

Self-determination theory argues that making people do things has the opposite effect to what we might want. Extrinsic motivation (which means, coming from the outside) is less helpful in learning than intrinsic motivation (coming from the inside). The research shows that people who are made to do things, whether by punishments or rewards, are less intrinsically motivated. They enjoy what they do less. When the control stops, they stop doing the activity. What this means is that we might succeed in getting a child to do something, but we can't insist that they either want to, or that they enjoy it. I explain this theory in more detail in my first book, *Changing Our Minds*.

The hidden lessons of school

When I was 13, I moved country and started at a comprehensive school in Bristol. Here, we had to line up outside the classrooms while waiting for the teacher. Because I joined in Year 8, no one explicitly told me this, it was simply assumed that this was what everyone did. I saw what everyone else was doing, and followed suit.

Except that I got it wrong. Waiting in line outside the music room, I found myself surrounded with giggles. I clearly was doing something weird, but all I was doing was standing still. I couldn't work out what was going on until the teacher arrived and looked down his nose.

'Are you a new boy?' he said.

Only then did I realise that there were two lines, one for boys, one for girls, and I was in the wrong one. My previous school would never have divided us up like that and so I had been totally oblivious. I literally hadn't noticed that everyone else in my line was male because it didn't seem relevant. I dashed to join the girls but it was too late, the only explanation my classmates could consider was that I fancied one of the boys and so that was all they talked about for the rest of the week.

Once in the music classroom, things weren't much better. We were all given little electric keyboards, a piece of sheet music and told to practise playing 'Downtown' by Petula Clark. Some of my classmates were accomplished piano players, I myself could read music but didn't play the piano, and about half the class had no clue how to relate the sheet music to the notes. No matter, we all had to work it out as best we could, and then one by one we went round the classroom, playing our little piece so that the music teacher could give us a grade while everyone giggled.

What was the point? No one was learning to play the piano here. Those who could play were bored, while those who couldn't were struggling to make some sense of the sheet music and work out where 'C' was on the keyboard before they had to suffer public humiliation in front of the rest of the class. The only reason we were doing it was because the music teacher had told us to do so. In order to waste our time in this way, we had to switch off our powers of critical thinking. We had to stop asking ourselves why we were doing this, because there was no good answer.

We were learning passivity. It wasn't important whether we thought we were learning or whether we found any purpose, the activity was predetermined and our task was to go through the motions as best we could.

I'd go so far as to say that this was one of the fundamental lessons of my schooling. If you aren't sure what to do, look around and see what everyone else is doing. Do it too and hope that no one will notice that you're out of sync.

I moved school several times, and each time I moved, the unspoken rules changed. Making a queue for girls only would have got you laughed at in my international school, unless it was a queue for the toilet. Getting it wrong meant you stood out. It was as easy as wearing your rucksack on two shoulders rather than one, or having an exercise book from Sainsbury's rather than WH Smith. You could never ask why it mattered, because that would simply result in blank looks or giggles.

We learn what we do

Why does it matter, if we take control away from children in order to educate them? Surely it's so important that they learn English and maths that we can't give them a choice? Well, I've already said that it damages intrinsic motivation. There is, however, another problem, and it's to do with neurological development.

Until quite recently, neuroscientists thought that most brain development occurred in childhood and that adolescence was a time of bodily changes and hormones. Theories of brain development were based on post-mortem examination of people who had died and left their bodies to science, or on people who had had brain injuries to a particular area of their brain and had survived.

Then, with the advent of magnetic resonance imaging (MRI) scans, it become possible to see inside the heads of living people. More than that, it became possible to ask people to do particular things, and then track their brain activity – functional MRI scans.

This was a dramatic development in neuroscientific research. Suddenly it was possible to compare how adolescent brains responded to events, compared to adults and younger children. And it quickly became clear that a lot was going on. Although brains don't change very much in volume from the age of ten upwards, there are dramatic structural changes taking place from puberty onwards. I'm not a neuroscientist and I'm going to focus on the bigger picture here rather than neurological detail. If you're interested in the detail, I recommend *Inventing Ourselves*, by Sarah-Jayne Blakemore (2019), which goes into fascinating details about teenage brain development.

One of the most important findings is that adolescence, if defined as the period of changing from childhood to adulthood, goes on for a lot longer than we usually assume. Blakemore, Professor of Cognitive Neuroscience and Psychology at the University of Cambridge, describes how the evidence now indicates that the brain changes associated with adolescence happen between the ages of 10 and 24, and that this is a period of great opportunity but also vulnerability – rather like early childhood. She suggests that late adolescence, in particular (by which she means early 20s) is a period of opportunity which is often missed, and when young people who have previously not done well in education may really benefit from a second chance.

As children approach adolescence, their bodies start to change and at the same time, their brains do as well. The emotional and motivation system in the brain – called the limbic system – becomes more attuned to rewards, particularly social rewards. Adolescent brains appear to react more intensely when something goes well. This intensity could explain some of the increased risk taking associated with adolescence – the emotional response if the risk pays off is literally more, in terms of brain reaction.

In addition, the adolescent brain appears to become more socially attuned to peers and the approval of peers, something which neuroscientists such as Professor Mary Helen Immordino-Yang describe as providing the fuel which propels adolescents outwards from the comfort of their families, powering them to explore new ways of being and challenge the assumptions of their parents' generation. There's evidence that adolescents are particularly likely to take risks when with their peers – and the more peers they are with, the more likely they are to take risks. One could see this as a bad thing, and take steps to isolate them from their peers – or one could see this as part of the natural developmental process of becoming an adult, finding your place among your peers and of pushing the boundaries of what you were previously able to do.

The limbic system isn't the only neural system which is changing during adolescence. Alongside it is the system responsible for self-control. The part of the brain which is responsible for this is located largely in the prefrontal cortex (the part at the front of our heads). Another term used for these brain functions is 'executive functioning', or sometimes confusingly 'non-cognitive skills'. This is the part of our brain responsible for higher-order thinking skills. It enables us to think through the consequences of what we do, to problem solve and to inhibit our initial reactions to something in favour of a more measured response. It allows us to plan for the future and set goals, and to hold those goals in mind while we put in the work we need to get there. It enables us to concentrate on learning things which we may not find that interesting now, because they are part of the purpose of some future goal. These skills are often something which neurodivergent children find harder or develop in different ways, and I'll be talking about this specifically in Chapter 11.

The self-control system matures gradually, throughout the whole of childhood and adolescence, and at very different rates for different people – and adolescence in neuroscientific terms lasts until the age of at least 24. This maturation doesn't just happen, it is experience-dependent.

Alison Gopnik argues in her book *The Gardener and the Carpenter* (2017) that schools are particularly bad at providing the right environment for the self-control system to mature. She suggests that before school and in pre-industrial societies, young people in middle childhood (the period from about 6–12 years) would have been learning meaningful skills, taking on some responsibility and developing mastery – perhaps in learning how to catch and prepare food, look after younger children, and do other tasks of adulthood which they would have seen around them. This would have given their self-control systems the experience that they needed to develop, meaning that by the time adolescence came along, the self-control system was relatively mature. The modern-day child, in contrast, will usually spend the period between the ages of six and 12 having almost every area of their life controlled and scheduled by school and their parents. This means that they have many fewer opportunities to develop the skills of self-control for themselves.

This means that when the 'motivational juice' of puberty arrives, making risk taking more rewarding and peer approval more important, the self-control system for modern teenagers may still be relatively immature. They haven't had the experience they need of having responsibility for real tasks. Young people may have an increased drive to go out and take risks, while still lacking the capacity to think through the consequences and limit their impulses. This is the dual-system model of adolescent brain development and it is one way to understand the changes we see in the behaviour of young people during this time period (Blakemore, 2019).

Brains are amazing things. They are acutely sensitive to the environment, and they develop in the context of that environment. The experiences that we have contribute to how our brain develops and literally form the structure of our brain. You have developed the capacity for language (and the specific languages that you speak) because of your experiences, and now, your brain will respond differently to languages that you understand compared to those that you don't understand. We can see those differences in a brain scan.

Sometimes when people start to talk about differences between brains, there is an assumption that this means that they are 'hard wired' (i.e. unchangeable). This isn't really backed up by science. Yes, there are differences in how brains develop, but those differences are a result of an interaction between the person's genetic make-up and the environment. There is very little which is 'wired in' at birth.

The process of a brain changing in response to the environment is called neuroplasticity, and it's thought to be one of the reasons that humans have been so successful in adapting to a wide range of environments across the planet. Babies are born with very immature brains compared to other animals. This makes them full of potential, ready to take full advantage of what their environment has to offer so that their brain can adapt to what is important. Very quickly they learn from the world around them what is important and what isn't. They learn to distinguish between the sounds of their native language or languages, while learning to ignore the distinctions which aren't important. The Japanese language does not have the distinction between 'R' and 'L' so Japanese babies do not retain the ability to tell the difference – meaning that in adulthood it can be hard to learn other languages where this distinction is important.

We retain this capacity for plasticity and adaptation through adulthood, although certain things – like languages without an accent which marks you out as foreign – are easier to acquire in childhood. This plasticity is reflected in brain structure – we can actually see the changes that occur as we learn. Studies with London taxi drivers studying for 'The Knowledge' – an exam which black cab drivers have to take that requires an encyclopaedic knowledge about London streets – have shown structural changes in their brains as they study for the exam (Maguire *et al.*, 2000).

Self-control or being controlled

Let's come back to the dual system of brain development. That self-control system which I talked about, the one which is located in the prefrontal cortex, develops slowly and gradually from childhood onwards, all the way through adolescence. However, it doesn't develop in isolation. Like the rest of our brain, it is acutely sensitive to experience. We develop the ability to control our behaviour by practising controlling our behaviour (and often failing). We learn to problem solve by solving progressively harder problems (or not quite managing). We practise these things in the protected environment of childhood, so that our brains develop the capacity to manage the higher stakes environments of adulthood. What we do influences how our brains develop these abilities.

Unfortunately, this means that the basic assumptions of the school system do not make sense in terms of brain development. In the name of education and acquiring knowledge, we remove chances to practise self-control from children. We replace this with lots of opportunities to practise *being controlled*, and then we confuse this with self-control.

This happens again and again. A child who is considered to have 'poor impulse control' often means a child who will not squash their impulses to do what they choose, as opposed to what their teachers choose. Poor concentration means not concentrating on what a teacher wants you to concentrate on. When it comes to children, the question of who is in control is often ignored, but it makes all the difference.

Freedom to make mistakes

Real self-control is about so much more than the simple choice of 'do what an adult says' and 'don't do what the adult says'. It's about the myriad of tiny choices that we make throughout the day – shall I get up, or stay in bed? Shall I read my book, or play on my iPad? Shall I have a snack now, or wait for lunchtime? Shall I shout at my sister or leave the room instead? For self-directed learners, it's about seeing the consequences of their choices over time. It's about seeing what happens when you choose *not* to do things, just as much as when you choose to do things. It's about having the freedom to experiment with learning things in different ways, and seeing what works for you.

This freedom is precious. To be real, it has to include the possibility of making what adults might consider to be 'poor decisions', or the choice to miss opportunities and say no. The right to miss out, we could say. All that gets taken away at school, because the 'right choices' have been decided in advance.

The idea at school is that adults make decisions until young people can be trusted to do so for themselves. Unfortunately, there's a flaw in this reasoning. For, as you may remember, a fundamental part of brain development is that we learn what we do – or as it is sometimes put, 'neurons that fire together, wire together'. And although compliance with being controlled is often confused with self-control when it comes to young people, they aren't actually the same thing at all. Volition matters. Choice and autonomy matter.

This is especially true for children with unusual developmental pathways. Neurodivergent children are particularly vulnerable to having control taking away from them in the name of education, because their abilities are out of sync with those required by the school system. This often means less time to choose what they do. It means extra reading lessons instead of art or music, or tutors after school instead of time to play. I often speak to parents who tell me that their child was stopped from doing the things they enjoyed at school to spend more time on the things they found hard.

There's something else that happens at school, and this is because of the focus on the curriculum over other forms of learning. When a child finds it very hard to organise themselves, it's tempting to simply do it for them. When they constantly forget to do things, it's tempting to set up systems so they don't have to remember anymore and other people do the remembering for them. When a child refuses to comply with instruction, some teachers will up the pressure and control in order to compel them to do so.

There's nothing wrong with setting up systems to help someone with things they find hard, or indeed setting up your own systems to help you remember things or organise yourself. However, when it comes to children it's important not to set up systems which effectively remove their chances to learn. I've heard of this happening in schools, when the 'support' organised for a child keeps them where they are, rather than helping them move forward and learn. An example would be organising a taxi to school for a child who is capable of taking the bus or train, but who would need support in learning to do so. The taxi is funded and so it keeps coming, and an opportunity has been lost to develop independence.

Coming full circle

At the start of the chapter, I talked about formal instruction and how children learn in school. I've then looked at the difference between what schools set out to teach children, and then the other things which they are learning alongside that. For the curriculum is only the visible part of what we learn at school. Slowly, gradually, over a period of years, schools take choices away from children and tell them that adult decisions are better, and that their own can't be trusted. They learn to ignore their own judgement about how to spend their time, and to passively take instruction. When children resist this, adults tend to call them 'resistant', 'oppositional' or 'defiant'. If they resist all control and are anxious, adults are likely to call them 'demand avoidant'.

Schools reward compliance. They do this because they believe that the aim of making sure that children learn the curriculum is so important that removing choices about this is justified. Unfortunately there are side effects to this. Young people need experiences of making meaning-ful choices and of problem solving in order to develop their self-control. Preventing them from doing so in the name of education is misguided, because brains mature through doing. If young people practise being compliant and ignoring their own judgement throughout their childhood and adolescence, why are we surprised if as young adults, they struggle to make meaningful choices for themselves?

We learn to make choices through making choices, there is no short cut to this. Experience matters as well as knowledge.

FIVE-POINT SUMMARY

1. Schools often define learning as understanding and remembering the curriculum which is delivered by a teacher.
2. Schools tend to prioritise formal instruction over other forms of learning and most recently have used cognitive science to justify this.
3. There are other cognitive science and psychological models which do not suggest that formal instruction is always the best way to learn, particularly when it comes to children.
4. Many of the things which children learn at school are implicit rather than explicit. These lessons are often about compliance and fitting in at school rather than academics.
5. Recent findings in cognitive neuroscience indicate that the control system is maturing during adolescence, and that this system is dependent on experience. Being controlled is not the same thing as self-control.

CHAPTER 4

LEARNING WITHOUT SCHOOL

Introduction

I push open the door. The house hums with activity. In the kitchen, two children are making cookies, to their own recipes. The floor looks sticky. One has added blue food colouring, the other has gone out on a limb and added chilli powder. Through to the living room and there's an animated game of *Mario Kart* going on. At the table, two girls are quizzing each other on capitals of the world and an older boy is reading a book. On the floor, a small child draws a penguin.

These children are self-directed learners, and their education is happening right now. They are choosing what they do, and learning as they do it. This isn't break time, or the holidays, this is what it can look like all the time. It doesn't look anything like school.

What happens when children aren't schooled?

I'm going to guess that most of you reading this think that schooling is necessary for learning. You went to school, everyone you know went to school; you have very little idea of what life would have been like without it. That is entirely typical. We find it hard to imagine what happens when children aren't *made* to learn. I certainly did, when my children first didn't start school. Surely we would have to insist on at least maths and English? And what if they never wanted to learn to write?

Turns out no, you don't have to insist. In self-directed education, children and young people choose what they learn and how they learn it. Really. Even if what they want to learn about is traffic calming methods and *Plants vs Zombies*. This is so far from what most people think is education should be that many dismiss it out of hand as impractical, without bothering to find out more.

Self-directed education starts with a very basic idea. Making children learn is unnecessary, and damages their relationship with learning and themselves. Instead, let's help them learn more about the things they are interested in. From this, everything else follows.

Most of us know what this looks like, because young children are exceptionally self directed and strenuously refuse any attempts to make them be otherwise. A good nursery provides an interesting environment within which children can choose what they do. In many ways, self-directed educators simply carry on with the same principles. The environment changes and becomes more sophisticated, but there is still an environment of opportunities, within which children can make choices.

As self-directed children get older, they take on more of that for themselves. Their parents stop structuring their environment in such a deliberate way. Young people find their own opportunities. They seek out people they like, things they like to do and find ways to learn.

What each child chooses to do will be different, meaning that they will learn different things. Variety of outcome is a fundamental part of self-directed education. One child may spend their time doing art, another may read or play games. Some will dive deeply into one interest for a while, explore every facet of it and then move on, others will have several interests running at the same time which will come and go. The interests they have frequently don't look like the things which children are taught at school.

This doesn't mean they can't and won't take exams or go on to higher education. It does mean that the person choosing whether and when they take exams should be them.

The difference between self-directed education and other forms of education isn't pedagogy. You can't necessarily tell from the outside whether a learner is self directed or not. It's about *who* is choosing what they learn, and who can decide when to stop. If a child chooses to learn maths through attending a lecture course, and can drop out at any time, they're self directed. If they feel pressured into doing so, or they are told they must do it, it's not self directed.

I was on a panel recently with Zoe Readhead, Principal of Summerhill School in Leiston, Suffolk, and when asked how education needed to change she said that young people need to be able to get up and leave. This single fact would transform how we do education. There must be the space to say no. If there was, then schools would work very differently.

Self-directed education, then, is characterised by the learner being in control. This means that it looks like play and experimentation, but it can also look like studying for an exam, following an online course or joining a tutor group. It looks like using Khan Academy, or Duolingo, and having many conversations. Choosing to study Japanese GCSE and following a curriculum because you choose to is self directed, even if you use an online class or a tutor. Being told you must take the exam but it's up to you how you study for it isn't.

Self-directed education goes on at home (where it is usually called unschooling) or in a variety of self directed learning settings, including democratic schools, Agile Learning Centres, self-managed learning centres and places which call themselves none of these things.

Self-directed educators do not deliver a curriculum unless children ask for it (and even then, they don't insist that the child follows through). Instead, they focus on creating an environment within which children can learn. They do this through facilitating intrinsic motivation – something which you can read more about in Daniel Pink's popular book *Drive* (Pink, 2010). This requires an environment of emotional and physical safety, within which the children can make choices. The environment isn't just about physical things. It's also about a space within which young people feel valued and listened to. You can see this in Figure 4.1. Self-directed education isn't about leaving children to get on with it. Adults have a very active role in facilitating this. There must be good relationships, and there must be interesting and meaningful opportunities. Within this context, the child has autonomy, but this autonomy is supported by the adults around them. They are supported to make choices, rather than left to figure things out.

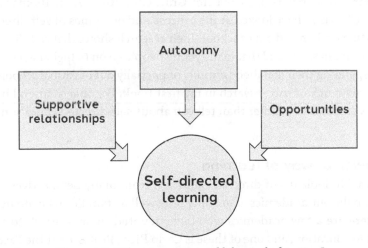

Figure 4.1: What goes into a self-directed education?

Does it work?

The first question most parents have about self-directed education is about outcome. 'Can it really work?' they ask. In fact, they often want guarantees that it will work for their specific child.

There's a problem with looking at the outcomes of self-directed education. A self-directed education isn't simply a way to end up at the same place as school but with less pressure. Traditional studies of education use standardised exam results as their outcome measure, but this makes no sense for self-directed education. We have to allow for diversity of outcome – for the young person who sets up their own business at 16, or another who takes exams at the age of 20.

This diversity of outcome makes self-directed education hard to evaluate, and certainly impossible to compare with more traditional forms of education. It makes no sense to give everyone a test or to compare exam results, because exam results are not the aim. The process and the aim are far more intertwined than that. Curious, engaged young people who are interested in the world and who feel that they can make a difference to their lives are what self-directed educators aim to facilitate, and also what might be considered a successful outcome.

Given this, the only way to really evaluate self-directed education is by asking adults who were educated in this way whether they felt prepared for life and whether they felt held back by their lack of formal schooling. This is exactly what researchers have done, looking at both unschoolers and at the outcomes of schools such as Summerhill and Sudbury Valley School. Academic researchers such as Peter Gray, Gina Riley, Alan Thomas and Harriet Pattison have looked at the process and outcomes of self-directed education both in and out of school. Their research shows that self-directed education can work, and that many young people go on to higher education after spending their childhood entirely or partially out of formal schooling. I covered much of this research in my first book. For this chapter, I hope mostly to show you rather than tell you about self-directed education.

A powerful way of learning

I wanted to look at self-directed education from many perspectives, and so I sought out academics who study it as well as families who are living it. There are a few academics who have devoted their research to self-directed education, and one of these is Carlo Ricci, Professor at the Faculty of Education, Graduate Studies at Nipissing University, Canada. We had a fascinating talk in the midst of lockdown via video call. He has spent years thinking and writing about self-directed learning (which he calls a range of different things, including self-determined and willed learning) and kindly agreed to tell me some of his thoughts. He starts off by defining it.

It's where the learner then gets to decide what to learn, when to learn, where to learn and for how long. They choose whether to opt in or opt out. It's about freedom and empowerment.

He told me about his experience working in education and academia and how self-directed education is often invisible.

Many people that I speak to with PhDs in education, they've never met an unschooler or a homeschooler. They've never been to a free school or a democratic school, but they do know one thing about it, and it's that it's 'not good'.

For those in positions of power, self-determined learning is just not one of those things that they choose to promote. Schools started about 150–200 years ago, and they were always about controlling people's minds and bodies. We can see the remnants of that today.

This has been my experience too. When I talk to educators about self-directed education they have very vague ideas about what it actually is, but very strong ideas that it doesn't work. People start to mutter about *Lord of the Flies* whenever they hear about children who can make choices about what they learn. Recently, someone asked me if I would allow my children to murder other people, in the name of choice. It's an insight into just how extreme these ideas feel.

Ricci's way of understanding education is fundamentally different from mainstream schooling. He doesn't think that everyone should be obliged to learn the same things.

There are people who want to do math, and people who want to do physics and chemistry and biology and singing and dancing, and all kinds of interesting things. We should be supporting all of those, rather than creating this fantasy that there's certain bits of information that every single human being in the world needs to know. It's just not true. In fact, it's harmful.

I always say that schools don't create opportunities, they actually limit opportunities. Those who are traditionally marginalised, continue to be marginalised. If you want to be a doctor, or a lawyer, schools are a gatekeeping mechanism to keep people out who are capable, but don't, for whatever reason, have the particular grade or whatever it is. Schools keep people out of professions that they could do very well in.

At the same time as traditional education not enabling people to learn the things they want to learn, Ricci feels that one of the downsides of schooling is that it doesn't allow much space for doing things that we enjoy, but that we might not be good at.

I don't think we should just focus on strengths. I think education should be focusing on whatever interests and passions we have. For example, I'm a horrible singer and I still want to sing. People shouldn't say to me, 'Well, you're a horrible singer. I think you should stop.' Same with swimming. If I'm not a very strong swimmer, but I love being in the water and swimming, I should be able to swim. Even though it's not my strength, if it's my passion, I should be able to do that as well because I love it and it makes me happy. Even though I can't paint or I can't do whatever it is, I can't do math, but I want to. Then, I should be doing it.

I think that's one of the things that school takes away from us, the pleasure of doing something that we don't do well.

I asked him about those who are disabled or have different abilities.

I think what we need to do for children with disabilities is to listen more and support. By support, I don't mean what is usually meant, which is, let's create a curriculum for them. I mean listening to what they are interested in and passionate about and allowing them to explore that if they choose to. Then if they realise that it's not something they're interested in, they can go in a different direction.

I think good pedagogy is good pedagogy for everybody. It doesn't matter if you're young or old, it doesn't matter whatever your abilities are and what your interests are, it's all the same. It's all about allowing the individual themselves to figure out what interests and passions they have and where they want to go.

I think school does a poor job of all types of learning. I think that being embedded in a natural environment is where you would thrive the most.

But, I asked him, shouldn't we teach children certain skills early on, or risk them never learning them? Might we let children down by not insisting that they learn reading and maths early on? What about those with dyslexia, shouldn't we be starting extra reading support as early as possible? Ricci doesn't think that we should take a different approach because a child has difficulties with a particular skill.

> Regardless of age, and regardless of who we are, what we need to know is what we need to know in the moment. There is no critical period for learning any academic subject. If you could learn it when you're in grade two, you could certainly learn it when you're 22. There's no urgency in any of this, we just need to know what we need to know, in this moment in our life.
>
> We might start with, do you need to cook for yourself, do you need to clean? How about laundry and getting dressed and personal hygiene? You could look at it as starting from the self and then moving out to the community. Then it would be about what you need to know that would be beneficial for your community. Do you have to shovel snow?
>
> Who knows what it is – but what it should not be is taking somebody and putting them in a classroom and trying to get them to do things that they have no interest or passion for. That makes no sense.

Ricci calls what he talks about 'holistic, self-determined education', learning that is always driven by the learner, and where therefore the learner spends their time doing what is important to them. He's clearly passionate about it.

The structure of self-directed education

There is no imposed curriculum in self-directed education. Seeing progress is not as simple as testing children and seeing them move from Year 1 to Year 13, via a few other classes in between. However, there is a wider structure, and it's one that is driven by child development. In my conversations with parents, clear patterns emerged as to how self-directed education changes as children grow. Children's way of approaching the world changes as they get older, and when they are outside school we get to see that process gradually unfolding. It happens at different ages and in different ways, depending on the individual.

Discovery learning

Young children learn though discovery. This doesn't mean they discover things without input – in fact, a crucial part of their learning is usually asking questions of everyone around them. It means that they are in a state of active enquiry, and they interact with their environment in that way – a process which Alison Gopnik, Professor of Psychology and Philosophy at Berkeley University, writes about in her book (Gopnik, 2017). They ask, they explore, they experiment. They are curious, and they look for answers. They do a lot of this through play.

Self-directed children often continue to spend most of their time in play at least until they approach their teens, and sometimes well into adolescence. Peter Gray, Professor of Psychology at Boston College, argues that the urge to play is a natural drive which enables children to educate themselves, alongside curiosity (which drives them to explore) and sociability (which enables them to learn from others) (Gray, 2013). Curiosity provides the stimulus and play is how they develop their skills.

Some children play very differently to others – and right in line with how our culture usually deals with difference, we have defined an apparently ideal 'norm' and we see deviations from that in terms of deficit, rather than as different but legitimate pathways of development. Self-directed education is an opportunity to do something different, and to embrace all sorts of play, at all sorts of ages.

Many children have really different play preferences and development to those expected by society. In early childhood, when they are expected to play with dolls and diggers, they may be fascinated with washing machines or spinning wheels. Or they may only be interested in very active play, tearing round the house or park and jumping over the furniture. Their play may be sensory, tearing up paper or chewing things. Some are really interested in letters and numbers early on, lining up magnetic letter sets and copying them out carefully. Others are fascinating by video games, or play the same thing over and over. Some children love to play with a group, while others only play alone.

Unschooling mothers gave me rich and vivid descriptions of their children's discovery learning. Sarah, an American unschooler, has four children under the age of seven. The elder two are both non-speaking autistic. She told me about watching her three-year-old son's way of interacting with the world and seeing the things he loves and finds joy in.

> My son loves to bounce all the time and he is obsessed with textures. He will go around and pick at paper and cardboard and plastic and rubber and silicone and all these different textures, and play with them. That's his favourite thing right now, which doesn't sound to you and me maybe as something that's useful, but for him, he gets such joy out of it. It's also

annoying because it means he rips up paper. We used to have the books out where anybody could grab them at any time. At the moment, they are sort of locked up in a separate room. They still have access throughout the day, but not unsupervised...

They love to just run around. My son especially loves to go on walks around the neighbourhood and look at the cars. The feeling of cars, the touching of textures. For a long time, my husband bought him dozens of little toy cars but he's not much interested in toy cars anymore. He loves to go and touch the tyres and the grills. He will stop and stare at ceiling fans or spinning things, fidget spinners or whatever. He was really into flicking on and off light switches for about three or four months. He doesn't do that so much anymore.

Schools move children on from their play, deliberately, in favour of formal learning, particularly if their play is not of a type which is valued. Parents of children whose play is atypical are sometimes coached on ways to encourage them in typical play. The focus is something we see across conventional education. When children do something different, the aim of adults is to pull them back to the 'norm', whether that is a difference in levels of activity, in how they choose to spend their time, or in how they interact with others.

This doesn't happen in self-directed education. Children play for as long as they want to, and when they are allowed to do so something interesting happens. Many of the types of play which society thinks about as for younger children, happen later in childhood and persist for longer. Unusual play is supported in the same way as any other type of play, because children are supported to do more of what they enjoy.

When this happens, we see very different and non-conventional developmental trajectories.

Go along to any home education group and you'll see just how different these developmental trajectories can be. You'll see children who started to play imaginatively for the first time when they were aged seven or eight, years, beyond the age when most children are said to start imaginative play (and when most schooled children are no longer spending hours in this type of play). This play is frequently connected to video games that they play. You'll see children who seemed to have no interest at all in narrative and books discovering *Minecraft*, where they start to make and tell stories and do role plays. You'll see children starting to invent games and invite others to play having never shown any interest in making things for others before. You'll see a really rich interaction between children's interests and their play, with games of 'Real-Life Minecraft' taking place in the local park. You'll also see mixed-age play, and how older children often scaffold the play of those who need more support.

Rebecca is a British unschooling mother of two. Her children are aged five and ten. Her five-year-old is autistic and also has complex medical needs. She describes how her older son Jacob scaffolds imaginative play for his brother Malachi and how Malachi's play has changed over time.

> For Malachi, video games are his main love. He really loves a good video game. He's very skilled at them. He likes watching YouTube videos about stuff. He really struggles with socialising. He actively avoids socialising, in fact, which can be tricky to balance. They have very different needs in that way. Even when we drop Jacob at the group, Malachi is anxious about it. He doesn't like to be there because of the other children. It can be tricky.
>
> He has things that he's really passionately interested about for a period of time and then that's kind of out the window. Then he doesn't really know what to do with himself for a while and he sort of wanders around. He likes being with me. He likes asking lots of questions, and just sort of

pottering around. He likes going on trains and bus rides. He likes to sit in a coffee shop. He likes things like shelling eggs and he really loves kneading dough. Then there's other things that he just really isn't interested in that you would assume he might be interested in, like watching TV shows.

He is quite sensory seeking in a lot of ways but then he's avoidant in other ways. We thought about Forest School for a while, and the idea of being outside and doing fires. We'd agreed that I would stay with him. He tried it for a little while. I think we had been three times and he said, 'I've done it now.' I said, 'You know, the idea is that you keep going.' And he's like, 'No, no, but I've done it. I've been there. I've seen the place. It's done. I know what's gonna happen.' So he doesn't do that anymore.

He loves playing with Jacob and they play together a lot: video games, or they make up games. Jacob frames the whole game, even down to when he'll say, 'And now you say this'. And then Malachi will say it. Jacob scaffolds the whole play for him and Malachi really loves that. But if you just say to Malachi, 'Do you want to just play?' Or, 'What do you want to play?' He'll say, 'I don't know. I just don't know.' But when Jacob is scaffolding things for him, then he'll say, 'Oh, yeah, I could say this.' And I can see that he comes out of himself a lot more than within that frame that Jacob has created for him.

Until Malachi was about five, he would only play independently. For the longest time, puzzles were the only thing that he wanted to do. He would do loads of puzzles by himself and he did not want to be helped to solve the puzzle. Before that, he really liked stacking things for a long time. This lasted a really long time. It's only been in the last year that they've played together like that. Before that, they used to do chasing games. They weren't really speaking, it was more just about movement and playing together. It's only recently that the more imaginative play has started. But it's not something that Malachi ever does independently of Jacob. He only does it when he's playing with Jacob.

Rebecca refers here to something which many parents told me about – how their children started doing things later on in childhood than many other children. Her son started playing collaboratively for the first time when he was over five, at a time when the school system has moved on from play and when children at school are being encouraged to think of playing as something for break time. We think of school as providing opportunities, but what if, through its standardised structure, it stifles them too? What if it prevents some children from going through the developmental stages which they would naturally go through in their own time?

There's a lot written in the child developmental literature about the importance of imaginative play, and lots of concern when children don't play imaginatively. It's thought to be an important way for children to learn skills such as social perspective taking, flexibility, social reciprocity and problem solving. Parents of self-directed children told me that imaginative play emerged in many different and natural ways in later childhood.

The imaginative play they told me about in later childhood is often more sophisticated than the tea-parties of the early years, and incorporates things they have learnt. It's less likely to be about playing shops than about complex social dramas or exploratory expeditions (although playing school did come up quite often, interestingly for those who never attended school). It may often take place within the context of a video game (particularly sandbox games like *Minecraft*), which means that parents are less likely to value or even notice it, or it may be a deep dive into a special interest.

Alice told me about her nine-year-old daughter, who spends hours playing imaginary games about dogs with her younger friend.

> My daughter is very sociable, but she doesn't crave being with other children. She has one friend who she met during lockdown here. It was our neighbour's daughter, who's six. They play together for hours. They play with these toy horses and things, huge kind of imaginary games. Her learning has been mostly dogs and animals. Her reading was all about signposts and cereal packets. We have a child's dog breed book and she would want to find out what breed every dog was. When she was little, she didn't want to go to the playground, instead she wanted to go to the dog park in the town. There's a dog park where people run their dogs and everyone knew her. We have a dog that we borrow here that we take walks.
>
> She likes to be in nature. She's very creative. She makes things. She loves David Attenborough, and she watches documentaries. And learning wise, she is different again. Her brothers are very interested in facts: history, geography, politics, economics – I mean, they're phenomenal. They'll debate for hours and hours. I think that is a bit too much for her. She's all about animals.

The research on the importance of play is seriously at odds with how we value play in the school system. Most of the research on play is with the under-fives. In the school system, children are moved on from play by the age of six or seven. Play is for playtime or after school. It isn't the way schooled children spend most of their time, and isn't valued in the same way as formal learning. Mastery learning is what schools aim for.

Mastery learning

The gradual maturation of the brain makes a different type of learning possible. Whereas learning in the earlier part of childhood is play-based, entirely based on interest and enjoyment and is very much about the moment, as the self-control system matures children become more capable of thinking about the future and planning (Gopnik, 2017). This means that they can start to learn more intentionally, rather than simply as a by-product of doing something that they love.

This isn't to denigrate discovery learning, rather simply to say that most young children do not set out to improve their fine motor skills or their handwriting. They set out to build a Lego house or draw a picture, and their fine motor skills improve as a side-effect. As children get older, learning becomes more deliberate, and they start to plan ahead when they would like to improve at something. Of course, there will still be incidental learning going on all the time – you might be working on improving your roller blading, and as a side product you learn to balance, and now you can ice skate too.

Clara is an American unschooling mother of four. She told me about her older children, now teenagers, and what she sees them learning.

My oldest son has been studying Japanese for about three years. He started with YouTube videos. Then he asked me for some flashcards. He got a bunch of books about Japanese and the etiquette there, all the things. Then a year ago, he finally said, I want to take some classes to talk to other people. He's now up to three classes a week. I've just noticed in my own life that with the kids who want more structure, they can create more structure. If they want less structure, they can create less structure. They all have structure, but it doesn't necessarily look like how I would have structured it. That's the whole thing. They create the structure that they need. When they need help, they ask for help.

This type of learning is called 'mastery' learning and it develops gradually throughout middle childhood and adolescence. You can see it happening when a child decides that they want to improve their skateboarding, and spends hours practising a trick. You can see it happening when they decide they want to beat the Ender Dragon in *Minecraft*, and spend hours planning out their strategy and then implementing it – and then trying again when they fail.

This is the type of learning which makes it possible for self-directed young people to study for exams or go to college, if they want to. Sometimes at the start of self-directed education, parents think that all learning will continue to be through discovery and play, as it is in early childhood. They wonder how a young person will ever learn the GCSE maths curriculum through spending their days playing video games or climbing trees. They think that mastery learning has to be forced or it won't happen.

The answer is that if they need to learn a curriculum for an exam, they can choose to do so by whatever means works for them, just as an adult might. They might attend a class, they might study by themselves from a book or they might work with a tutor. They don't have to go back to the start of the primary school curriculum because a lot of that will have been picked up along the way. They are likely to make rapid progress because they will be motivated.

Katharine has five autistic children and is autistic herself. She told me how thinking about the future has changed how her teenagers set about their learning.

It's been different this year, because my older two are now 15 and 13. They're thinking that they do want to access college at some point. We've been looking at the options; we're quite lucky that there are some colleges nearby that have a 14–16 provision. As a result, my eldest, who's now 15, has made a concerted effort and started doing more formal learning.

We're really hoping that come September, my oldest two will attend a college. My eldest just wants to focus and do his maths and his English GCSE. That's our big goal at the moment. That's given them a bit of focus. And they've chosen, therefore, to do a bit more formal learning.

Many self-directed young people do not choose to take exams at the same time as schooled young people, and will instead have other priorities.

India, 14 years old, has been out of school since she was six. She told me about how she learns.

I have really got into books. I've actually just finished a series called *Murder Most Unladylike*. I really enjoy reading those. I don't read that often. I do want to, I just don't. I don't have as many strong passions as most autistic people do. I have phases of what I like. If I like something else, I sort of space it out and still remember my other stuff to do while doing that.

I just decide I want to learn about something. Whether or not I do is another matter, but if I do it, then I think I'm aware of it. I think it all falls quite nicely into place. When I decide I want to learn or do something, it's usually because that thing is perfect for me right now, it would be really useful and I'm interested in it.

Alice's son is also not planning to take exams any time soon, but is deeply committed to learning, particularly languages. He has also become interested in attending groups and clubs, having found this difficult before.

He's just turned 15. At the moment, he's learning languages, and it's quite incredible. He spends about three to four hours a day on these languages. This is a guy who pretty much gamed for two years. Now, he was concerned on Christmas Day about taking the day off his work. And he's learning to code.

The last year between the lockdowns, when we were allowed out, he started going to quite a lot of different clubs and things. I can see that his sense of safety is increasing. And he's able to do things on his own terms. He knows himself. Now he wants to start study groups. So now he wants me to set up some kind of study group that he can be a part of, so he can learn with other people.

Practice is a strange thing. School puts a lot of emphasis on practice, and requires children to practise skills by repeating them. Reading, handwriting, number skills, all of these are learnt through enforced repetitive practice. Homework is often about repetitive practice. However, school children are typically not practising because *they* want to improve their skills. They are practising because someone else wants them to do so.

Psychologically, there is a significant difference, even though they may look the same. Writing out a hundred words because someone else makes you feels very different from writing out a hundred words because you yourself want to improve your handwriting. The first case is tedious, the second has purpose. Practising because you've been made to is going through the motions, practising because you want to improve is like switching the power on. It wasn't unusual for parents to tell me that their self-directed teenagers practised things like languages, coding or writing for hours every day, and that they could see a dramatic improvement in their skills. They described their teenagers setting themselves highly challenging goals – fluency in several languages, for example, or spending a year in Asia.

Several parents told me that when they were younger they weren't sure their children were learning, but when they looked back, they could see how development was always happening. Sallie's daughter Madeleine is now 17 and studying for A-levels at home. Sallie reflected on the process.

> I think that it gets easier as you see it working. The reality is if a child wants to achieve something, they'll find the way. Mads did not really write at all until she got to her GCSEs. And now she sits down and does it. Yes, it's a slow process. But you know, she does all the research for her essays.
>
> The most important thing is giving them the tools so they can do it. It helps if you've got people around you and home education groups that are like-minded.

I think there has to be an honesty in home education groups because school parents will say things like, 'Oh, yes. Well, mine is doing Pythagoras.'

In home education, there often is that honesty of 'Oh, well, you know, mine just sits down and wants to paint with red paint this week.'

Just wanting to play with red paint...many parents told me how this stage went on for far longer than they had anticipated when they started self-directed education. At the ages of nine and ten, children were still spending most of their time in play, and showed little interest in setting any sorts of goals or systematic practice.

In schools, children are moved on from the discovery stage of learning early because mastery learning is valued more highly. Children are made to practise skills, in the belief that this is how they will learn best. In self-directed education, this change happens when the child is ready and not before. Parents reported a qualitative shift in how young people approached learning, which usually started around puberty. Without being forced, young people start to learn in quite a different way as they mature. They practise skills because they want to improve. Teenagers and parents of teenagers described this change happening, whether they chose to do exams or not.

FIVE-POINT SUMMARY

1. Self-directed education involves learners retaining control over what they learn, how they learn it and when they stop.
2. Self-directed education changes over time, from play-based/discovery learning to mastery-based learning in middle childhood and adolescence.
3. Self-directed learning means that different developmental trajectories can have time to unfold. This may be particularly important for children who do things in a very different order from other children.
4. Parents report the change from discovery to mastery learning occurring naturally and not needing to be forced.
5. Self-directed teenagers set themselves challenging goals, use a variety of ways to learn and see themselves as active agents in their learning.

CHAPTER 5

THE SAFE TO LEARN PYRAMID: FOUNDATIONS OF SELF-DIRECTED EDUCATION

Introduction

This is when this book becomes practical. The first four chapters have been about theory and experience of neurodiversity, learning and self-directed education. From now on in, it's more about actually how to do it. You may have turned here directly, although I think you'll get more out of it if you have read the other chapters first. If your child is not attending school you probably want to rush in with what you think of as 'learning' – perhaps signing your child up for courses or joining groups, because you are feeling anxious about how little like school their life looks. Relax. It's okay. Give yourself some time. This is a very common experience of parents when they decide to try an alternative to school. They want to be doing something, showing that it is working. If your child has had assessments done, you may be worried about those recommendations and whether what you offer ticks their boxes.

Many of the parents I talk to in my clinical practice or on the courses I run are confused and worried. They often have a vision of what self-directed education will look like, perhaps based on reading on online groups, or books about unschooling – and that isn't what is happening in their homes. They want to start exploring the world, but their children aren't doing what they expected. They pay for fun courses, buy entertaining books or suggest days out at the beach, but their children say no. Parents ask me whether self-directed education can really work for autistic children, or those with ADHD or a PDA profile. They expected their children to explore the world – but instead they are stuck at home watching YouTube videos on repeat.

I'd like to encourage you to take a deep breath and put your great ideas on hold for a while. The parents I talked to told me a consistent story about how self-directed education worked with their neurodivergent children. They said that while they might have started with expectations of how their children would be learning which involved lots of adventure and activities, in fact they had to step back and start with focusing on relationships and safety.

Talking to these parents led me to develop a model which I use to encapsulate the process of self-directed education. This model applies to all children, but particularly to those who experience life in a different way or who have had a very bad time at school (these two things often come together). Through the following chapters I'm going to suggest that you think about approaching self-directed education as a pyramid. At the bottom of that pyramid comes safety, connection and acceptance, and that's where you have to start.

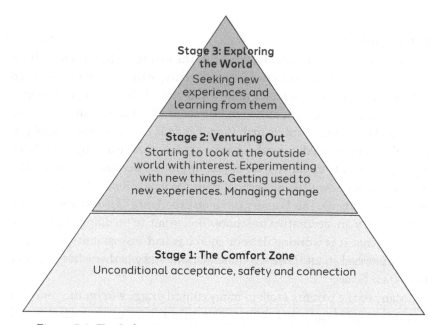

Stage 3: Exploring the World
Seeking new experiences and learning from them

Stage 2: Venturing Out
Starting to look at the outside world with interest. Experimenting with new things. Getting used to new experiences. Managing change

Stage 1: The Comfort Zone
Unconditional acceptance, safety and connection

Figure 5.1: The Safe to Learn Pyramid: A model of self-directed education

At the top of the pyramid is what we often think of as 'learning' – a child engaged in an activity or process which challenges them and which they are finding stimulating. New experiences and information. Questions and interaction. But many children can't start there, particularly if they have recently left school, or if there are other reasons why their nervous system might be on high alert. Challenges need to come later because at first anything outside the comfort zone feels like a threat.

I call this the Safe to Learn Pyramid (Figure 5.1), and the rest of the book can be seen through that lens. This chapter runs through the pyramid, explains it and gives some examples. Chapters 6–7 are about how to establish the sorts of relationships which help children to self-direct their learning. Chapters 8–9 are about starting to expand beyond the Comfort Zone (and particularly about ways in which parents can work with children to do this), and Chapters 10–12 are about what self-directed learning can look like when it's working and how children acquire new skills.

This chapter gives you an overview of the model and how children progress through the different stages.

Free to learn – but why aren't they?

When you read books and internet discussions about self-directed education, it can be easy to get the idea that when given the chance to do so, children explore freely, and when they do that, they will learn. There's sometimes a kind of utopian picture painted, of children engaging in hours of unstructured-by-an-adult mixed-age play, and through this acquiring all sorts of skills and knowledge. For some children, this is exactly how it works. For others, it isn't so simple. They just don't seem to know what to do with unstructured time. They don't want to spend hours hanging out with others. They don't enjoy being outdoors for extended periods and they prefer to play alone or with an adult. They don't want to try anything new because it makes them anxious. Some of them seem bored and unhappy, but don't like the idea of any new activities.

Their parents worry that self-directed education just won't work for these children, that they need school. They think that maybe they need to be made to learn, or at least made to comply with a structure.

In my experience, these children do benefit from a self-directed education (and also often find hardest to access a conventional school education), but it requires some extra thought and patience on the part of their parents. They need a lot more support to be autonomous. There isn't a short-cut to self-directed learning. It must start with the child and their environment, emotional wellbeing and physiological state. This is part of why it is so valuable for children whose development is unusual. It starts with the child, exactly as they are.

At school, education is mostly about the academics. It's about learning information and remembering it over time. It's about reading and writing, skills and knowledge. If a child is succeeding at learning academic subjects, they may be successful in the eyes of the school, even if they are desperately unhappy.

In order to keep children focused on learning, schools often use a system of control, with incentives and sanctions. These strategies oblige the children to comply, no matter how they feel about it. This means that how the child feels about it all is less important – they are being made to comply, regardless of their feelings. It can look like children are really engaging in learning – at the top of the pyramid – when in fact they are going through the motions because they feel they have no choice. That's the short-cut school tries to take to learning, using control by extrinsic motivation instead of nurturing intrinsic motivation.

In self-directed education, the whole thing is flipped around. The child remains in control of their learning, just as they were when they were very young. Adults are very involved but they don't control what the child learns. Instead, they work on creating the circumstances for intrinsic motivation to flourish, for young people to follow their interests and to grow and explore. The very nature of this means that learning can't be forced. It will happen when the children are ready and interested and not before.

For some children, this is easy – give them opportunities and they are off. For others, it's harder and takes more time. Learning comes naturally to all, but some children find the world itself more challenging and just managing day-to-day living takes up more effort. They need more support, and for them, establishing the base of the pyramid takes more time and effort.

The Safe to Learn Pyramid

Instead of starting with maths and reading, the Safe to Learn Pyramid starts with emotional wellbeing, the Comfort Zone. Getting that in place means that children can be freed up to focus on other things, and that's when the learning starts to flow. This can happen both in the short term – over the course of a few hours – and in the longer term. When a child doesn't feel safe, they may temporarily not be able to explore again, and need to re-establish safety. Parents sometimes see this as regression, but it doesn't mean that children have lost their skills. It means that right now, they don't feel safe enough to do the things they were doing before.

Stage 1: The Comfort Zone

How do we help a child feel safe? It's about far more than the physical environment. It's about them feeling safe with the adults around them, and safe in the knowledge that whatever they do, those adults will be there for them and will still care about them. Carl Rogers, psychologist and founder of person-centred counselling, called this 'unconditional positive regard'. This doesn't mean that the child can do anything or have everything they want, but it does mean that they are not shamed or punished for not meeting expectations. They get the message that they are acceptable and they can be themselves, just as they are.

The three 'P's
The Comfort Zone has three components which all need to come together. These are the physical, physiological and psychological (Figure 5.2). In the middle is the sweet spot, where a person feels safe and is able to learn.

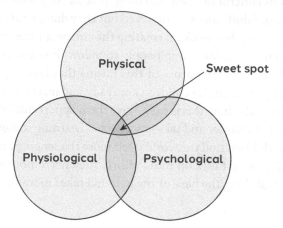

Figure 5.2: The three 'P's (based on the biopsychosocial model by George Engel)

The physical space is the environment and there's no quick way to get this right. There is no one environment which fits all. For many children, it means having a private area where they will not be interrupted, or having noise-cancelling headphones or ear defenders so they can get away from noise. Others might prefer noise and bustle, and lots of other people around.

For some families, this means setting up their house in such as way so as to support their children's needs, perhaps with a gaming room, or a simple soft-play room with mattresses to bounce on. When my children were young we had a room designated the 'calming room' with indoor swings, exercise mats, a mini DVD player and soft toys. Whenever anyone came over to visit, this room was reserved for the children to use if they needed a calming space, no questions asked and no pressure to come out. Other families have small tents for the same purpose, or a den under a child's bed. The physical space is also about finding groups where the child's behaviour is accepted, or finding friends whose approach aligns with your own. It's not an easy process and there will be plenty of mistakes along the way. You don't have to get everything right from the start, and their needs will change as they grow. It's a constant process of refinement and experimentation.

Many children find that sensory stimulation or exercise helps them to regulate their emotions. Indoor swings or climbing equipment, mini-trampolines, baths or sensory play with things such as slime or playdough are all things that children can find calming, depending on their sensory needs. I can't tell you exactly what your child will prefer, because that's something which you will only find out by watching your child. If they like to rock, find things which they can rock with. If they like to climb, find safe ways to climb. If they like water, have lots of baths. If they like to wrap themselves up tight, find ways to do that safely. There are books you can find with different sensory activities – if your child will try activities, give them a go. If they won't, then you could try them for yourself and see if they help you!

The physiological component is about biology – is the child getting enough of food that they can eat? Are they able to sleep and if not, can something be done about that? Can they rest when they need to? Can they eat and drink when they need to, and go to the toilet whenever they want? If a child isn't eating or sleeping enough, their body is going to be under stress and it will be harder for them to learn. Some schools have food policies which mean that children cannot take in the food they prefer to eat – these policies are well meaning and usually focused on health, but they can make it harder for a child who is already struggling to cope with their day.

The final element, and often the hardest for parents, is the psychological. This is about relationships and whether the child feels safe in their relationships, particularly with their parents but also with siblings or other frequent visitors to the house.

Alice is a highly experienced mother of three self-directed learners. She told me about holding the space for her 15-year-old son. She first talks about establishing safety and unconditional acceptance.

We've given him space and support. I see it as just a nurturing space. It's really about just saying, he is who he is. And me not being triggered by him, giving him space and not imposing on him my own issues. So if he says something like, 'Be quiet', then I have to go. He's not being rude. He's saying that he's overwhelmed. I'll say, 'Okay, I'll move.' Then a minute later he'll come, he'll give me a big hug and go, 'Oh, I'm really sorry. I just got really overwhelmed.'

He needs space to allow him to just be. It's like a little dance really. He'll say, 'Oh, I'm really interested in this', or, 'Did you know that?' And then, it's that dance of me grabbing something. I might say, 'Oh, yeah. Sounds interesting. Can I help you in any way?'

When I go too far, he says, 'Oh, no, no, I don't want to do that anymore.'

Because I push, he will say, 'Yeah, definitely don't want to do that. Because you want me to do that.' Then I back off.

Please, thank you. Good boy

When I was a trainee psychologist, I worked on an in-patient unit with an autistic boy. He had very little spoken language, and he was highly anxious. Whenever he felt under pressure, or when asked a question he couldn't answer, his reply was always, 'Please, thank you. Good boy'. Sometimes he would say it even when not asked. He'd learnt that the words 'please' and 'thank you' were often what adults were looking for, and that this would be followed by 'Good boy' if he got it right. He was trying to offer the adults what they wanted, in a confusing world full of demands.

A lot of conventional parenting and education is about control. Parenting books advise parents on how best to control their children, whether that is through praise, punishments or star charts. Some behaviours are desirable, others are not. For some children, this isn't a big deal, because they naturally fall in line with what their parents expect. For children who don't fit the mould, this can mean that their whole life becomes a litany of the ways in which they should be behaving differently or responding differently. They are surrounded by negativity. They start to be on edge, waiting to get something wrong, or they try really hard to get it right, even if they don't really know what 'right' means.

Stepping away from the 'Please, thank you. Good boy' paradigm is hard. Parents need to provide an environment that is psychologically safe – which means that children know that they are loved, no matter what, and that their choices are valued. This doesn't mean that they can do whatever they want, nor that they can always make the choices they want to make. Hitting other people, for example, doesn't make for a safe environment, and parents need to be clear that these behaviours aren't acceptable and they must intervene (more about behaviour in Chapter 9). But it does mean that children know that their choices will be respected when possible, and that they will not be shamed for simply being themselves. It means that they can say no to suggestions, knowing that their parents will take that on board, even if they can't always accommodate every request.

Stage 1 doesn't look a lot like what others think of as 'education' and so it's easy for parents to underestimate how important it is. This is about preparing the ground, building the foundations for both children and parents. It's the stage when parents have to get alongside their children, right where they are, and join them without judgement. Learn to see the world through their eyes, and you will become better able to plan for success.

This is particularly difficult for parents who have been focused on interventions and skill development – or who have got used to seeing their children through a deficit model. It's easy to get used to thinking about the things your child can't do, and to spend your time trying to help them learn those things. Starting at the base of the pyramid requires letting that go, and focusing on them just as they are.

Stage 2: Venturing Out

When the Comfort Zone has been established, it can be tempting to stay right there. Everyone is calmer and safer, after all, and things are often a lot better than they were in the past. Some families live for years without doing anything that might rock the boat, it just doesn't seem to be worth the risk. They know they don't want to go back to how things were before the Comfort Zone was in place.

The problem with this is that children need new experiences and opportunities to learn. The Comfort Zone can start to feel like a padded cage when you can't leave it. Staying inside and doing the same thing for ten years is not going to have as much potential for learning as having new experiences and leaving the house. One aim of self-directed education is that children can learn about the things they care about, and we need to help them develop skills so they can do that.

This is a challenge, and many parents find it makes *them* very anxious, particularly if they have managed to establish an equilibrium after some very unstable years. It's like walking a tightrope, finding new ways to help children learn while also keeping a foot in the Comfort Zone. Often, the easiest way to do this is to start with what the child values and enjoys, and to do more of that, find new people to do that with, or find an extension of something they already do. It might be as straightforward as finding a new YouTuber and watching that together.

What counts as a new experience for each child will be different; for some, it might be that a first step is sitting in a different place in the car, or going to a different bus stop. Sometimes just thinking about doing something differently might be enough for a while, and then when the idea becomes less unusual, it's the time to actually do it.

For many families, venturing 'out' in fact starts at home. Home is usually a safe place, and so bringing new experiences into home can often be less overwhelming than jumping right in with outside events. If a child has a special interest, that is a great place to start. Is there a new person who could come and talk about their special interest with them? Or maybe play their favourite game, or watch their favourite programme? Another child might be possible, but often an adult will be a more predictable new person to get used to. Home-educated teenagers are often free during the day, and may be able to come and hang out with younger children, joining them in what they do. Relatives are another possibility. You need someone who will come regularly and who will be unfazed if they are totally ignored the first few times they come, or told loudly to go away. Taking things personally isn't an option.

Katharine told me about the process of gradually doing new things with her five children, and how she found that low pressure was essential.

I know that what works for us is low pressure, basically, following their lead. Even to the extent of being able to drop stuff. The few things we did do, we always did in a very ad hoc, optional kind of way. So, for example, with PE I organised it at the community centre. It was lovely, it was a drop-in event and it was very chilled. Mostly it was me making brews for other mums. The way it would work is that we would all go along as a family. I knew for sure my older two would join in but my younger ones may or may not. It didn't matter. There wasn't that pressure of 'we're attending, we're paying, you're expected to do this'. Everything has always been optional. I swear that's the key to our success.

EXERCISE: EXPANDING THE ZONE

Observe your child again, but this time, look to see if you can identify places where you could change things a little, just to expand what they are experiencing and their opportunities. Don't focus on what you think they should be doing, but on how you could help them to do more of what they enjoy. Write down any ideas you have, even the silly ones. Then go back and look, are any of them realistic? Might your child be ready to give any of them a go? If they like playing on an iPad, could you find new apps? If they like particular games, are there extensions? Is there anything that they themselves say they would like to do, and how could you help that happen? Sometimes children prefer suggestions from other young people to suggestions from parents, so finding people to hang out with is part of this too.

Alice, who you heard about earlier, told me how this started happening for her son.

Over this past year, it's been like moving out into the world, slowly moving out into the wild. To see that person functioning in that way is phenomenal. Part of the reason he can is because he knows he has choices. He can come to me tomorrow and say, 'I'm not doing carpentry anymore' and I'll say, 'That's great'. Everything he does is free choice. What we've given him is autonomy, which is what he has to have. If he doesn't, he's out of control. He's learning to live with his autonomy. And I think sometimes it is too much for him. There's too much to choose, he gets overwhelmed by who he'll be in the future and where he will go. And that's when perhaps it's just time for a big hug and to let him know that you know it's all okay.

Some parents find it helps to think about this stage as a ladder, with small steps all the way up (Figure 5.3). Each rung needs to be repeated so that everyone is comfortable enough before going on up to the next stage. In this way, the Comfort Zone can be gradually expanded. Break things down into small steps, and practise each step until it feels easy. Be prepared for setbacks and for progress not to be linear. Some days it will be all about comfort and that's fine. This is one of the huge advantages of self-directed education – it can fit the child each day. There is no expectation that just because they did something yesterday, they'll be able to do it again today. If a child sleeps badly or just isn't feeling good, having a pyjama day is always an option.

Figure 5.3: A ladder of new experiences. This is only an example, the ladder itself will be specific to the child and what they find hard

Trying again – and again

Some children can have very strong reactions to a new experience – and then their parents back off and don't offer the experience again. The problem with this is that having a strong reaction is just how some children react the first time, and so if this means their parents stop trying this can mean that they are not able to do things.

Rosie came to see me about her daughter Lara, who was having a hard time doing anything new. She gave me an example. Lara had been wanting to go to the inflatable indoor play park for ages. Finally, the day came. They bought their tickets, went in, and Lara froze. It was noisy, echoey and unfamiliar. She panicked and started to cry. Her mother Rosie was devastated, they had been building up to this for weeks – and now it was all for nothing. They turned around and went home, with Rosie vowing never to try something like that again. Lara cried all the way home. This was happening again and again when they tried something new and Rosie was worried that Lara was being traumatised by her experiences.

The problem here was that Lara was someone who often panicked in new situations. Her mother was frightened by her panic, because she thought that meant Lara was being traumatised. Lara was never getting a chance to learn that actually she could get used to new situations even if she felt anxious at first. I encouraged them to go back to the play park on a quiet day, and not to worry if they didn't get through the door, but just to go and get familiar with it. Two weeks later Rosie rang to say they had been back three times to get used to it, and on the fourth time Lara had been able to go in and had had a great time. She couldn't wait to go back.

Table 5.1: Tips for venturing out

Plan for success	Don't be too ambitious. Going out for ten minutes and coming back happy is better than trying to get out for a whole day and everyone being miserable
Start where they are	What are they doing, and is there any way to gently expand on that?
Don't give up	The first time you go anywhere might be terrible. That's okay, it's the first time. Try again and reassure your child (and yourself) that lots of people find first times difficult
Reduce other stresses	If you're going out with a group of people and you know it will be hard to talk to them as well as manage your child, warn them in advance. Apologise and say you won't be able to talk and it isn't because you're being rude

Take enough food and drink	Trying to buy food and drink is intensely stressful with a hungry child. Take it with you if you can, and have an extra snack for emergencies
Don't push things too far	It's tempting when things are going well to try to stay longer or try one more thing – resist the urge to go too far. Better to leave when they still want to come back next time
Gradually extend what you are doing	When you're all able to do one thing, now is the time to try something just a bit more challenging
Talk about the process with your child	Make the process visible. Tell them that it gets easier to do things when we are familiar and that often the first time is hard. Don't make them feel that it's a failure to choose to go home when you've had enough

Are they ready to go back to school yet?

Oliver had been at school and was really unhappy there. His parents had decided to take him out to home educate, and immediately Oliver had appeared to regress. He stopped wearing clothes, would scream at visitors and refused to leave the house. His parents worked hard to help him feel safe at home, and to turn their relationship from one of control to one of support. It all went well, Oliver was visibly more relaxed and happier. Friends started to visit and they were even able to go out during the day. He was more responsive and started to express himself. As this happened, Oliver's father (who had never been totally convinced by the idea of home education) started to think that maybe he was ready to go back to school, that this time it would be different. He told Oliver that he thought he could manage school now. Things changed overnight. Oliver stopped getting dressed and refused to leave the house. It felt as if they were back to square one.

There's a pattern which often emerges with children who have been to school, and it's one which parents will need to deliberately set out to break. As a child feels more secure and confident, and is able to venture out more, the reaction of the adults around them is often to think that this is a sign that school (or a school-at-home curriculum, or 'proper learning' as it's sometimes phrased) can be reintroduced.

This puts the child in an impossible situation. They are feeling better because they are away from the pressure of school – but if they show signs of being happier, they will be made to go back to school, or made to follow a school-like curriculum. Then things will get worse again. They're stuck on a hamster wheel, unable to get better because of what it will mean for their lives.

In order to break this cycle, children need to know that they will not be made to go back to school, no matter how well others around them think that they are doing. If they want to go back to school that's different, but this should never be enforced on them as a result of an improvement in their wellbeing.

Stage 3: Exploring the World

When the bottom parts of the pyramid are securely in place, a young person can make decisions based on what they want to do and what interests them, rather than needing to prioritise safety and comfort, or pleasing a parent. It's at this point that learning can really start to flow and connections will be made. When this happens, sometimes the learning comes so fast that parents are dumbfounded. Children reveal things they have been learning, or rapidly acquire new skills such as reading, playing a musical instrument or making friends.

Emily told me about what this looks like for her youngest son, who is non-speaking autistic and has never been to school. She described how he seeks out new opportunities and loves to read.

> Liam, my youngest, is incredibly intelligent. It's really hard with Liam because obviously he can't talk to you, He taught himself to read as a baby, he was picking up letters and things and even before the age of one he was doing the left-to-right reading. He is obsessed with reading. He loves his books. I think that opens up an awful lot for kids for the self-directed learning.
>
> Liam is very much directing his own learning, even with his difficulties. He reads anything and everything that he can grab hold of that he likes with the pictures and things. All of the Julia Donaldson books are favourites. We've got the illustrated versions of Harry Potter. The night is terrible for sleeping. He only needs a couple of hours' sleep. But he's learnt that when it's bedtime, he stays in his room and reads about 10 or 15 books a night.

Her older son is a teenager who is autistic as well as having cerebral palsy. He spent several years in a specialist unit in a school before leaving to be home educated.

> Learning at home with him was about enabling him in different ways, you know, finding those different resources, those paths, those different ways

to allow him to learn. He's so creative. He loves *Lord of the Rings* and *The Hobbit* at the moment. He's creating characters from Lego figures. He's extending the story out, and then we're using the Clicker software word processing to allow him to get his stories out. They are phenomenal, to the point where he's like, 'I want to be a storyteller. I want to be a voice actor.' And I'm like, 'Oh, you have communication difficulties, and you'd like to do that? You chose a hard one!'

The space to make choices

When do we get to the 'real learning', you might well be asking yourself at this stage. When can we start the curriculum and use the textbooks I've already bought? This is when it gets hard for some parents, because one of the most important features of a self-directed education is that young people make their own choices about what they learn. You can't measure the success of a self-directed education by how much it looks like school. Outcomes are always going to be variable and those textbooks may never be opened.

This doesn't mean that self-directed children won't take GCSEs, or decide to study school subjects. Many of them will, but they tend to decide to take exams when they have a reason to do so – perhaps because they want to go to college to study something – rather than simply because it's what all the other teenagers are doing. What is more likely is that at this stage children will start to really explore the things which matter to them, whether that is Pokémon, piano playing or astrophysics. These interests will then lead on to other things in ways which are impossible to predict from the start. It's the interest and engagement which show you that learning is really happening, not the particular topic that they have chosen to explore.

Having the foundations in place doesn't mean that a child will suddenly be a different person, although it does mean that they will learn things you might have never thought possible. Part of the philosophy of self-directed education is that we learn best through doing – and so children learn about making choices through making choices. They might sometimes make what adults consider to be 'poor' choices, but that's part of the process of learning. They will sometimes 'miss out' on things, and they may regret some of their decisions. As long as those choices aren't dangerous or harmful to themselves or others, being able to make them is an important part of the learning process. Far safer to practise making mistakes for the first time when you are eight or ten or 12 than when you are 20, away from home for the first time.

Learning is everywhere

The top section of the pyramid is learning and thriving, and this can come from all sorts of directions. Netflix series, *Minecraft*, YouTube videos, *Dungeons and Dragons*, other people – they are all sources of learning. Parents need to value these, join their children in their activities, and provide opportunities for development. For younger children, parents need to be proactive, while older children and teenagers will often seek out opportunities for themselves (although some children will need support with this for longer).

Perhaps at this stage you're thinking, but my child doesn't have any interests! They don't do anything! Where do we start? I haven't yet met a child with no interests at all, nor one who is doing nothing at all. I have met children who have no interests that their parents value. Their interests are usually things like YouTube, a video game or a TV series. Possibly something like slime making or My Little Pony. Some children I've met have interests in traffic-calming measures, locks or washing machines. All of those are great places to start. Traffic-calming measures, for example, are everywhere. You could go and visit some in real life. You could make models with cardboard or draw them. You could find videos of their construction or of how traffic changes when measures are put in place. You could invent your own. You could make games about them, write stories – there is so much to do when you start to think about how to embrace the interest, rather than how to pull them away from it.

At this point, people often ask, but how do you make sure they all learn what they need to know? There are many answers to this, but first is that there is no way at all to ensure that all children learn what they need to know, and school is definitely not a way to guarantee this. Many young people leave school without the basic skills they need, and without any idea of how to acquire these for themselves. Self-directed children do all learn different things, although they will develop some of the same skills, particularly skills which are important in our society such as reading (of which more in Chapter 10).

It's a big mind shift for parents. One child learns about dogs while another learns about *Oliver Twist* and that doesn't matter? Really?

Yes, that is what I'm saying. What matters is that they learn about things they care about. They learn what has value to them, and through this process they learn about themselves. They learn to manage themselves and their individual characteristics. This makes learning more efficient, and it means that for many children, they can learn in a way they just couldn't at school. The lack of pressure makes it possible.

At this stage, you will probably have more questions than answers. You're probably asking yourself how this can ever work for us, how will they learn to read, for example, and will they ever choose anything difficult? Won't they spend their whole life gaming? I'll talk about these things in the rest of the book. But before you can get there, you need to slow down, back off and ask yourself whether the foundations are in place for your child and your family. If they aren't, start there. Right beside your child.

FIVE-POINT SUMMARY

1. Self-directed education needs to start from a firm base, and this means starting with emotional and physical safety.
2. For some children, this takes a lot longer and takes far more work on the part of adults than it does for others.
3. The Safe to Learn Pyramid of self-directed education starts with emotional wellbeing and acceptance and then moves upwards towards challenge and exploration when the child is ready.
4. Over time, children can gradually start to expand their Comfort Zone and then over time will be able to self-direct their learning from a place of security.
5. Adults are involved throughout but as facilitators, helping the children do more of what they find interesting, rather than as teachers.

CHAPTER 6

RECOVERY

Introduction

Jack has been unhappy at school for a long time. He found it hard to fit in with the other boys and was always being excluded by them. He hated the schoolwork and would often refuse to go to school in the mornings. When he was 12, his parents decided to take the plunge and told him he didn't have to go back to school and could be home educated. At first, Jack was delighted and the whole family felt good. But after a month or so, Jack started to complain. He missed his friends. He missed the routine. He didn't know what to do with himself and he was bored. His mother started to worry, maybe Jack should go back to school? Had she made a terrible mistake pulling him out?

This chapter is about what happens when a young person stops going to school. It's about the process of recovery, and how families start to question many of the hidden assumptions of schooling in order to focus on self-directed learning. In this chapter, I'll discuss the things which families talk to me about in those early weeks and months after they leave school for good. I'll talk about the skills a child needs to develop in order to be self directed – and how some of what is learnt at school makes a self directed education more difficult. I'll talk about how the relationship between parents and children needs to change from one of control to one of collaboration, using the example of screens. Finally, I'll discuss school trauma.

Leaving school

Coming out of school is almost always a destabilising process. No matter how much children (and their parents) dislike school, it provides structure and a routine. Even the routine of trying and not making it into school each day provides a focus. When school is no longer there, it can feel as if there's nothing to take its place.

It's very common for children to have an initial honeymoon period after coming out of school, and then for there to be a time where they feel very anxious and upset about what they have lost. They may withdraw, and parents think that they are regressing. They stop doing things they did before, and may refuse to go out of the house or get dressed. This can happen even for children who didn't particularly dislike school.

Katharine told me about her son who came out of school in Reception after a very difficult time when he stopped talking or interacting at all at school.

> After October half term, he didn't go back. He'd always been a child who couldn't tolerate socks, couldn't cope with clothing labels, all the usual stereotypes. But when he left school he went from that to being a child who had to be naked and couldn't dress at all. The demands of school had been so intense and left him so traumatised that he couldn't even put on pants.

At this point, many parents panic. They start wondering what on earth will happen next, and consider whether they have just made the biggest mistake of their lives. Their children seem to have no interest in anything, and are often withdrawn. Some young people seem exhausted and burnt out by their years of school. Many parents also feel burnt out after their years of trying to support their child to attend school.

In the self-directed education world, the process of recovery is called 'deschooling' and it's a well-recognised part of the transition from school. Lucy, a long-term unschooler whose daughters are now teenagers, described how her older daughter was when she came out of school aged six.

> She would get really upset if I mentioned the word learning in any capacity. I can remember her crying and crying. She really did believe she had learnt nothing. She thought her friends were getting cleverer and she was being left behind. If I made any mention of the word learning she just collapsed in a heap and couldn't bear it, she was so stressed. It was maybe two or three years before she would even pick up a book and read. She had been reading at school and was quite advanced academically. Most things would end in tears, I think it was because of the pressure of what she felt she wasn't doing and I think unschooling was actually quite hard on her.

Deschooling is about finding a different way to live, but it's also about recovering from what might have happened at school. It's about remembering how to live and learn in the way that you did before your children started school, and about decompressing from the demands and requirements that school imposed.

Learning how to do school

Think back to when you started school. Do you remember what it felt like in those first few days? My first primary school was in Bristol and I remember being confused by all the loud noises. My classroom door was off the big assembly hall, and there were always other children coming past our door. Our door had a window in it, and they peered through as they walked past. I had to learn to ignore them. Outside we had to line up in our classes before school and march in. I had to learn how to find my class and where to stand. Then there were assemblies, lunchtimes, and the rhythm of each day. There was the way that the playground felt when all the children were in it, and how deserted it was in between breaks. I loved reading, but there wasn't any time in school for me to read the books I liked. At playtime, I wasn't meant to be reading, and during lesson time, the others were learning to read.

Children learn many things at school beyond academics. They learn how get by at school. They are taught to wait for instructions rather than have a go. They are told that the things they really enjoy doing are best kept for playtime or after school, and they are told that learning works best when you are sitting still and keeping quiet. They learn that learning is most important when it's going to be evaluated by someone else, and that it's up to an adult to say whether you've done well or not. They learn to ignore their own thought processes if they are 'off-topic' – you can't start to investigate the history of domestic cats during a maths lesson, just because you saw one out the window and it made you wonder if the Ancient Egyptians kept cats. Schools call this 'keeping on task'.

Children learn at school that this is how things should be, and when they stop going to school, it can be hard for them to manage the change. When Jessica's son stopped going to school in Year 2, he wanted to recreate carpet time.

> I facilitated this and I actually found a local carpet person who kindly donated some carpet squares for us.
>
> We never actually used them. It was his initial need to recreate school and his anxiety was quite high. But he let it go quite quickly. It really made me realise how responsive I needed to be, and that from now on meeting his needs was going to be a moving feast. It was going to be what he needed rather than a fixed plan I had in my head.

Many of the things children learn at school are in fact skills for managing at school, rather than skills for learning. Many of those skills aren't useful in self-directed education. In fact, many of the things children need to learn in order to get along at school make self-directed learning more difficult. How so? To be successful in school, children have to learn a certain degree of passivity. They wait to be told what to do. They follow instructions. In self-directed education, you can't wait to be told. Learning is an active process, children often dive straight in, and the topics which interest them are the best place to start.

Relationships are different too. Relationships with adults at school are often based on evaluation. What the teacher wants to find out is whether a child is making progress and understanding, and that's the hidden (or not so hidden) agenda behind many of their interactions. Children come to expect that this is how their relationships with adults will be. This runs deeply through the way in which adults and children communicate.

Think of the teacher who asks a child 'What's ten times five?' The child knows that this isn't a genuine question of enquiry because the teacher already knows the answer. What they want to know is whether the child knows the answer – it is, in fact, a test. Children quickly work this out and start to react accordingly. They come to expect the adult to already know the answer to questions they ask, and to think that their task is to guess what the adult wants them to say. This affects how children relate to adults in all areas of their life – something which may only become visible when children aren't educated in school and you see how differently they relate to adults.

Table 6.1 shows you some of the ways in which school skills and the skills of self-directed education are not only not the same, but work in opposition. In order to comply with school requirements, a child has to stop practising the skills which enable them to educate themselves.

Table 6.1: Skills learnt at school vs skills needed for self-directed education

School skills	Self-directed education skills
Waiting for instructions	Having a go, even if you're not sure how to do it
Sitting still and keeping quiet	Moving around and asking questions
Inhibiting your desire to play until playtime	Following your desire to play, whenever it takes you
Showing your learning so an adult can evaluate your progress	Evaluating your progress for yourself
Staying on-topic	Following connections, cross-topic and cross-subject
Following the goals set by the system	Setting your own goals
Accepting what someone else has decided you should learn and do	Deciding what you yourself want to learn and do
Knowing your place in the social hierarchy	Talking to adults and children of all ages as equals
Only asking questions when it's your turn and you've been called on	Asking questions all the time
Controlling your emotions outwardly until the end of the day	Managing your emotions when they arise
Doing what you are told	Working out what you want to do for yourself
Compliance	Collaboration
Sticking at something you've started	Decided when you've had enough and stopping

Parents learning how not to do school

When children stop going to school, their parents often have assumptions about how things will go. The parents try to implement this, and then it quickly becomes clear that this isn't working and no one is happy. Then parents back off, and the family finds a new way of learning. There are great real-life examples of this in *How Children Learn at Home* (Thomas & Pattison, 2008). Children have much more power when they are out of school, and so the process of learning is collaborative in a way which education at school is not.

Katharine told me about how that happened in her family. She has five autistic children. They were at school before she withdrew them to home educate.

> When I started I had ideas about what we should be doing even though I said we would go with the flow. I thought, what you have to do is this. When they show an interest, you get everything together, and you create a project around it. If your child dares to look out the window and say, 'What a beautiful moon tonight', before you know it, you've printed off 20 worksheets and we've got them in a folder. Then that's what we're doing for the next week. I genuinely thought that was what we were meant to do, because that's what a lot of the other home educators in our area were doing. 'Lap booking' at the time was a big thing.
>
> They sold the idea as if it was radical, as if it was somehow different from the school system. I bought into that to an extent. I looked at these things, and I downloaded them, and I printed a few out. Then I went, 'Actually, this is just more of the same. Yes, we've loosely tied it to something we were passingly interested in at 10 o'clock last night. But our reality is that those interests, they come and go because we're just switched-on humans, we just have conversations and opinions. Not everything we talk about has to become a project.' For me, that was such a revelation, because I genuinely still felt like I had something to prove at that point. I think that that was the last weight. Once I removed it we just became happier individuals all around.
>
> I realised that they've been in an institution doing this stuff every single day, and they were all 'behind'. The institution had failed to get them to that point, so why was I copying it? Actually, if I take that pressure off myself, and we just start actually living our lives and having a nice time, let's see what happens. That's what we did.

Rebecca had a similar experience. Her son only attended school for a short while and they started off being play-based when he left, but she told me how she had assumed that school-type work would have to start once her son reached the age of about seven.

I'd seen all this stuff that says that you start academics when they're seven. They talk about these countries where they don't start teaching them these things until they turn seven. That's the time when you're meant to do it. I was like, okay, we're going to start doing work now. So we sat down. I read a ton of books about dyslexia and how to help dyslexic people to learn things. I was quite heavily in learning about Steiner Waldorf. The child-led curriculum, all of that kind of stuff.

We tried some academic learning and it became clear quite quickly that he was not engaged in that. I decided, okay, let's just go back to what we were doing before, and that worked.

Screens and technology

I wonder how many of you have turned directly to this section. This is one of the issues that comes up most when I talk to parents. Parents who have had strict screen time limits find that these are impossible to maintain when their children come out of school, and then their children start spending all day, every day on their device. Their parents panic.

A lot of our societal angst about young people gets projected onto screens and 'screen time'. Screen time is regularly blamed for young people's mental health difficulties and there is much hand wringing about the amount of time that young people spend in front of a device or computer.

Screen time in itself is pretty well a meaningless concept. Over the last 20 years, more and more things have been accessed via a screen. I now read books on a e-reader, talk to my family via a video call, play board games with my children across tablets and write and send letters via email. All of those things I might have done in the past using different means. It's hard to see what has changed about the activity to turn it from something beneficial to something harmful, simply because we are using a computer or device rather than paper, cardboard or a telephone. During the COVID-19 lockdown, I started to exercise using a programme on the Nintendo Switch, met up with friends over videos and played online escape rooms with family. I would have preferred to do all these things in person, but I don't think they became harmful because I had to do them via a screen.

However, the real reason why screens are such a big part of deschooling isn't to do with what 'screen time' means or doesn't mean. It's because of our relationship with our children and their relationship with screens.

Screens are a bit of a test case for how we relate to our children, and the shift from control and coercion to collaboration and connection.

Most parents control their children's screen time because they think it is in the child's best interest. In fact, having strict screen time limits is almost a marker of a 'good parent'. The logic is that screens are something which children cannot be trusted to make their own decisions about, and so parents step in, with timers and complicated systems which everyone has to keep track of.

The problem is that when something is limited and controlled by a parent, it affects the child's relationship with that thing, and their relationship with their parent. The aim, as self-directed educators, is for children to be able to choose to spend time doing something on a device or computer, and then to stop when they have had enough. The aim is for them to be able to work out their own relationship with these things.

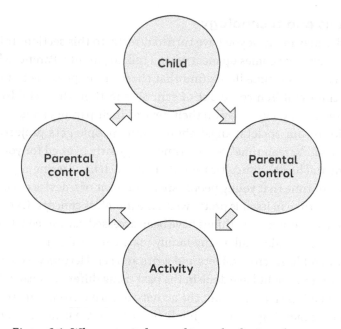

*Figure 6.1: When parental control is used to limit and restrict,
a child's relationships with what they are doing changes*

When parental control comes into the equation, suddenly the child's relationship to it changes. Now it's not just a device, it's a rationed and special thing which they can only use for an hour a day. It acquires a specialness and rarity, quite apart from what can actually be done on it. This will make the child more likely to want to use it for their full allocated time, even if they actually might have better things to do. Scarcity has such a powerful effect that advertisers use it in marketing to make something more desirable – when you're told that you only have two days to use your discount code, or that there are only three items left in stock, it makes you more likely to buy something. It makes children more likely to value screen time over other things because it has a cachet, a rarity value. I know children who refuse to go on days out to places they want to go, so that they don't miss their screen time. The child's relationship with what they do has been changed.

Then many parents do something else which also alters a child's relationship with technology. They also use it as a reward. They will allow their child to use the device more when they have been cooperative, and they remove this privilege if the child is non-compliant.

When something is used as a reward, it becomes more attractive. Through associative learning, when something is paired with approval or the feeling of 'doing well', it becomes more attractive, more desirable – this is why gold stars make us feel good. It's not because of the shiny paper.

Most parents are doing two things which make screens more desirable to a child. Limiting and using as a reward. Both of these have the reverse effect to that which the parent wanted. They will both affect the child's relationship with the screen, as well as the child's relationship with their parent. They will mean that a child is likely to want to spend more time on a screen.

The third thing parents often do with screens is that they denigrate them. Sometimes even while using a device themselves, they talk about what rubbish their children do on their devices, and how much time they 'fritter' away.

Table 6.2: Things that parents do with screens and how they affect children

Things parents do	What it looks like	Unexpected effect on child
Impose strict, inflexible limits	30 minutes a day and 60 minutes at the weekends	Makes it more desirable through a process of rationing and created scarcity
		Limits opportunities for learning and social play
		Means the child may prioritise getting their full quota of time over other activities
		Child may resist ending their time because they are in the middle of a game or activity, which will be seen as 'bad behaviour'
		Child may avoid getting into flow as it is so painful to be pulled out of it at the end of their time

cont.

Things parents do	What it looks like	Unexpected effect on child
Use as a reward	'If you behave yourself at Grandpa's house, you can go on the iPad for another 30 minutes afterwards'	Associates it with doing well and feeling good Makes it more desirable through a process of associative learning Leads to conflict if they do not behave 'well enough' and are not allowed the reward which has been promised
Use as a punishment	'Now you've done that, you can't go on the iPad again for the rest of the week'	Makes the iPad more desirable through scarcity Makes child feel angry and resentful (and reminds everyone all week about whatever it was that they did wrong)
Denigrate what their children do on screens	'He's just wasting his time on that device' 'They're just playing mindless garbage on the console again, I wish we'd never got that thing'	Makes child feel bad about their choices and the things they enjoy Makes child anxious about their choices Makes it harder for the child to trust their judgement Makes them feel angry with those who say these things about the things they enjoy Makes it less likely that the child will share their enjoyment with their parent, or tell their parent what they are doing
Stop children playing together on a screen in favour of alternative play	'Come on, it's time to go and play outside now, you've been on that long enough'	Disrupts social play Disrupts connections For some children, limits the best way they have of forming relationships with other children Makes them angry

When children want to do something a lot and they are preventing from doing so, they protest when it's taken away. They may argue, or shout or become physical. When this happens, parents use their children's behaviour as a reason why they must limit screens. They say, but when I tell him to stop, he screams and kicks! It's like he's addicted! Those screens themselves must be dangerous and I must continue to limit them.

This puts children in a really difficult situation. Something which they enjoy doing has been limited (which makes it more desirable), used as a reward (which makes it more attractive) and now they are also told that it's bad. They learn that their choices can't be trusted and that their parents don't approve of their choices. They want to use technology, but when they do they know their parents aren't happy. This makes it hard for them to see themselves as a competent decision maker, someone who can make good choices. It makes them feel bad about their ability to make decisions.

In addition, for many children who find school and other aspects of life challenging, technology has a special role. They often use devices to decompress from their day, creating a space with familiar activities where they can feel competent and autonomous. Then there is the aspect of learning and mastery – for many children, video games can be a place where they excel. They feel good about themselves as they fight the Ender Dragon, or build a new civilisation. They can connect with other young people in way that is much harder offline. This is extremely important for children and young people who may not be feeling good about themselves in many other places.

All of this explains why many children, once they leave school, want to spend much of their time on a device, and how this becomes a source of conflict. Children know that their parents want them to do other things and this pressure sometimes makes it harder to say yes to other choices. Their parents panic and try to control things again – and before you know it, the family are stuck in a cycle of constant asking about screen time, and constant monitoring by both the child and the parents of exactly how much time has been spent doing what.

The big problem for self-directed education is that the child can't make free choices about using technology when there are so many other associations connected with it, and particularly when it is so loaded with parental approval or disapproval. This is something that some children are far more sensitive to than others. What can you do instead? Treat it as you would another interest. Join your child in their playing and seek out ways to help them explore the things they enjoy.

Pressure detectors

When I first met Anastasia, she was 14, refusing to go to school and she wasn't speaking to her mother Rachael. She was playing online with her friends and Rachael could hear her laughing and chatting to them, but whenever her mother talked to her – nothing. She looked right past her or gave monosyllabic responses.

They lived alone together and Rachael cried as she told me that she didn't know what was wrong. She said Anastasia told her she was controlling, but she put no pressure on Anastasia, none at all. She said she never told her to do anything and she had given up even asking her to lay the table.

Anastasia told a different story. 'Everything my mother says is pressure,' she said. 'No matter what she says, I feel her disappointment and I know that she doesn't know what to tell her friends about me. When I come down for breakfast and she says "Morning", I can hear in her tone what she's not saying. "What sort of time do you call this? For how much longer are you going to sleep the day away and waste your life?" I hate it. It makes me feel terrible. So I keep out of her way.'

School is full of pressure, and a lot of that pressure is passed on to parents, who pass it on to their children. However, when pressure comes home it sometimes goes underground. It hides itself, in apparently innocuous phrases and wistful words. It is unspoken, but nonetheless present and powerful.

Often parents equate 'pressure' with 'explicitly trying to make a child do something' while ignoring or simply not acknowledging hidden pressure. The child – like Anastasia – feels constantly under pressure, while the parent thinks that they aren't putting on any pressure at all. These parents communicate with their children mostly in subtle demands – saying things like, 'Have you done your homework?' if they see them playing or watching TV, thus showing that they would prefer the child to be working. Or they say, 'It would make me so happy if you could do your job without complaining' thus adding emotional pressure to the situation and making the child feel annoyed and resentful whether they complain or not.

Some children, like Anastasia, are particularly good at picking up these hidden agendas. They are pressure-detectors, able to sniff out the hidden agenda a mile away. As young children they may pick their parents up on every hidden message, every attempt at manipulation or control, while as teenagers they may be more likely simply to refuse to communicate. These are the children who will absolutely not be bribed out of the house by the promised reward.

These children are a gift. Their super-sensitive pressure antennae mean that their parents have a great advantage in becoming aware of the indirect pressure in what they say, and therefore an opportunity to change. If they don't do this, everyone can be stuck, sometimes for years. The child feels pressured, the parent can't see the problem and blames the child for seeing pressure where they believe there is none.

Parents in this situation can find that their children lead the way towards change, faster than they might have pushed themselves. If parents are able to drop their defences and hear themselves through their child's ears, then this can be a fast-track for parents into deschooling. These are the children who insist that their parents embrace self-directed education. There is no way to force them to be compliant. The challenge is for parents to hear what they are saying and adjust their behaviour, even when it feels personal and upsetting.

School trauma

When I was five, I started primary school. I'd happily attended nursery where I'd been one of the Big Children, tasked with important responsibilities like getting the milk bottles back when we'd all drunk our school milk. Primary school was different. The hall was echoey and the playground hard and concrete. There was no play equipment or bushes to hide in like there was at nursery, just hopscotch painted on the floor. Our classroom was small and cramped and the other girls pinched me when our teacher wasn't looking. My friends from nursery had gone elsewhere. Sometimes I was scared to ask to go to the toilet, so I hung on, feeling increasingly desperate. When I went, they smelt horrible and there were wads of toilet paper stuck to the ceiling and walls where other children had thrown them.

Everyone else was learning to read and I could already, and so I was bored. I had to sit at a table copying words from an orange folder while they sat on the carpet reading *Jennifer Yellow-hat*. I felt different, not one of them, and I hated it. In assembly, we would sit cross-legged on the hard parquet floor, with the youngest children – us – in the front row, right by the headteacher's legs. Our teacher would sit on a chair at the side, hushing us when we whispered. I felt tiny and insignificant. The bigger children felt like giants, rushing around the playground and towering over me. It felt like an unfriendly place to be, and I didn't want to go. I protested. Each time I went in, I felt worse. Each night before, I worried about going.

I was lucky. My parents decided not to force me to keep going. By the end of my first term they had found a Waldorf kindergarten instead. Here, everything was soft and friendly. We called the teachers by their first names and they wore flowing robes. The garden was full of trees and I was back to hiding in the bushes with my friends. No one pinched me. We drew pictures on wet paper with no corners and drank camomile tea at break time. And the Waldorf system doesn't teach reading until children are older, so it wasn't a problem that I already could. This school felt like (and of course was) a totally different place, somewhere where I felt safe.

Nothing really terrible happened at my first school. I wasn't being badly bullied, and I wasn't struggling academically. There was nothing you could put your finger on. But it felt like a hostile place to me. I couldn't see the point. I was unhappy each time that I went and it had an immediate effect on my wellbeing. Going every day to a place you don't like and that you cannot leave is a very quick way to feel terrible about yourself and the world.

For many children, schools feel like a threatening situation, even if from an adult perspective no threat is present. Being without your parents, being surrounded by other children, being required to conform with adult expectations, dealing with frequent transitions, not being able to go out and run around when you want to, not understanding the rules but knowing you'll get in trouble if you break them, having no space to get away from everyone else if you need to calm down, the smells and chaos of the dining hall – all of these things can send a child's nervous system into overdrive. They don't feel safe, and their bodies respond as if it's a threat.

Then, unfortunately, many schools recommend that parents should force their children to attend. This is partly because of the strong focus on attendance in government policy. Parents tell me that they have been encouraged to bring their children into school in their pyjamas if they refuse to get dressed, that they are told they must bring them in every day even if they just sit outside or touch the school gate. They tell me that they have terrible memories of feeling trapped between their distressed child and the teacher, and that when they decided not to keep insisting, the teachers said things like, 'Well, if you give in to her then of course it will never change.'

In my experience, schools justify this approach in one of two ways. Either they use a behavioural justification – they frame school refusal as 'bad behaviour' and tell parents they must not give the child what they want as this will make the child's behaviour worse, or they use an emotional justification. They say that if the child is anxious about school, then they must be made to go every day as otherwise the anxiety will get worse. In later chapters, I'll discuss why both these reasons may be misguided, but for the meantime, all that matters is that this means that parents are encouraged to ignore their children's distress. Parents are told to force a child repeatedly into school, in the hope that they will stop protesting and start complying.

I don't know if you've ever been forced into a situation where you felt unsafe by someone you love and rely on, but it can have exactly the opposite effect to what the school is hoping for. Rather than learning that school isn't as bad as they thought, children learn that they can't trust anyone to listen to them. Rather than become less fearful, they become more anxious.

They have repeated experiences at school of not feeling safe, and not being allowed to leave, no matter how hard they try. The result of this is that some children get sensitised to school. They start to feel unsafe every time they see anything which reminds them of school. They may respond with panic to anything which resembles school at all – perhaps a playground of children, or a person who sounds like a teacher.

It's not just about bullying

When people hear the term 'school trauma' they almost always assume bullying. That's what I would have assumed, before I started hearing from families. For most of the families who tell me about distressing experiences at school, bullying is only one part of it or may not feature at all. For many, there are many small distressing experiences which accumulate. There's the time that the other children ran away from them in the playground laughing, or the time that they forgot to do their homework and got told off. There's the morning that there was an unexpected supply teacher, or the day when PE was cancelled with little warning. There's the lunchtime that the dinner lady wouldn't allow them to eat their crisps because they hadn't finished their crusts. There's the way that the toilets smell, and how chaotic the classroom feels sometimes. For older children and teenagers, there's often an increasing sense of anger about how much their lives are controlled – down to how they cut their hair and the colour of their shoes and coat.

Then there is the personal element. Children who struggle at school hear a lot of negative things about themselves. Over time, these affect how the child feels about themselves; repeated experiences of feeling worthless at school, for example, can lead to a child coming to believe that they really are worthless. Things which teachers say such as, 'Why can't you just fit in?' or, 'You just need to stop being so lazy and try harder' become critical voices which follow them around. I've worked with adults who still have the voices of teachers ringing in their ears 20 years later.

Many autistic adults tell me that for them, school involved repeated experiences of feeling wrong and that their reactions were shameful. They tell me that they feel that it was their fault, and that they were always being measured up against a yardstick and deemed to be lacking. Dyslexic adults tell me how stupid they felt when they just couldn't learn to read in the way that everyone else did. They tell me of teachers who would get frustrated and shout things like, 'What is wrong with you?' and they didn't know the answer. For them, each of these experiences felt threatening.

Over time, this accumulated and led to longstanding feelings of inadequacy and failure.

The third part of school trauma which is often missed is how parents are drawn into it. Parents are expected to persuade their children to attend school. When a child is refusing to attend school or is very unhappy, pressure is usually put on parents to make sure their children continue to attend. Parents are the ones who have to get their children up every morning and get them off to school. They are the ones who are around at the end of the day to pick up the pieces. They have to calm their children down, feed them, get them to bed, and do it all again the next day. They are deeply involved with trying to make school okay for their children, and in trying to keep a positive relationship with the school. They often feel caught in the middle between what their child is saying, and what school is saying that they must do. Many parents tell me that they are called into school repeatedly and they feel blamed. They are scared that they will be reported for truancy and taken to court if their child doesn't attend school regularly enough. This all has an impact on the relationship between parents and children. Children can be very angry if they feel that their parents have prioritised school over them. School trauma becomes something which is deep within the whole family and many parents need to heal just as much as their children. Rebuilding relationships and showing your child that you have their back is an essential part of recovery.

In the next chapter, I'll talk more specifically about trauma and how parents can help. For now, I'd like to finish with Jessica. Her eldest son Luke came out of school in Year 2 after a really distressing time. He's the one who wanted to recreate carpet time. He showed signs of school trauma, which re-emerged when Jessica tried to do anything that resembled school. For them, a crucial part of recovery was Jessica really listening to what Luke was saying and changing her approach.

By January, I thought we'd be ready to do some 'proper learning'. It was horrendous; the whole school stress came straight back into the house. I just tried to do a nice topic – the skeleton, the human body.

I have a very vivid memory of him. Me: 'Can you just sit and listen for five minutes?'

I was pleading with him to try and do this.

He turned to me at the age of seven and said, 'You want this, I don't.'

I had tried for a few weeks to get this semi-structured thing to work, but that was the pivotal moment.

Good on him for speaking up, and I'm proud that I had learnt from my previous mistakes and this time I listened to him. I had to cast aside my preference for semi-structured learning. The more I learnt about education and about PDA, the more I realised that unschooling/SDE/autonomous education was the most aligned philosophy for him.

I was *totally* out of my comfort zone. It has taken a huge amount of change, faith and trust to move *me* from structure and control to respect, connection and autonomy, and not just in education but in parenting too. A total 180-degree change in direction. It was one of the best things I have ever done. And we have *never, ever* looked back.

FIVE-POINT SUMMARY

1. Recovering from school is usually not a quick process for either parents or children.
2. The period after leaving school is often called 'deschooling' and each family's experience is different.
3. It will always take time to get used to a new way of learning, and to establish new relationships which are not based around school and control.
4. Recovery has to happen not only for children, but also for parents who often have to give up their ideas about what education would be like.
5. Many children and families experience school trauma, which can be made worse when parents are encouraged to force their children into school.

CHAPTER 7

TRAUMA AND ANXIETY

Introduction

Some families come to self-directed education following life-changing events and trauma, after which they have to re-evaluate their whole lives and find a different way to learn. Others find their way there because their children become so anxious about school or experience trauma there. Mental health is an important (and often under-recognised) part of the pathway to self-directed education for many families.

In this chapter, I'm going to explain some of what goes on for children when they experience trauma, and also discuss how anxiety develops and is maintained. I'll talk about the ways in which parents can help their children to learn to tolerate their emotions, something which many children find difficult, particularly when the way in which they express their emotions is unconventional or seen as 'bad behaviour' by those around them.

I'll start with a real story of self-directed education after trauma. I met Nicola when she was a participant on one of the courses I run for parents. She had been a self-directed educator for over seven years by that point, and her son Isaac was 16. When I heard her story I asked her if I could share it in this book. Isaac had a traumatic brain injury at the age of eight, after which everything changed for him and his family. Nicola ended up withdrawing Isaac from school against the advice of professionals, because she felt so strongly that being there was not helpful for him. I'll let her tell their story in her own words.

Nicola and Isaac's story

Isaac had an accident in November 2013 when he was eight years old. He was kicked in the head by a horse and knocked unconscious. In hospital, he was diagnosed with a skull fracture and bleeding in the brain. He was unconscious for approximately a day and then started to speak quietly on awakening. He was in high dependency for three nights, then stayed three further nights in a children's ward.

On release from hospital we were advised by the neurosurgeon that he could return to school the following week. When I contacted the neuropsychological team a month after his accident to query the state of his mind/health, they listened but encouraged me to wait until our appointment which was due in February, three months after the accident.

Isaac returned to school in January 2014 because he wanted to. I regret this now. He attended school for about two days a week from January to July and it got steadily less manageable. He lost his belongings every day (having never previously done so), he lost his close friendships, he started fighting and his academics dipped. After the first day, he never wanted to go. He was psychologically better when he had two weeks off at Easter, and during other longer breaks. He developed night-time anxiety. He was banging his head after school. He was so lost after school and it took hours to calm him down. It was unbelievably hard and stressful. I did not feel that school listened to my concerns although I wrote to them regularly. One teacher had taught Isaac for two months before the accident and had known him for longer, but she claimed not to notice any difference in him afterwards. He was very different in many subtle and not so subtle ways.

By our appointment in February I had worked out that he had a brain injury, but they wouldn't confirm. it. His tests indicated that his verbal and comprehensive abilities were low, but maths and non-spatial logic were exceptional (top 4% for his age) and therefore they concluded that there couldn't be a brain injury.

Following that appointment, we had three more neuropsychology appointments (from March to September). These were highly frustrating as the neuropsychologist seemed unable to compute that although his teachers didn't see anything wrong with Isaac, they were not being observant enough, did not have the right expertise or interest, and that my accounts of the situation were true.

The neuropsychologist drummed home many times that since Isaac didn't apparently struggle in school he should spend more time there. He convinced me in June to push him in for three full-time weeks. It was completely awful. Isaac developed nervous tics (a walking tic and a verbal tic). The hardest thing was not being listened to or believed, despite my obvious desperation.

In September 2014, Isaac really couldn't face returning to school.

He found it so traumatic. He attended for three non-consecutive days, but was very unwilling. One day I was reading a fairy book to him and his sister (he had regressed in interests by two or three years) and we all had to make a wish. He said that he didn't think his wish could come true, but he wished not to go back to school. I told him he didn't have to go again. It was apparent to me that there wasn't really any choice. My only reason for him to attend school was if it was beneficial to him, and it clearly wasn't. He wasn't who he had been, he couldn't maintain friendships or schoolwork, it's hard to even conceive what that is like for an eight-year-old boy.

The confirmation of brain injury came in September 2014, when occupational therapists from The Children's Trust came to assess Isaac. He had already stopped going to school by that point. They spent two hours at my house interviewing me and Isaac separately in his room. They told me that they knew within five minutes that he had a brain injury.

I don't know if Isaac is autistic or has autistic tendencies. He was assessed in 2015 by child and adult mental health services (CAMHS), and they said no he wasn't, but the whole diagnostic process relies on recall, and I didn't have an accurate memory of him as a young child. He had become so confident at school that I'd kind of wiped out the memory that he hadn't settled at nursery and actually we had held him back from attending school until he was nearly six.

Isaac spent two years living in the lounge after leaving school. I read to him during the day and we played cards, but he liked to spend quite a bit of time watching TV both alone and with his sister. He needed to keep the TV on at night-time to stay calm enough to sleep. He was a psychological mess and so was I. He was referred to CAMHS by the neurological team, but unfortunately this was specifically for an autism assessment. That assessment took a year, and then he was referred back to CAMHS for mental health support (another 18-month wait), which never amounted to anything since I couldn't get him to visit and he wouldn't engage on video chat.

It's been a fragile story of small steps forwards and many steps backwards. Forming relationships has been so tough. In 2015, I started a mentoring scheme where sixth formers would come and spend a few hours a week with Isaac. We had some great kids. Some encouraged him to play sports including basketball, football and even martial arts. I also paid a sports coach who was amazing – he also had a tragic brain injury story from having encephalitis when he was 15.

Isaac gradually became less angry and reactive as the years passed. It really helped to have the connection with other kids as they treated him very nicely and helped him to feel less isolated and alone.

Isaac has had regular sessions with an online mentor for approximately two years now, playing computer games and doing some games design. I think that has taught Isaac how to be more confident in his abilities, and how to have fun and relax again. He's also had a maths tutor for the past three years and he gets an hour a week of maths with him. Isaac plays bridge with the family. He has a number of great friendships locally and they meet at a games club I set up last year.

In 2021, Isaac enrolled in Cheney School which was offering home educators the chance of a flexi-scheme – school tuition online and part time if required. It was an amazing scheme and has been so positive for Isaac. He has built bonds with his teachers and is loving working towards GCSEs in maths and science. Oxfordshire local authority has told the school that the scheme must come in line with normal school set-ups from September onwards, which means that the kids will have to attend their lessons in person. This is sad for many families, although I think Isaac will cope and will probably attend many of his lessons in person in the school.

I honestly cannot think about the future. My brain is fixed in the present now, because anything else seems pointless. I hope that Isaac manages to keep stepping forwards and that he goes on to do A-levels and maybe even a degree.

He's chatty and very humorous; he'd like to do games design – but who knows? Life is a tightrope for someone like him. He'll always have a mum (hopefully) who has become imaginative and creative in helping him and finding pathways.

Nicola and Isaac's story is a hard one, and Nicola told me how she felt unsupported in her choice to remove Isaac from school to home educate. Despite his obvious trauma and signs of distress, professionals advised her to continue with 'school as usual', apparently under the belief that doing so would help Isaac recover.

Isaac's story is one of major trauma, but it's also a great example of the pyramid model of self-directed education I introduced in Chapter 5. He completely withdrew from the world for several years after his accident, re-establishing his sense of safety, and then Nicola started to bring in people from outside to expand his horizons and relationships. As he became able to do more, she found ways for him to make new connections and learn new skills, until he was able to do online lessons and start to study for GCSEs. Being out of school gave him the time he needed to recover from his experience, while being in school was keeping him in a state of high distress – which is never a good place to start learning.

So what happens to us when we experience trauma – and why are some children so emotionally reactive when they have apparently never experienced a major traumatic event? To understand this, we need to appreciate how hard our brains try to keep us safe.

The survival system

When our bodies feel under threat, we respond by going into survival mode. This isn't dysfunctional, or pathological. It evolved to keep us alive. This is a very basic brain reaction, shared with most other animals. It's not under conscious control and it's not a cognitive process – in other words, it's not something that we think about and choose to do. It's a physiological and emotional response.

Think about our ancestors from millennia ago, living in the savannah. A major source of danger would have been wild animals. In order to stay alive, it would be extremely important to recognise threatening wild animals and to respond appropriately. Our ancestors didn't have many choices when they met a wild animal. They could either fight, flee, freeze (and hope the animal didn't see them), or fawn (submit). Our brains evolved to do this. You can't have many encounters with a lion before you come off worse.

An important part of this survival system is threat detection. A small part of our brain called the amygdala acts as our alarm system. It looks for clues in the environment which might indicate danger, and then sets off the internal alarm. This sends us into survival mode, ready to fight, flee, freeze or fawn. This reaction involves our whole body being flooded with adrenaline – you need it, to survive an encounter with a lion. This reaction isn't pleasant when you don't have to fight. It means that you feel suddenly highly aroused, maybe like you want to run away or fight. Sometimes this feels like a panic attack.

Keeping us safe

The amygdala is over-inclusive. In survival terms, it's better to set off the alarm system more often when it isn't needed than to miss the one time when it might be needed. With lions, this might mean that the alarm is set off by a lion-shaped rock, or a yellow-looking bush, or even a harmless cat that just walks in a similar way. This makes sense, if your priority is survival. It does, however, mean that your body can be flooded with hormones which prime the body for fighting or running, when there is really nothing there.

Our threat system collects memories of experiences in order to better protect us in the future. When we are very highly aroused, the situation feels dangerous to us and the memory is stored in the amygdala. This memory is then used to identify future dangerous situations, by looking for matches with past events. If you are in a car accident involving a red car, you may find yourself responding to the colour red as if you're about to be hit by a car again. You may start feeling highly anxious and as if you want to run away, even if that red is on a Coca-Cola advert billboard and no threat.

When the amygdala is triggered by something which isn't actually dangerous, then another part of our brain comes into play. Our fastest response is the survival response, but slightly more slowly our medial prefrontal cortex kicks in – and this can be thought of as the Watchtower (terminology from Bessel Van der Kolk's 2014 book, *The Body Keeps the Score*, a great book if you want to understand more about responses to trauma). The Watchtower has an overview of the entire situation, and can stop the quick firing danger response. We can feel this working when we realise that the thing we thought was a snake actually is just a stick, and so we don't need to get out of there so quickly after all. Our body relaxes, the urge to run disappears – but we may still feel shaken and find our heart is beating fast for a while afterwards.

Many children who have struggled to survive at school for years are left with an overresponsive amygdala alarm. It is triggered in response to situations which aren't actually dangerous, but which remind them of how vulnerable and powerless they felt at school. They become very reactive and volatile, angry or upset at apparently minor occurrences. One way to think about this is through the lens of the 'window of tolerance'.

The window of tolerance

The 'window of tolerance' is a term introduced by Dr Daniel Siegel in his book *The Developing Mind* (2020, but first published in 1999) to describe the optimal arousal zone of human beings. It's a way of thinking about the state where humans can function well, manage a certain amount of stress and regulate their emotions. When we're in our window of tolerance, we can learn and interact calmly, and cope with a certain amount of disruption and distress without over-reacting.

Table 7.1: Window of tolerance (based on work by Daniel Siegel)

Zone of hyper-arousal
Feeling overwhelmed, anxious or angry, so much so that you can't function
Body wants to fight or flee the situation
Window of tolerance (optimal zone of arousal)
Flexible, grounded, able to self-regulate
Open, curious, engaged with the world
Zone of hypo-arousal
Shutting down, freezing or fawning, lethargic, unmotivated

Our window of tolerance isn't fixed. It's affected by all sorts of things, including individual characteristics and the environment, and the interaction between the two. It changes through the day, and between days. When we are hungry, tired, frustrated or under any sort of stress, our window of tolerance shrinks.

Invisible stressors can make the window of tolerance smaller. For many children, managing the demands of a day at school puts them under stress which they cannot show, meaning that by the end of the day it takes almost nothing to push them over the edge. Having trouble putting their seat belt on, or the wrong flavour crisps will be enough to do it, and then the meltdowns can last for hours.

Young children often have a fairly narrow window of tolerance – they can be pushed out of the zone by frustration over the wrong colour cup. And once they are hyper-aroused, it may take a lot of parental soothing and emotional containment to bring them back. They can't yet do that for themselves.

When children are very inflexible, it can be a sign that the demands of their environment are exceeding what they can comfortably cope with, and so their window of tolerance is narrow. A clue that this is happening is when you get apparently over-the-top, extreme reactions to minor events – perhaps the child who appears to have been managing fine, and then suddenly there are no chicken nuggets left for supper and the idea of sausages instead is just too much, resulting in a meltdown. Parents say things like 'we're walking on eggshells' or 'it's like tightrope walking'.

This can leave adults confused and trying desperately to solve the apparent problem, either by making suggestions: 'Maybe we can go to the shop and buy more chicken nuggets? Maybe we can have chicken nuggets tomorrow?' or asking questions, 'Is there something you'd like better than sausages? Can I make something else for you?' Or finally, when all of those have failed, getting annoyed, 'You usually like sausages. Lots of children don't have enough to eat at all and here you are making a fuss about chicken nuggets. Stop it.'

All of these are doomed to failure because the problem was never really the chicken nuggets. The problem is everything that has happened over the whole day, culminating in the chicken nuggets which have pushed the child over the top into hyper-arousal. Their nervous system just can't cope with any more demands, and the suggestions and questions can actually make that worse because the child feels under more pressure, which makes them more aroused. Their distress is the signal that the child struggling to manage and needs more help.

What's the alternative? It's thinking in terms of emotional arousal, rather than in terms of what the apparent problem is (like the chicken nuggets). When a child (or adult) is hyper- or hypo-aroused, they need soothing. They need compassion for how they are feeling, empathy for how hard this is, and a calm containing adult who shows that it's okay to get emotionally overwhelmed sometimes, and that they can cope.

This means getting alongside the child, even when they are at their most frustrated and frustrating, and empathising with how hard it feels. Once they are out of their window of tolerance, they aren't open to learning or rational discussion. In the moment, there's no point in trying to rationalise with them, or trying to teach them that their behaviour isn't acceptable. That can come later. In the moment, connection and empathy come first. It's not always easy to tell if a child is outside their window of tolerance and you'll need to observe your child closely to find their cues. Some examples of this are given below.

What are the signs that a child is outside their window of tolerance?
Hyper-arousal (fight or flight)
- Aggression
- Trying to escape
- Headbanging
- Agitation

- Being very loud
- Meltdowns
- Pacing around
- Fighting
- Hitting
- Punching
- Shouting
- Running away
- Inflexibility
- Very fast talking
- Rocking
- Tone of voice
- Not seeming to be able to hear
- 'Not listening'.

Hypo-arousal (freeze or fawn)
- Unresponsive
- Withdrawn
- Not seeming to hear what is being said
- Not answering questions
- Repetitive behaviour
- Inability to make choices or decisions
- Compliance
- Passivity
- 'Glazed eyes'.

Repeated experiences of feeling under threat result in a narrowing of the window of tolerance, and therefore even more reactivity and less flexibility. All of these experiences are collected in the amygdala, the part of the brain which acts as the alarm system. It looks for matches between threatening memories and things in the environment which might indicate that the threat is there again.

When fear becomes anxiety

Many parents tell me that their children seem to be fearful all the time, and they don't know how to help. Anxiety sets in when that feeling of being under threat becomes chronic. There are two parts to anxiety – the feeling of being under threat, and the feeling that we will not be able to cope. Both of those things are important. A threat which we know we can manage doesn't make us anxious and as we grow up, many of us become able to manage things which initially made us anxious – riding a bicycle, for example, or swimming.

This is why doing something for the first time is so much more anxiety-provoking than doing it later on – we don't actually know if we will be able to cope or not.

Children draw on their parents to help them feel safer, and to help them cope with feelings of threat. When children don't think they can cope with much, and they constantly feel under threat, their parents provide an anchor. The parents' emotional stability reassures the child that things will be okay, and that they will get through this. It provides an underlying sense of safety.

What can go wrong? Well, sometimes parents can't maintain their emotional stability. The demands are just too great. Many parents have told me of how threatened they feel when they are caught between the judgement of other adults and their child's distress. This often happens if a parent has been told they must force their child in to school, and the child resists. One mother told me how, when she decided to take her son home after an hour trying to peel him off her, the teacher said, 'Well, it's not surprising he behaves like this, if you give into him after that sort of behaviour.'

When a child becomes violent, or attacks their siblings, it's really hard for their parents not to feel under threat and to react accordingly. The world can feel very unsafe for a child if they think that their parent is scared too. This is illustrated in Figure 7.1. The system gets out of balance and more anxiety is the result.

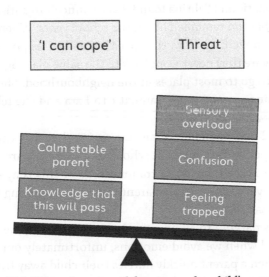

Figure 7.1: When the sense of threat exceeds a child's perception of their ability to cope, then anxiety is the result

You'll notice that there are two possible areas which could change here. We could help the child feel less under threat, and we could also help them increase their capacity to cope. This is where parents can make a big difference. Many children learn that their emotions are dangerous and think that they must be avoided because they feel so intense. If parents can show them that emotions are just part of life, and that they will pass in time, then children feel that they can cope better, and that they are in less danger. If a child is scared of their own emotions, they are very likely to be anxious a lot of the time. When we increase their belief that they can cope (or give them lots of experiences of coping and not feeling overwhelmed), then the inevitable threats will feel less anxiety-provoking.

Will I re-traumatise them?

Sabrina got in touch. 'I'm so worried about my two boys. I think they have school trauma,' she said. She told me that her oldest son, Ezra, aged nine, had been at school for two years, and had left school after an awful year of refusing during which Sabrina had been encouraged by the school to force him to go. This was two years ago. They were now home educating, which Sabrina described as a relief for everyone.

The problem was that now they couldn't do anything or go anywhere. Ezra would become extremely upset at anything which reminded him of school – a person who looked like a teacher, a book he used to read, even a car that looked like the headteacher's could set him off. Ezra's upset was loud and dramatic and Sabrina found it very difficult to anticipate. It made her feel terrible and reminded her of the school years. When it happened, she would remove Ezra from the situation as fast as possible and they would make sure they never went back to the same place again. They were now unable to go to most places in the neighbourhood. She was worried that everything seemed to be traumatic to Ezra and she felt that things were getting worse, not better.

I have had many parents contact me saying that they think their children have experienced trauma at school, and that they are afraid to take them places in case they get re-traumatised. By this they usually mean that they get very upset. Many parents worry that getting very upset in itself is traumatising.

This leads parents to avoid situations which make their child upset or afraid. And when we avoid emotions, unfortunately our fear of them can grow. When a parent quickly hurries their child away from a group of children who are reminding them of school, what that child learns is that they are right to feel anxious, that their parents also feels anxious – and that their anxious feelings are something to be avoided as much as possible. This cycle is outlined in Figure 7.2. They may also learn that their anxious feelings are dangerous – which will make them more anxious. They can get sensitised to their own feelings.

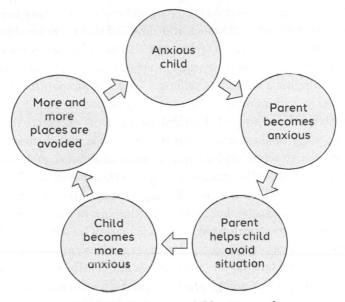

Figure 7.2: The parent-child anxiety cycle

This is a problem for many reasons, not least that feeling anxious is part of trying out new things, and if a child learns that their feelings are dangerous, they won't be able to explore the world. It's also a problem because it prevents the child from having new experiences, which help them to feel safer in the world. It prevents any new learning from taking place, and the child gets stuck.

So what makes the difference between an experience which is traumatising (or re-traumatising) and one which is healing? Both can involve intense emotions. The key difference is that in a healing experience, the child has the chance to find out that things are not as bad as they thought they would be, and that over time, their emotions reduce in intensity. This reduction in intensity can happen because a trusted adult is there to soothe them, or because the situation turned out to be less bad than they thought. In therapy, we sometimes use the metaphor of dipping your toe into the river of difficult emotions. We need to help our children dip their toe in and tolerate a bit of discomfort, while keeping the other foot firmly on the safety of the bank.

Unfortunately, if a child leaves every situation when they start to get anxious, then any situation can become re-traumatising – particularly if you leave at the worst moment. That's because the brain will learn to associate the experience with a high level of anxiety, and it may get stored as a threat memory. The child (and parents) needs the chance to see that the feelings of anxiety will reduce over time and that there are things they can do which will help them feel better. This can't happen if they always leave when things are at their worst. They effectively stay on the bank of the river, dipping a toe in and pulling it back the moment they get wet, while the river grows more and more terrifying and turbulent.

At this point you are probably thinking, but hang on, you're saying that avoiding things makes anxiety worse – but this is a book about finding an alternative to school and my child is anxious about school! Aren't you implying that I should be making them go to school? Well, no, I'm not, but I don't blame you for being confused. I'm going to go into more detail about this later on in the chapter but there are two important things to remember. First, anxiety is frequently used as the explanation for why many children do not and cannot attend school, but it is usually a reaction not a cause. By which I mean, let's say there are things about school which make the child unhappy, perhaps things which the child is not very able to articulate. When they tell their parents and teacher they don't like it they are told they must continue to go. Over time, as they are made to attend, they become anxious about it, because having to go somewhere that you are unhappy day after day is anxiety-provoking. The anxiety is a reaction, caused by being made to go repeatedly into a situation where they feel unhappy and uncomfortable. It isn't the root cause of the problem. The real problem is that the child feels uncomfortable and unhappy at school and that is where any intervention should start (and for some children, that may be because school as it currently works just isn't a place where they can thrive).

Second, forcing a child into a highly anxiety- and distress-provoking situation day after day in the hope that it will lead to them becoming less anxious is never a good idea and I would never advocate doing that. It's likely to have the opposite effect, because the child will become sensitised to school. Being forced to do something which makes you unhappy is not therapeutic. Their brains will learn that school is more dangerous, rather than less so.

In addition, any intervention for anxiety should be time limited. Parents sometimes tell me that they have been on reintegration programmes for years, with the child going to school just to touch the gate or sit in the corridor, and it never gets any easier. In therapy, if something isn't helping, the answer is not to keep going regardless. If an intervention for anxiety hasn't helped at all in the first few weeks, it is not likely to suddenly work several months or years in. You should be able to see progress if it is working. It should get easier each time.

Come back to Ezra. Last week Ezra went to a playground with his family. When they got there, there were a few other children. Groups of children remind Ezra of school. Ezra started to panic and wanted to leave. His mother Sabrina wanted to help him feel better, and so started to pack up, even though her younger son Nathan wanted to stay and play. Nathan started to protest 'Why do we always have to do what he wants? It's not fair!'

Sabrina stopped, took a deep breath and tried a different approach. She was pretty sure there was nothing scary in the playground and the reason Ezra was scared was to do with his past experiences, not the present situation. 'Ezra,' she said, 'it's okay to feel anxious around new people, lots of people feel this way. Our feelings won't hurt us and they don't mean we have to leave.' Ezra was confused but his brother was delighted. He had left a lot of places before without having had a chance to do what they had come for. He ran off to play.

Sabrina stayed with Ezra. 'When I'm feeling anxious, sometimes it helps me to exercise,' she said, and did some running on the spot. Ezra laughed at her but wasn't fooled. 'I still want to leave,' he said. Sabrina listened and empathised, and said they would leave soon, once Nathan had had a chance to play. She told Ezra again that feeling anxious was okay and it wouldn't hurt him and she knew he could manage to stay for a while. After a few minutes Ezra asked to move from the bench and she and Ezra walked around the outside of the park, with Nathan in sight. They talked about Pokémon, something Ezra felt passionate about and which helped him calm down. Sabrina focused on being with Ezra in the moment, rather than trying to avoid his feelings. After another 30 minutes they all went home after some negotiating with Nathan, but Sabrina felt quite differently about their outing than usual. The playground had not become off-limits, and she planned to go back. Each time they went, Ezra felt a bit better about it. They took tablets and card games and set them up on a picnic table so that Ezra could play while Nathan ran around. It became a time for Sabrina to focus just on him. Then one day Ezra felt brave enough to go down the slide and chase Nathan around, and came back exhilarated.

Ezra is learning that his feelings aren't dangerous, and that they don't have to be avoided. He's learning that Sabrina can tolerate his feelings and isn't scared of them, and that feeling anxious sometimes is part of life. He's learning that he can cope with some anxiety and there are things he can do to help himself. This will mean that he is able to gradually learn that the world is a safer place than he feels, and he will be able to expand what he is capable of managing. It isn't re-traumatising to feel emotions when the situation is in fact different, particularly if you have someone with you who can help you get through it and you are helped to retain some control over the situation. Paradoxically, there would be more risk of re-traumatising if Sabrina behaved as if the park was dangerous, and Ezra left at his peak moment of anxiety and then never came back again.

Table 7.2 shows some of the ways in which parents often (with the best possible intentions) show their children that their anxiety is to be avoided or ignored. Table 7.3 gives some alternatives.

Table 7.2: Ways in which parents respond to anxiety

Ways parents instinctively deal with anxiety	Unwanted consequences
Avoids the situation	Child learns that it was indeed a dangerous situation, and feels more anxious about it Life is more limited
Becomes anxious themselves	Child feels that their anxious feelings must be right, since their parent feels the same way. Anxiety increases
Becomes angry	Child becomes more aroused. Anxiety gets worse
Forces child to do thing they are anxious about	Child resists more strongly the next time round. Child feels trapped which increased anxiety
Tries to stop child feeling anxious or talk them out of it	Child learns their feelings should be got rid of, which makes them more anxious. Child resists these attempts and becomes more anxious
Dismisses child's anxiety	Child learns their feelings aren't acceptable and stops telling their parent

Table 7.3: Alternative ways to respond to anxiety

Alternative ways to deal with anxiety	Consequences
Acknowledging that feelings are hard sometimes	Child learns that feelings are part of life, even negative ones
Commenting on your own feelings of anxiety in new/different situations	Child learns that everyone has these feelings

Not leaving immediately when child becomes anxious but helping them calm themselves and remaining confident that the anxiety will pass	Child learns that they can tolerate the feelings
Sharing anxiety management strategies such as exercise or slow breathing when the anxiety is misplaced	Child learns that this is something they can do something about
Returning to places where the child became anxious	Child learns that feelings are not catastrophic and that their parents aren't afraid of them
Predicting that anxiety might show up and that's okay	Child learns that it's okay to choose to do something which makes you anxious. Anxiety is less frightening when it is predicted
Keeping calm and compassionate	Child learns that their parent can tolerate their feelings
Starting with small steps and gradually increasing at a rate the child can manage	Child gradually becomes more able to manage new situations
Using distraction	Child learns that they can focus on other things, even when they feel anxious

Do you mean I should be forcing my children to do things they are anxious about?

No. These principles of anxiety and trauma come with some important caveats. It will not help an anxious child to feel safe if they are continuously put into a situation against their will where they feel unsafe with no option to leave. There is a big difference between a child agreeing to stay somewhere for a while longer with a trusted adult, and being repeatedly forced to do so.

Many parents I have worked with whose children were very unhappy at school were told that they must force their children to go to school, or their children's anxiety would increase. They went through the process time and time again, leaving a screaming child at the classroom and picking up a child who was either shut down or went immediately into meltdown. The anxiety never reduced and instead the child's refusal got worse. I have talked to parents who have done this for years.

So it's not surprising that they tend to avoid all signs of anxiety once their children are out of school. Why are the two things different, encouraging an anxious child to stay a little longer at the park, and forcing an anxious child into school?

Sometimes anxiety is given as a *reason* why a child doesn't want to do something, when in fact it is a reaction. Here's an example. Imagine you really don't like your job. Maybe you find the work tedious, or you have a boss who shouts at you. Maybe you have ethical concerns about what is going on there. Soon you start to feel anxious each day and you don't want to go in. You stop sleeping well and you start dreading Mondays. You are certainly anxious about work. However, I hope it's obvious that the real problem here isn't your anxiety, it's your workplace. Insisting that you go every day won't make you less anxious about it. Instead, something needs to change at work, or you need to leave. Anxiety is a reaction to not liking your job, not the reason why you don't like it.

The approach of helping children learn that their anxiety is not dangerous only works if the anxiety is irrational (i.e. it's not a reaction to being made to do something which makes them unhappy) and if you have some degree (even a tiny bit) of buy-in from the child. If those children at the park had been horrible to Ezra, or if they had been shouting names at him, then staying there would not have been the right thing to do. To be anxious about going somewhere where you are being badly treated or where you have been repeatedly very unhappy is not irrational.

This is different from feelings of anticipatory anxiety which prevent a person from ever being able to find out whether they like the experience or not, or feelings which are actually leftovers from the past. Ezra didn't know whether he disliked the playground with other children there, but his body was telling it that it was frightening and his anxiety was stopping him from ever finding out whether he liked it or not. When Ezra stayed at the playground for a while with his mother helping him keep calm, he started to feel less anxious – because there wasn't actually anything distressing there, and his mum was there to help him calm down.

Encouraging a child to practise tolerating their emotions should never be a process of forcing them, or telling them they have to become more resilient to doing things they don't like. It's about holding the space for their feelings, showing them that their feelings don't frighten you and that emotions are simply part of life.

Compassionate imagery

This has been a heavy chapter. Let's finish with something positive and lighthearted. There is hope, you are taking positive steps towards restoring your child's mental wellbeing. You need to start by looking after yourself, even if your child isn't up for doing anything different yet. Increase your capacity to cope, and you will do the same for your child.

It's not easy for parents to change their approach from trying to fix things for their child to holding the space for their child's difficult emotions. Most parents feel their child's distress intensely, and they want to make it go away. It makes them feel like a bad parent. Sometimes this is reinforced by the looks and tuts from those around them, who also seem to think that the child's behaviour means that the parent isn't doing a good enough job.

One of the ways to help with this is to develop your own compassionate imagery, to help you stay calm in difficult situations. Parents I have worked with have imagined themselves as roller-skating waitresses, jugglers, ice-skaters and surfers. The idea is that you imagine the feeling of competently managing the situation, and when things are hard, you draw on that imagery and the feelings that it brings up.

COMPASSIONATE IMAGERY EXERCISE

Think of a metaphor for managing and keeping your cool when things get hard.

Some that parents have thought of are:

- Putting on a performance on stage
- Ice-skating
- Flying overhead like an eagle
- Juggling
- Swimming like a swan
- Being a polar bear.

Choose one of these, or imagine one of your own.

Imagine this and let yourself focus on how it feels in your body. Flesh out the image. What can you see, hear, smell or feel? Are you moving? How does that feel?

Now introduce a challenge to the imagery, and see yourself managing it. Maybe you are skating around a hole in the ice, or

---

catching a ball which you almost dropped. See yourself coping as things get hard and tough and you keep going.

Notice how that feels in your body. Focus on your emotions and the sensations.

If you want, you can slowly tap your knees or the side of your thighs about six to eight times, and notice if the feelings grow stronger.

Now give your image a name to remind yourself of it. Practise it over the next few days at times when you don't need it but are feeling relaxed. Over time, you can bring up this image in moments of stress to help you keep calm at the hardest times.

FIVE-POINT SUMMARY

1. The survival system is triggered when a person feels under threat. This can put someone into a flight/fight/freeze or fawn response.
2. Repeated experiences of feeling under threat mean that a person's survival system is triggered more easily. They become sensitised.
3. This results in a narrowed window of tolerance, which can look like challenging behaviour or shutdown.
4. Anxiety results when the sense of threat is greater than a child's feeling that they can cope.
5. In order to help children feel safer, we need to show them that emotions are part of life and not something to be scared of. Over time, this will lead to children feeling safer and their emotions will be less frightening.

CHAPTER 8

WHEN PRESSURE IS TOXIC

The adults around Jamal were confused. 'I don't know what I'm doing wrong, but nothing seems to work,' his mother told me. 'Whatever I say to Jamal, he does the opposite. Even when I'm praising him! Last night, I thanked him for eating his dinner so nicely and he said he'd never do that again and then he kicked his sister. I never know when I'm going to say the wrong thing. I thought he was interested in space, so I got a workbook about planets, but he was completely uninterested, and then he ripped it up when I wasn't looking.'

I meet a lot of children like Jamal. Children for whom the usual parenting strategies don't seem to work. Praise their clay sculptures, and they never pick up the clay again. Ask them to sit at the table, and they react as if you tried to force them to eat a mouldy banana. Bribes and persuasion have no effect, they have a deep aversion to reward charts and they definitely won't go near the naughty step. The more parenting manuals their parents read, the worse things seem to get.

In the last decade or so in the UK, these children are often identified by their parents or others as having pathological demand avoidance (PDA). PDA is a new arrival on the diagnostic scene. It is usually understood as part of the autism spectrum, but with quite different characteristics. The first paper on PDA was only published in 2003, and it is something which is better known in the UK than in other countries, where children with this profile may be given a diagnosis of oppositional defiant disorder (ODD) or simply told they are 'badly behaved'.

The central feature of PDA (a term coined by Elizabeth Newson) is an anxiety-driven need to avoid the demands of everyday life, which often appears to others as resistance. Some children are now being given a diagnosis of 'autism with a demand avoidant profile'. PDA is not an official diagnosis, meaning that it isn't in the psychiatric diagnostic manuals, which means that many professionals won't diagnose it. It is a description. It brings together a group of characteristics and gives them a name.

The concept of PDA has spread extremely fast, perhaps partly because it is not an official diagnosis and therefore is likely to be something that parents recognise in their children, or adults recognise in themselves, but which is frequently not also assessed by a health professional. This doesn't mean those people are wrong, but it does mean that a much wider group of people are now identifying themselves as PDA than was originally conceived by those who drew up the criteria. It has what consultant child psychologist Phil Christie, who has been involved with PDA from the beginning, has called a 'strong recognition factor' (Christie *et al.*, 2011). People hear about PDA, and they have a lightbulb moment. For many parents, it describes what they are seeing in their child, and it explains why none of the strategies they are using have been working. For adults, it gives them a new way to understand their experiences and to think about their difficulties. Some people prefer to think of PDA as standing for a 'persistent drive for autonomy' since this puts a different lens on the behaviour. Others feel that this doesn't capture the realities of life for some children, who aren't so much asking for autonomy as too anxious to participate in things they might enjoy.

Many children avoid demands at different stages in their lives, particularly following bad experiences at school or elsewhere. Demand avoidance is a natural and common response to stress and trauma in adults and children. The approaches in this chapter are not only relevant to one group of children, and just because your child avoids demands now does not mean they will be the same forever. Brains are developing throughout childhood, very little is 'hard-wired' and what you do as a parent can make a difference. The aim of the strategies I'm outlining in this chapter is to create an environment within which your child can thrive and grow, and we really can't predict what that might mean for the future. We can only do the best we can do right now.

I suggest not worrying about whether you think your child fits the criteria for PDA or not, but instead reading this chapter with an open mind and trying things out. Thinking through the lens I offer here might help you to help your child, no matter what diagnoses they do or don't have.

One way that I think about these children is as pressure-sensitive. It's as if they are born with an in-built coercion detector and they are acutely sensitive to hidden agendas and manipulation. Many pressure-sensitive children are exceptionally clear-sighted. They challenge their parents in so many ways, because much of what we think of as parenting involves controlling children. They ask the questions which haven't occurred to anyone else and this can mean that they challenge the conventions that need to be challenged.

Children and adults like this have always existed. Describing PDA didn't bring them into existence, but it did give a name to a developmental trajectory which previously might have been understood in different (and often negative) ways. One of the reasons PDA has become so popular (apart from the lightbulb moment) is because it offers an explanation to parents for whom traditional parenting techniques aren't working. It gives another way of understanding the problem to families who have often been blamed for their children's behaviour. It offers a rationale as to why mainstream parenting isn't not working, and it can lead families to an alternative way of parenting and educating. This often isn't an easy journey.

To start with, here's Chloe's story.

Chloe's story

Chloe was 14 when I spoke to her with her mother Tracey. Chloe is a social influencer and has a YouTube channel @chloemejustme. There, you can see videos of Chloe explaining how she feels when people tell her what to do, and how she has to get around her brain. She's fantastically articulate and funny, and a great advocate for a different way of doing things.

Chloe started school and tried two different schools before the second school suggested that they home educate – a suggestion which Tracey says was less of a choice and more like the only option they had left. School was always hard for Chloe, and Tracey said that looking back she wouldn't have sent her if she had known there was a choice.

Chloe told me about what she remembered of school before she came out when she was seven:

It's just constantly being stressed. It's just a new place away from the people you feel safe around. Being someone who is neurodivergent, it's just terrifying. It's been so long, so I can't really remember exactly, because all I can remember now is waking up early in the morning and feeling the weight and expectation to get ready and go to school. I don't know why school expects you to wake up so early. And then they complain that you don't do homework – like, take away my sleep and then complain that I'm tired!

Chloe was reading and writing before she started school and wasn't allowed to read books at her level at school, something else she found nonsensical.

> They used to try and stop me from reading certain books saying, 'No, you have to read this really easy book, because we don't want you getting ahead of the others.'
>
> They would say, 'It's not ABCD. It's Aa ba ch.' And a year later, they would say, 'Oh, now it's ABCD.'
>
> They tell you not to do joined-up writing and then as soon as I learnt that way they said then we had to join up.
>
> I thought, 'Well, why didn't you tell me?' They undid everything I knew.
>
> They would say, 'Oh, no, we need to keep it easy. Because if you learn too much, then we can't teach you.'
>
> Basically, they'd make you completely forget everything you've learnt. Just hold you back. As soon as I got to the age where I did actually need to know the stuff that I used to know, they had to reteach me. It was so counterproductive.

Things got really bad for Chloe and her family when she was at school. They told me that she would have 'instant meltdowns' when she left school each day. She remembers complaining about everything and not being able to sleep. She talks about it as offloading her trauma. Her mother said she wouldn't leave the house at all and it felt as if their house became a prison. Doing anything required enormous amounts of preparation so that Chloe felt safe enough to manage.

Chloe left school to be home educated when she was seven. You'll hear more from her at the end of this chapter, but let's start now by thinking about what sensitivity to demands means for children at school – and what is going on underneath.

The demands of school

The central idea in the concept of PDA is that children (and adults) resist demands because of anxiety. 'Demands' are actually a bit of a misnomer. We're not talking about demanding that a person does something, like a sergeant major. What is meant by 'demands' are the expectations and requirements of everyday life. Getting dressed in the morning, for example, or answering someone when they speak to you; lining up at school, or sitting down at your desk; making yourself food, or cleaning your teeth.

The idea is that children resist demands because they make them anxious, and they often express that anxiety in ways which those around them see as anti-social behaviour. Violence, for example, or swearing at other people. Or simply outright, inconvenient refusal.

This response becomes particularly problematic at school because many mainstream parenting and educational strategies rely on provoking anxiety. It's commonplace to try to motivate children to 'behave' by telling them that that if they don't do what they are told, they'll get into trouble. That's anxiety-provoking. Schools sometimes tell young people that if they don't pay attention and do what they are told at school, they won't get good jobs and might end up 'under a bridge', as one of my teenage clients told me. That's anxiety-provoking. At primary school, children who are disruptive sometimes have their names written up on the board for all to see. That's anxiety-provoking, not just for them, but for everyone else who can see what might happen to them in the future.

Anxiety is actively used to control children, often by adults who have not thought about what they are doing in these terms. Parents and teachers do this because it works. For many children, it does change their behaviour. They want to avoid anxiety and so they comply in order to get away from the uncomfortable feelings. Many children can manage this anxiety and so for them, there doesn't (externally at least) seem to be a problem.

Other children can't manage it. Their anxiety spirals. They start to worry so much about ending up under a bridge that they can't think about anything else. They start chewing their sleeves or fingernails to shreds and can't sleep at night. And for some of these children, the way they express that anxiety is by shutting down (or refusing), or through anti-social behaviour. They try to avoid more demands, because that over-loads them even more.

Unfortunately, what often happens then is that schools and parents increase the pressure. They try to push children to stop behaving in those ways, perhaps by forcing them to attend school when they don't want to, or by punishing them for their behaviour. That's when everything can go wrong, because the more parents and schools try to get them to conform, the worse their anxiety becomes – and the more avoidant their behaviour is.

This means that for these children, most traditional parenting and behavioural advice not only doesn't work, it actively makes things worse.

Nothing we do seems to work

Sophie's mother Beth got in touch. 'I don't know what to do anymore,' she said. 'I've tried so hard to get things right, but we can't do anything at all. Our life is a minefield. Sophie can throw a tantrum about anything – yesterday it was because her little brother had had a haircut! I don't know what to do.'

Sophie was home educated. She had started school and had managed Reception, but things had got progressively worse in Year 1 and then in Year 2 she had a strict teacher and was constantly in trouble. After one particular incident which had ended in Sophie climbing the fence, running away from school and getting half-way home by herself, her parents had decided to home educate. They did not trust school to keep Sophie safe.

However, things had not been easy at home. Beth explained how Sophie resisted things which they hadn't even thought of as requests. She wouldn't sit at the table for meals, let alone eat her greens. She would strip her clothes off whenever possible, and she really disliked leaving the house, to the point where she would bar the door and scream if Beth tried to insist. Recently, she had started to stop Beth leaving too, insisting that they all stay at home. But while at home, she didn't seem that happy either. She was bored and frustrated, and didn't seem to be able to get into anything except playing on her iPad, which her parents restricted to one hour a day. They had terrible fights over that. They were locking the iPad away as otherwise Sophie would find it and hide away. 'The only way our life is liveable is if we do exactly as she wants, all the time,' said Beth. 'I feel like I'm in prison. And the worst thing is, I feel she is calling all the shots and she's stopping us living our lives, but she isn't happy.'

I've met many families like Sophie's. Some of the children have diagnoses, others don't. The reason I meet a lot of them is usually because school has gone wrong for them. Not because they can't do the academic work, nor because they don't want to learn, but because for them, all the other demands around going to school make them so stressed that they cannot function. Some of them refuse to go to school, kicking and screaming in the mornings. Others show extreme behaviour at school, doing things like throwing tables at teachers or out of windows. Some of them get excluded or suspended.

Not all children who find the non-academic demands of school intolerable show it at school. Some of them appear to be 'fine' while at school, but collapse when school is over. This group are perhaps the most challenging for parents and schools to understand. They get to the car after school and start shouting or kicking their parents, or they arrive home and immediately strip all their clothes off and run around the house screaming. Or, as they get older, they disappear into their bedrooms and the X-box, refusing all attempts at communication or interaction. Schools tend to assume that the problem must be home, and recommend parenting classes. Parents feel terrible, wondering what they have got so wrong that their child, so well behaved at school, is so distressed at home.

Sometimes, when these children finally stop going to school, they seem to have lost all interest in anything. They refuse all suggestions, but are bored and frustrated. They are so sensitive that even the suggestion of pizza or ice-cream is enough to trigger distress. Their parents don't know what to do.

The more we try, the worse it gets

Children like Sophie are acutely sensitive to being controlled. They have specialist detection antennae for it, with the sensitivity threshold set about a thousand times lower than other children. They can sniff out a hidden agenda a mile off, and generally tell their parents so. They are unpersuadable and unbribable. All the usual parenting and school behavioural tools make things worse, because most parenting tools are in fact techniques to get children to comply. These are the children who see through these manipulations. They are exceptionally clear-sighted.

These are the children who will absolutely not be persuaded to cooperate at the doctor's with the promise of a sweet afterwards, but instead will have insisted that you give them the entire bag, abandon the whole doctor visit idea and go home, before you even get out of the car. The more their parents try to 'be consistent' the more their children resist. Table 8.1 summarises some of the ways in which parental strategies don't work as parents hope. Not all children will find all of these strategies anxiety-provoking. There is no one-size-fits-all.

The reason why things get worse is because so many of the strategies that parents use are based on anxiety, and it is anxiety that drives many children to behave the way they do. Increase the anxiety, and you'll get more of the behaviour that you're trying to prevent.

Table 8.1: Common parenting strategies and their effect on anxiety

Parenting strategy	What it looks like	Possible effect on child
Rewards	'If you do this, I'll buy you an ice-cream afterwards'	Emotion: increased anxiety Possible thoughts: 'What if I don't do this? What if I can't do this? What if I don't get the ice-cream?'
Punishments/ consequences	'If you do this, I will take the X-box away for the rest of the week'	Emotion: increased anxiety and anger Possible thoughts: 'What right do they have to take away my X-box? I need the X-box, but what if I can't stop myself doing that?'
Telling off	'That was a horrible thing to do and you must never do it again'	Emotion: increased anxiety, shame and anger Possible thoughts: 'Am I a horrible person?' 'Why do I do these things?' 'What happens if I do do it again?'
Emotional pressure	'It makes me sad when you fight with your brother'	Emotion: increased anxiety, sadness, guilt, confusion Possible thoughts: 'I make my mum sad. Am I a bad person? What do I do when my brother kicks me?'
Non-specific threats	'If you make me angry, you'll regret it'	Emotion: increased anxiety, fear, anger Possible thoughts: 'What will happen? How might I make them angry?'
Disapproval/ disappointment	'I am really disappointed in your behaviour. I thought you knew better than that'	Emotion: increased anxiety and shame Possible thoughts: 'Does that mean I'm a bad person? I did the wrong thing, does that mean I can't trust myself?'

Giving warning (including, for some, visual timetables, counting to three)	'Tomorrow we are going to do this, then this, and then this.' 'When I count to three, I want you to get in the car'	Emotion: increased anxiety Possible thoughts: 'What if I can't manage that? I don't want to do all those things. What if I want to stay at home instead?'
Star charts	'If you get five stars then you can have a reward'	Emotion: increased anxiety Possible thoughts: 'What do they want me to do? What if I don't get five stars? Can I have another star now? Why can't I just have the stars? When can I have my next star?'

This basic paradox – that some children are highly prone to anxiety, and most parenting strategies are based on using anxiety – can mean that the harder parents try to 'take control' the more highly aroused a child gets. And the more highly aroused they are, the less they can cope, and the more rigid their behaviour becomes. Their window of tolerance (see Chapter 7) shrinks.

Parents find this very difficult, particularly parents who have tried to take a peaceful, gentle approach to their children. Children respond to a mild request to put their socks on with 'NO, YOU CAN'T FORCE ME' at the top of their lungs, and the parents is left wondering what they are doing wrong. Why are their children so angry, when forcing them is the very last thing they want to do?

The result can be that everyone feels bad about themselves: the children because they are constantly being told they shouldn't be reacting in the way that they are, and the parents because they can't understand why they are getting such extreme reactions.

The demand avoidance continuum

As with pretty well every other type of neurodiversity, there's a tendency for some children to be categorised as 'PDA' and then seen as different from everyone else. While there are definitely children who are (much) more sensitive to demands and have more extreme emotional reactions than others, demand avoidance is something which varies not just between people, but also between contexts.

We all have a level of background stress that we can manage and what exceeds that level will differ for everyone. When our background stress levels are too high, we cope less well with day-to-day stressors. Our window of tolerance shrinks. Each demand can start to feel painful, like being poked, even if it's something as commonplace as replying to a text message or making a meal.

Think back to some of the most stressful times in your life. Did you become less able to manage the other tasks of life? Did it become harder to deal with people who were slightly annoying, or to manage a bit of frustration? That was certainly the case for me when I was taking my university exams. I lived on instant noodles because shopping and cooking were just too much, and I holed myself up in my room much of the time because being around others (who might talk or ask about exams) just added to my feelings of being overwhelmed. I often didn't answer the phone or respond to emails. There were others whose response was more extreme, and their ability to meet the demands of looking after themselves while dealing with the high levels of stress reduced to the extent that they could not cope at all. Everything was too much. We all have a different capacity to manage demands, and that capacity will change depending on the environment.

Some children's ability to cope is exceeded by being at school or nursery. They find the school day so demanding that they don't have anything left for other things. Just getting through that door, being surrounded by other children, having to wear uniform and separate from their parents already puts them in a state of high anxiety. This can just be because of developmental differences – some children mature more quickly than others, and we know that maturity makes a big difference to how well a child fares in the education system.

When the demands exceed their ability to cope, this blocks those children from learning, because they spend their days outside their window of tolerance. That is never going to be a good place to learn. They are constantly in a state of high arousal, and the smallest things may make them distressed. It often mystifies those around them, because it doesn't seem as if anything should be so distressing. It's just school, and everyone else 'seems fine'. So, as with so many things, we locate the problem in the child and say that *they* are different, or 'pathological'. We blame it on their brain.

This takes our attention away from the context and focuses it on the child, but actually the context is what makes all the difference. A child can be highly anxious in one place, while relaxed and happy in another. The problem arises in the interaction between the child and their environment. Some children can't thrive in some environments.

Working hard to stay okay

Most demand avoidant children I have met work really hard to keep themselves in their window of tolerance. This work is not recognised nor appreciated by those around them. Many of the strategies that they find for themselves aren't valued by the adults as attempts to keep themselves balanced. This is because children often try to control the world outside them, in order to make themselves feel okay. This is perceived as 'bad behaviour' and so the children get told off or punished, which then pushes them outside their window of tolerance – and off we go again. The lists on the following page summarise some of this.

How children try to keep themselves in their window of tolerance

Signs of being hyper-aroused

- Meltdowns
- Violence
- Shouting
- Trying to escape
- Running
- Agitation
- Swearing.

Signs of being hypo-aroused

- Not responding
- Glazed eyes
- Passivity
- Appearing not to hear what is said to them
- Lethargy
- Tiredness.

Strategies children use to try to keep themselves within their window of tolerance

- Avoiding everyday demands
- Trying to control other people
- Refusing to go to places which might overwhelm them
- Getting away from sensory input – taking clothes off, hiding in duvet, covering ears
- Refusing to let the people who help them feel safe leave (often their mothers)

- Refusing to try anything new
- Trying to keep adults focused on them (rather than talking to each other)
- Refusing to let their parent be distracted from caring for them
- Telling visitors to leave if they arrive at a time where there is already too much going on
- Asking visitors when they will leave or telling them it's time for them to go now
- Refusing to put down a device
- Showing behaviour which they know will mean they are excluded from an activity
- Titrating what they can do at one time – e.g. if at a new place, don't want to also meet new people.

It's great that children try to keep themselves in their window of tolerance. This is something that will be extremely useful to them as adults. However, the problem arises when their efforts cause problems for those around them, or for them themselves. Our job as parents is to help them find other ways to manage their emotions which don't limit their lives and opportunities in the same way.

What do parents do in response?

When a child resists their parent's demands in an unusually intense way, parents tend to go two ways. They either refuse to accept the child's resistance, becoming strict or authoritarian, or they totally accept the child's resistance, rearranging their lives to avoid anything which make the child anxious.

Both have drawbacks. In the first scenario, life is a series of battles and there is a lot of shouting and unhappiness. In the second scenario, the parents severely constrain the lives of the whole family, and accept that one child will control what everyone else can do. This is not going to work well in the long term. It's important that the voice of every child (and adult) in the family is heard – and that reducing demands and increasing autonomy doesn't become 'we all have to do whatever she says'.

It's also common for families to veer between these two approaches, and for one parent to take on the more authoritarian role, while the other parent takes on the more accepting role. The parent who is around less is often more inclined to fight the battles, while the one who is around more (often, but not always, the mother) is often more likely to take on acceptance, perhaps after first trying out the authoritarian approach and finding that it didn't work. It's also common for families to find that they have to go for no demands at all at home while their children are at school. This is because school creates such a lot of anxiety that the child is essentially in recovery mode when they are at home, and they can't tolerate anything that causes extra stress – which includes all demands.

As children recover, the aim is that over time they can practice managing new experiences – and in order for that to happen, parents need to make sure that those opportunities are there in the environment. In Chapter 9, I'll discuss in detail how to go about introducing change for a child who finds change anxiety-provoking. Here, I'll discuss what self-directed education can look like and how it's different for pressure-sensitive children.

Ultra-low demand self-directed education

Self-directed education is already a far lower demand way to parent than school, and for some children being outside the pressures of school is enough for them to relax and to be able to explore new things.

For others, this isn't enough. Some kids are so sensitive to pressure that even a new toy or book is too much, if it is perceived as coming with an adult agenda attached. The parents of these children find that just suggesting something is enough to ensure their children will not try it, possibly for years. I know people who managed to put their children off *Minecraft* by being too enthusiastic about it. I've met children who loved to paint – until their pictures won competitions, whereby they immediately stopped. For these children, enthusiasm from a parent can feel like a demand – the child thinks, how am I expected to respond? What if I don't respond appropriately? What if I don't like it? It feels safer to simply not engage.

Self-directed education with these children is an art form. While other parents talk of 'strewing' workbooks around, or organising educational trips with other home educators to the local history museum, parents of demand avoidant children have to develop a whole new set of skills. Even making a suggestion can be enough to rule out an opportunity, because the child feels that is an expectation. Suggesting a video game can be enough to ensure that the game is never played. Being given something as a gift can be enough to make it a demand, meaning it will never be used.

I have met many families with piles of unopened activity boxes or magazines, ordered in hope or given for birthdays and then never touched. These parents can never get away with printing off worksheets whenever a child expresses an interest, because they learn fast that creating those 'teachable moments' is enough to kill the enthusiasm. Much of the advice they are given by other home educators just doesn't seem to apply. Their problem is not finding the right resources or local groups, it's how to introduce those to their children in a way which doesn't get an automatic 'No'.

As always with self-directed education, you need to start where the child is, and join them there. If your child has been in school or you have been parenting in a controlling way, you and they have some recovery to do. It will take time, possibly years. You need to rebuild their trust that you will not try to force them to do things and that you are not secretly trying to get them back into school or following a curriculum. Even if your child hasn't been to school, however, you will need to spend a long time establishing that you aren't there to force them to do things. They need to really believe that they will be able to say 'No,' before they can risk saying 'Yes'.

Some parents find that they can introduce new ideas by doing things that they themselves are interested in – but this has to be genuine. Your child will notice if you feign an interest in fractions or photosynthesis. However, if you're genuinely interested in baking chocolate cakes, learning mosaicking, or practising the oboe, then give it a try, for you. Don't wait for them to show an interest. If you want to order a subscription activity box, do it for you and open it yourself. Your child may join you, or they may not. No matter, you do it anyway. You are bringing new ideas and energy into the house even if your child doesn't join you. Parents of only children have to work harder on this one, because siblings naturally bring a different energy into a house. Put on background music (if they can tolerate it). Buy magazines which you are interested in, listen to podcasts or audio books. Learn a new skill. Bring in different people to your house to see you, not your child. Think about how you can make sure there are opportunities for new experiences in your family life, even if your child isn't ready to take you up on them. Seek out new connections. At the very least, it will make your life more interesting, and that is important in itself.

The expectation that something will be 'fun' can be felt as a demand, and so it's often best to be offhand about any organised outings or events. 'We could go, but we don't have to' can go a long way. Or, 'We could go to see what it's like and then come home.'

When choices make things worse

Self-directed education involves allowing children autonomy in what they do – but this isn't always straightforward. Many parents think that autonomy means 'lots of choices', and then they discover that choices send their child into a tailspin. Some children really don't like choice. They get easily overwhelmed by questions like, 'What would you like to do today?' or, 'Would you like sausages, soup or nuggets for supper?'

Autonomy isn't the same as 'lots of choices'. It's more important to have the chance to make choices you find important and meaningful than having lots of options. Autonomy means that children can make decisions about their lives, but some children will need a lot more support to do this than others – and some won't want to make lots of decisions. It's important to meet each child where they are.

One way to support autonomy is to reduce the demands associated with choice. Rather than asking 'Would you like to go to the zoo or the seaside?' it might be better just to ask about one at a time. 'I was thinking of going to the zoo.' If there's no response, you could wait a bit and then try the same for the seaside, at which point they may say, 'But I thought you said the zoo.' For these children, it can be less stressful if they are just asked whether they would like a packet of Monster Munch rather than choosing between all the packets of crisps. An autonomy-supportive environment isn't the same as lots of choices. Table 8.2 outlines some of the ways in which well-meaning parents can add to their children's stress, and offers alternatives.

Table 8.2: Reducing the demands

Instead of....	Try...
Choices (Would you like Quavers or Cheesy Wotsits?)	One option at a time (Quavers?)
Persuasion (Come on, you'll like it when you get in there)	Backing off (We can decide not to go if we want)
Expensive days out (I've paid a lot for this, we're going to stay until this afternoon)	Annual memberships (We can leave after 20 minutes if you want, and come back another time)
Bank holidays out at the beach	Bank holidays in the garden (or the house)
Building up the excitement/anticipation before Christmas and birthdays	Playing down the anticipation/build up Opening presents when they arrive
Buying things you think they'll like in advance	Waiting until they see something and ask for it

Planning activities for them (We're all going to make cupcakes)	Planning activities for you (I'm going to make cupcakes, you can join me or not, as you wish)
Enthusiasm (It'll be great!)	Being off-hand (It might be fun, or it might not)
Expecting them to join you (Let's all play Monopoly)	Joining them where ever they are (You're playing Minecraft)
Expecting them to make connections in groups	Making individual connections with other families who understand
Rationalising (Last time you did this you enjoyed it, so why not this time?)	Empathising with their feelings (You're feeling worried about it this week)
Pushing their limits (This day has gone well, let's top it off with a meal with friends)	Quitting when you're ahead (This day has gone well, let's go home to decompress)
Big gatherings with lots of people	Smaller gatherings and space to get away
Hoping that they'll just join in	Providing space for them to choose not to join in
Reacting personally (Why do you always do this to me?)	Breathing and holding the space (It's hard at the moment)
Meeting to chat with other parents while the children play	Letting other parents know in advance that you may not be able to chat and you'll catch up with them another time
Insistence that if we have paid, you're going to do it (We can't afford to pay for you not to do it)	Flexibility even when you have paid (If we can afford to pay for you to do it, we can afford to pay for you not to do it)

When it comes to outings, you need to build up credibility. Don't waste time on things you might regret. Noisy, busy trips to theme parks with lots of queuing and expectation of enjoyment are not the right places for most pressure-sensitive children; in fact they may be more like torture for everyone. Find interesting things to go to, try to go out of season and be ready to leave quickly, or for a child to say 'No'. Start small and local. Rainy days might be the time to head for an outdoor attraction, while sunny days could be ideal for doing things inside.

The aim is for children to be relaxed enough so that they can start to engage with the world on their own terms. None of this should be done so that children can then be returned to school (unless they themselves want to go). The aim is learning, not school. If we can reduce the demands enough, they can be freed up to learn whatever interests them. In the longer term, they will have the time and space to learn to manage their emotions and to look outwards as well as inwards. That can't happen if they are in crisis all the time.

So what happens when families adopt a low-demand, low-pressure lifestyle? What does a different way look like? I asked Chloe, with whom I started this chapter.

When Chloe came out of school, aged 7, things did not improve immediately. Her mother Tracey said she felt that it took about a year before Chloe was ready to start to meet people. They couldn't go anywhere before that, particularly since Tracey doesn't drive and so they would have had to take the train. Tracey described how they started going out for short walks in the park, and how it took a long time for Chloe to realise she wouldn't have to go back to school and wouldn't be made to do things.

> Eventually we did go to a few things, but it had to be no pressure. I'd say, 'If you don't like it, we'll just leave straightaway.' And we did that a few times. It helped her realise, okay, if I'm stressed, I can go. If I'm stressed, we can go somewhere else. We can do this, we can sit down and it will be okay.

The difference in Chloe now is dramatic. She says she feels she hasn't been properly stressed for a long time, and can't remember the last time she had a real meltdown. She'd like parents to know that a PDA profile doesn't have to mean stress and meltdowns.

> I sometimes read parent forums, and parents say, 'Oh, yeah, they cry a lot and have meltdowns.' And I want to say, 'That's not a normal thing. You're doing something wrong! If they are having violent rages when you say things, it's clearly something to do with how you bring it up, it's not enough to say, "Oh, that's just their nature".'

Chloe is taking courses in cookery and art, as well as maths and English and would like to take GCSEs. She knows that when she is told directly to do something, she feels anxiety, which prevents her from doing the task. She's finding her own ways around this, a process she called 'looking for loopholes'.

If I am given something direct to do then the anxiety attached will be too crippling and I will be unable to even try it out. Having options, freedom or just the safety of knowing that I can explore different ways allows me to actually do something!

I like to look for the loophole. If they said we had to make a book, for example, I don't see a specific loophole. So I'll just make it bigger or smaller, or different. That way I can somehow make it work in my head. Then I'll panic because of time management and that's my own downfall. I made it way too big and way too extravagant.

Tracey said that now that Chloe is older, they are finding that there is more flexibility in courses that she does. Over time, activities of daily living have become more possible but Chloe still does them in ways which feel easier for her. Tracey explained:

She finds a way around it now rather than refusing or procrastinating, which was pretty much what she did in her younger life. Yeah, she now just goes, 'Okay, so in order to do this thing I want to do, I have to find a way around it.' I can imagine it being very taxing and tiresome in her brain and she needs to find ways that help her feel in control and safe. I hope the environment and the way we help her allows her to do that.

Chloe talks about the other ways in which Tracey and she work together to make it possible for her to do things.

My mum has found a way that helps me do certain activities by putting a bunch of things out on the table. Then I walk up and I go, 'What's that? I want to do that!' My curiosity always gets the better of me. I know why she has done it but there is no pressure, just choices of what I can do.

Tracey agrees that she does plan things to avoid a direct demand.

When she was young, I would start doing something and she would come and say, 'What are you doing?' I'd say, 'Oh, it's really hard' and then she'd be like, 'Oh, Mummy's really stupid, I can help you.'

Chloe is quick to tell us that she's onto this, and the approach no longer works.

Tracey and Chloe feel that PDA is strongly environmental, meaning that how much Chloe is able to learn is down to her environment. They work on trying to get the environment right, so Chloe is free to learn. The transformation is obvious. She's not just learning, she's learning how to manage herself in the world. She's looking for loopholes, so she can work with how her mind works, rather than fighting against it.

That's what we need to be doing as parents. Helping remove barriers so that our children can find ways to achieve the things that they want to do. The difficulty that many of us have is that mainstream parenting culture routinely uses pressure to get children to do things. Rewards, punishments, shame and anxiety, all are different forms of pressure. For pressure-sensitive children, the more pressure there is, the less likely they are to be able to join in or make a real choice.

To help them learn, we have to back off and give them the space, which includes the space to say 'No'.

FIVE-POINT SUMMARY

1. Some children are very sensitive to pressure and emotion.
2. Traditional parenting techniques do not work for these children because they make them anxious, and this makes avoidance worse.
3. These children are often exceptionally clear-sighted and self-determined.
4. Self-directed education provides an alternative way to learn, but parents will need to be aware of hidden pressures and agendas.
5. There is likely to be an extended period of recovery when a pressure-sensitive child comes out of school.

CHAPTER 9

MAKING CHANGES: STOP AND SMELL THE COFFEE

Sara's story

Sara found it hard work going to the playground with Amal. Her behaviour could suddenly escalate, for no reason that her mother Sara could see. She'd told her off multiple times but it just seemed to make things worse. She was eight now, and other children her age seemed to be able to control their behaviour in quite a different way to Amal. Sara hovered nearby, ready to swoop in if she was needed and watching out for signs. Then another mother came up behind her.

'Hi!' she said. 'How are you?'

Sara turned to chat. Three minutes later there was a howl. Amal had pushed another child off the play digger, hard, so that she could have a turn. Sara was there in an instant, apologising profusely to the other child and his mother. Amal was clinging onto the digger with both hands.

'It's my turn,' she said.

Sara didn't know what to do. If she told Amal off, Amal would start screaming and they might be there for hours. If she asked her to get off the digger, she would cling on tighter. She could try to pull her off but that would involve a full-on physical struggle, watched by half the playground. But clearly she was 'meant' to get Amal off so that the little boy could get back on, while telling Amal off and making sure she 'got the message' so she never did it again. Sara felt paralysed. The other mother looked at her and then looked at Amal.

'Some Mummies don't teach their children how to behave. She needs a proper telling off,' she said to her son.

Sara crumpled inside.

In this chapter, I'm going to talk about behaviour. Behaviour is a huge part of education. It's something which prevents thousands of children every year from attending school, leading to exclusion or suspension. There are many books devoted to children's behaviour – how to manage it, what it means and how adults should respond. You've probably read several of them, and tried the strategies.

For this book, I'm going to define behaviour as what we can observe a person doing: their actions, whether that is refusing to go to school, tapping their pencil on the desk or hitting other children. In school, behaviour is often considered something which mostly gets in the way of learning, to be managed through behaviour policies and systems of incentives and consequences. It's seen as a distraction, something which stops learning from happening and which needs to be controlled so that the school can get on with what they see as the real business of education – transmitting academic skills and knowledge.

For many neurodivergent children, however, behaviour is not just a distraction. School expectations for behaviour are a barrier for them, and the way that schools address behaviour can also be a barrier. They are unable to behave in the way which school expects, and in particular, they do not respond well to the strategies that the school uses to control behaviour. They become highly anxious about whether their name will be written on the blackboard, or they refuse when told to get up off the carpet and go to their chair. They intensely dislike having to raise their hand to go to the toilet, and so they don't go at all and end up wetting themselves. They worry about breaking the rules so much that it keeps them up at night. They feel threatened and overwhelmed by groups of children, and they respond by hitting out. Then when the teacher shouts to stop them, they are so afraid that they run away. For these children, it's not academic work that makes school so challenging, it's all the ways in which they are expected to behave, and the ways in which that is enforced.

Many children are excluded from school due to behaviour, and behaviour is one of the main reasons why parents contact me asking for help. They find their children's behaviour unpredictable and challenging, and they don't know how to manage it. Their children react very badly to mainstream parenting techniques such as the naughty step, time out, gentle reminders, star charts or telling off. Many parents have tried autism-specific techniques such as visual timetables, giving lots of warning and social stories, but these don't work for all children either.

In self-directed education, behaviour is not separated from learning, or seen as distraction from learning. It's not seen as something to be controlled and managed. Instead, it's seen in context, as a response to the situation. Behaviour is a way in which children communicate, and one of the things which they communicate through their behaviour is that they lack the skills to manage the situation. They need our help. As with other areas of learning, they need us to work with them and get alongside them.

How do I get them to...?

Most days I will get an email with some variation on the following. 'Our nine-year-old daughter is autistic, and dyslexic and has ADHD. She has been out of school for a year and life is much calmer than it was. However, she won't leave the house unless we insist. We don't want to have to make her but if we don't, she just sits at home. What can we do?'

When it comes to behaviour, most of us think that being a good parent means getting their children to do what they want with minimal struggle. Society tells us that whether you are strict or gentle, authoritative or connected, the proof of the pudding is whether the child will do what you say, ideally the first time and with a smile. This is why the question most parents ask when they contact me is usually some variation on, 'How can I get this child to…?' How can I get them to leave the house without protest, or allow me to have a shower in peace? How can I get them to stop fighting with their sister? How can I get them to stop using their phone so much? How can I get them to eat something other than sausages?

Some parents get in touch for a different reason. Some say that they feel that one of their children is controlling everyone else in the family, and that this doesn't feel right either. They say that they have stopped trying to impose their will on the child, but now they have no idea how to have any influence at all. Not only will their child not leave the house, no one else is allowed to leave the house either. No one else can choose where they sit around the table, even, or whether they have a haircut or change their clothes. Some of these parents even say that they themselves are fine with never leaving the house, but there's a younger sibling who definitely isn't fine with it, and they need things to change for them.

This dichotomy – either the adult is in control of the child or the child is in control of the adult – is mirrored in our attitude to education. I've lost count of the people who have said to me when I am describing self-directed education, 'So you just let them do whatever they want?' Self-directed education is continuously confused with adults doing nothing or very little while the children run amuck. People think that the only alternative to a controlling education system is no adult influence at all.

Self-directed education is not about parents checking out or giving up. It's not about leaving kids to figure things out for themselves. Parents are deeply involved in the educational process with their children – but they don't do that through controlling them. They collaborate with the children to help them learn the things they find interesting. Strong relationships with adults are essential – remember back to Chapter 5? A self-directed education requires relationships, opportunities and autonomy. This approach applies to behaviour just as much as to other forms of learning. Behaviour is an integral part of a self-directed education, and just like other types of learning, parents need to find a third way. An alternative to being controlling or being controlled.

The most helpful practical approach I have found to this is collaboration, where both sides can express their preferences, and adults and children work together to find a solution to a shared problem. Dr Ross Greene is a pioneer of this approach between parents and children, which he calls 'collaborative and proactive solutions'. His book, *The Explosive Child*, outlines his approach in detail (Greene, 2021). He asks parents to think about their children's behaviour in terms of 'lagging skills' rather than 'bad behaviour' and to develop strategies to help their children develop these skills. His basic philosophy is that 'children do well if they can' and therefore if they aren't doing well it's because they lack the skills to do so. It won't help someone acquire skills if you punish them for not having them, particularly if they don't actually know what skills they are lacking – which will be the case with most children. Remember Amal and Sara at the start of this chapter? If Amal lacks the skills to wait for her turn on the digger, telling her off isn't going to help her acquire them, even if we think she really should have them by this stage and even if other children her age do have the skills.

This is a great approach which fits well with self-directed education. However, Greene's approach does assume that children will be at school, and that there are certain non-negotiables such as homework and getting the school bus. Lots of his examples are to do with these. He also puts a lot of focus on 'unmet expectations', which are expectations that adults have of children. I'd take a different approach here. I think that a lot of the time, the problem is that adult expectations are unreasonable. If a child thinks their homework is pointless, my starting point would be that maybe they are right and to find out why they think that (rather than starting with, how do I get them to do their homework?).

For this reason, I have adapted Greene's approach, while retaining his basic principles. It is still collaborative, but my version is suited to children who need things to go a lot more slowly, and whose instinctive reaction to being asked a question is usually 'No'.

A good cup of coffee

Greene's book *The Explosive Child* gives a detailed account of how he uses collaborative problem solving and when I read it when my children were small I laughed. He recommends starting by asking children something like, 'I've noticed you aren't doing your science homework, what's up?' and then having a 'drilling discussion' with them when you find out exactly what the problem is, so that you can solve it together. The parent asks questions like 'I don't understand. What about it is hard?' so that the child and the parents have a clearer idea of what exactly is the problem.

That would be fine, except that for many children a question like that is enough to tip them over the balance and they either ignore us entirely or shout, 'No I'm not' and that is the end of that.

The method I'm outlining here is an alternative and much more low-demand approach. Heidi Steel, a trained teacher, unschooling coach and unschooling mother of four, and I developed this approach for our popular online course for parents – you'll hear more from Heidi at the end of the chapter.

I'm going to use the metaphor of a coffee machine throughout this chapter. I am selective about coffee. I'd rather not have coffee at all than have bad coffee. Making good coffee always has several steps, and it's just not worth rushing it. Instant coffee is a completely different drink. I'd suggest that you remember this as you're working towards collaboration with your child.

This approach is a step up from the base of the Safe to Learn Pyramid. It introduces challenge and change. For this reason, it isn't suitable for all children at all stages. Before any change can occur, the environment needs to be safe, relationships need to be secure, and the child needs to feel that you're on their side. This involves acceptance of the child, their needs and where you are right now. It involves everything you have read about creating a low-demand environment and about working in your child's window of tolerance. Whatever works to increase calm, do it. This is like buying the coffee machine and getting the coffee – you have to do it before you can start.

Setting things up

Throughout this section, I'm going to use the example of Jade and her son Elijah to demonstrate how this process works. Jade came to see me about her son when he was ten. She was finding life very difficult. She was a single mother and she and Elijah were alone together for most of the time. She said he was very controlling, she felt she had no influence at all and she felt trapped in her house. She was doing everything she could to implement a low-demand life, but the more she did this, the more she felt that she had no power.

The first thing I asked Jade to do was to identify all the things which really stressed Elijah.

EXERCISE: WHAT'S THE STRESS?

- Identify the stressors.
- Make a list of all the things which stress your child, no matter how minor or irrational they seem. Then see what you can do to reduce those stressors, and to accept that this is how things are right now.

This is Jade's list:

- Too much talking by adults.
- Questions – feeling 'put on the spot'.
- Any quick changes to plans.
- Getting changed to go to bed.
- Lack of choice.
- Sirens in the street outside.
- Being rushed.
- People arriving at the door unexpectedly.
- People who come to visit and don't say when they are leaving.
- Adults talking to each other and not concentrating on children.
- Clothes with buttons.
- Unfamiliar food.
- Certain tones of voice which sound like a 'telling off'.
- People with funny laughs.
- Sitting at the table with a group of people.

Jade tried to be really honest when writing this list – it wasn't things she thought it was reasonable for Elijah to feel stressed by, it was *everything* that he found stressful, even things Jade found upsetting or rude, like the way that he strongly disliked Jade's sister's laugh and would run away from her or tell her to leave immediately when she came to visit.

Then Jade thought about what she could do to help reduce these stressors. Clothes was an obvious one – they moved over to jogging trousers and t-shirts. Food was fairly easy to deal with too; she stopped trying to make Elijah to try new foods and cooked him his favourite, Quorn nuggets or sausages. He could still have other food if he wanted and the food was on table, but there was no pressure.

Then she started to think about what happened when other people were there, and realised that Elijah was much more relaxed when he knew exactly when people were going to leave. In fact, Elijah would often greet visitors with 'When are you leaving?' – a question which Jade found embarrassing and rude, but which she could reframe as Elijah trying to work out how long he had and how to pace himself. Jade started to say to visitors, 'Elijah likes to plan his day, so we were wondering how long you'd stay?' when he asked, rather than apologising and 'shushing' him. She started to do this more with things which Elijah said which before she had thought of as rude, but which now she reframed as him being honest about his needs.

Elijah often greeted visitors to the house with 'Go away' and Jade realised that Elijah really hated being interrupted in the middle of something and expected to talk to a visitor. She started to say that, in a matter-of-fact way, and to tell Elijah that he could keep going with what he was doing and did not need to come and talk until he was ready.

Jade tried to work with how things were right now, rather than how she wished they were. When she met up with other adults with Elijah there, she warned them that she probably wouldn't be able to talk to them as Elijah would need her. This took the pressure of expectation off her. She finally told her sister that Elijah didn't like her laugh, and that it wasn't that he didn't like her. Her sister was a bit upset, but also saw the funny side and laughed (out of Elijah's earshot).

All of these things made life easier for both Jade and Elijah. Elijah relaxed, and as he relaxed he became able to manage a bit more each day. He wasn't using all his energy coping anymore and Jade noticed he was less reactive, less volatile and (sometimes) a bit more flexible. Jade was more honest with people about the things Elijah found hard, and this helped too. She felt less stressed because she wasn't trying to manage other people's expectations and minimise Elijah's differences. They started to do more things together which they both enjoyed, mostly playing *Roblox* and *Minecraft*.

As Elijah and Jade became more relaxed, Jade started to think about the next stage. This was Plan A, Plan B and Plan C.

Introducing change

Sometimes there are just so many problems and things you would like to change. It can feel overwhelming, and you don't know where to start. The good news is that you don't have to do everything at once, and you don't have to take the same approach to anything. In fact, when it comes to parenting, you have three basic choices. Ross Greene calls these Plan A (imposing your will on the child), Plan B (collaboration) and Plan C (putting that problem on the back burner for now and not insisting).

All three of these approaches are appropriate at different times. If your child is about to run under a car, Plan A is appropriate. If your child is refusing to wear pyjamas and prefers to sleep in their clothes, this might be something you could simply stop worrying about or insisting on – Plan C.

But if there are things which are causing problems for others in the family, choosing Plan C isn't always a good option because it doesn't involve helping the child take account of the perspective of others. It reduces tension and conflict, and it helps the child feel more in control – these are all good things, and in the short term when a child comes out of school, Plan C may be appropriate for most things.

However, what often happens is that parents let go of many things, but then when something happens which cannot be let go of, they don't know what to do. Or they find themselves uncomfortable with just how much they have let go of, and so they revert to Plan A – imposing their will on the child. And just as it didn't work before, it doesn't work now.

Finding a middle way, one where both adult and child voices are heard and where they collaborate, is essential. But it doesn't come easily. Most adults have lagging skills in the area of collaborating with their children, and need to gradually build up their skills.

EXERCISE: PLAN A, PLAN B AND PLAN C

Make a list of the various problems you would like to solve in your family. Try to frame them in neutral language. Then go back and divide them up according to how you think they could be approached. It's fine to put a lot of things into Plan C, and some of those things might be in Plan C for good. But try to put at least a couple into Plan B, because this is where change can start to happen. Be realistic, don't put things which you think there is no hope of changing right now in Plan B – better to place them in Plan C and start with something with a reasonable chance of success.

Jade made her list, and divided everything up. Her lists are given in Table 9.1.

Table 9.1: Plan A, Plan B, Plan C

Plan A (parent imposes control)	Plan B (collaboration)	Plan C (let it go for now)
Elijah, in a spirit of exploration, has climbed out of his window on the second floor onto the roof outside several times. He has continued to do so when asked not to. Jade has decided to put window locks on. Elijah is not happy about his window being locked at night but Jade has decided this is non-negotiable.	Elijah hasn't left the house for several months and will not allow Jade to go alone, which means that Jade is also confined to the house.	Elijah has a very restricted diet. Elijah doesn't dress himself but waits to be dressed. Elijah will shout at other people when they don't do what he wants.

Plan B is proactive, not reactive. This means that it is not a quick plan, particularly with children who need a lot of time to get used to new ideas. It is not something to be put into practice when a child or parent is upset or angry.

In fact, when a parent or child is distressed is the worse time to try and make a change. It's not a time to make your point, stand your ground or have a discussion. It's a time to soothe and calm everyone down.

We call our Plan B 'drip and percolate', because each stage needs to be first carefully dripped in and then left to percolate. Set the coffee machine up, start with dripping in the new ideas, wait out the response (or lack of response) and then let it percolate. Smell the coffee. No need to rush. It can take weeks at first, and it's really important not to push it. The steps to this are shown in Table 9.2 and then I have elaborated on them below, using the example of Elijah and Jade.

The length of the percolation stage depends on your child. You need to let the idea percolate until it has become routine, something that everyone is familiar with. This means you need to be ready to wait out their initial response, which may be dramatic and loud or silent, depending on how they express their emotions. It's fine for them to be anxious about you bringing up something. You then need to empathise, back off and try again another time.

Table 9.2: Plan for Plan B

SET IT UP: Identify the problem without blame and gather information. State it to yourself in neutral language	'We can't leave the house because Elijah bars the door if we try'
DRIP: Introduce this issue to your child and ride out the reaction	'It is hard to leave the house at the moment'
PERCOLATE	Listen to what they say, don't try to solve anything. Empathise. Keep the idea around, don't stop saying it because they get upset. Drop the idea in, and then stop talking. If they are into playing, you could bring the idea of finding it hard to go out into their play, if they allow you to
DRIP SOME MORE: When the issue has been around a while, introduce another perspective (or the dilemma). Ride out the reaction	'It's hard to leave the house *and I would like to sometimes*'

PERCOLATE	Listen out for ideas, empathise, gather information. Wait. Back off if they are upset but don't give up. Listen to see if they are telling you anything about what the problem is from their perspective
DRIP AGAIN: Invite solutions. Let it be	'It's hard to leave the house and I would like to sometimes. *I wonder what we could do about that?'*
PERCOLATE	Don't expect answers to the question when asked. Ideas might come at unexpected times. Keep it in your general family discussion as something that will happen in the future
POUR IT OUT: Make a list of ideas	What might you do about this problem? Does your child have any ideas? Do other family members have ideas? Don't dismiss anything. Write any ideas down (but don't expect to sit down together and write a list). Be creative!
DRINK THE COFFEE: Try something new	Expect it to be difficult at first. Ride out the reaction.
If it doesn't work, don't catastrophise. Go back to inviting solutions and find something else to try	

The basic idea behind the percolation stages is that children need time to get used to each new idea, and that you don't have to keep talking to enable them to do this. In fact, lots of children find lots of talking by their parents highly stressful. If you have said it once in ear shot, I'd assume they have heard it.

Introduce an idea, wait for their reaction, and then back off and let it be. Be confident that they have heard, don't check. Don't let their reaction be a reason not to keep bringing something up again, but wait to do that for a few hours or even days – this issue is important, that is why you have decided to Plan B it. Expect a first strong negative reaction, and wait it out. It's a sign that the idea is new, rather than that they can't manage the change.

Here's a detailed example with Jade and Elijah so you can see what it looks like in practice. This is a very flexible method and the steps are not rigid, you will work it out alongside your child. The basic structure is: introduce the idea, give the child time, introduce it again, give them more time.

Step 1: Identify

Identify the problem and think for yourself a bit about what could be causing it.

Jade identified that leaving the house was really important to her and that she was feeling low and miserable because she could not go out. It wasn't just that Elijah did not want to go out, he would bar the door and fight her when she tried to go out alone, sometimes even just to take the bins out. She felt trapped.

Jade started by observing Elijah's behaviour, and formed some hypotheses for herself about why he didn't like going out. She remembered that in the past when they were out, she had had a habit of trying to add in 'just one more thing' as she hadn't known when they would be able to go out again, and so trips had got longer and longer. Often as they were almost home she would try to pop into the local shop to buy milk. At that point, Elijah would have a meltdown and she would struggle to get him out of the local shop and back home. She guessed that Elijah felt out of control when they were out, and that he didn't know that he would be able to go home when he needed to.

Step 2: Drip

Introduce the issue to the child. Empathise with their response. The technique here is brief, to the point. Initially, at least, expect a strong negative response.

Jade said to Elijah, 'It is hard to leave the house at the moment.' Elijah shouted, 'No, I'm not going' and walked out of the room. Jade left it. She didn't comment on his reaction, she didn't shout back and she didn't mention it again for a while. She didn't need to, Elijah had heard.

Step 3: Percolate

At this stage, continue to bring up the same idea, with nothing new, until the child's reaction becomes less intense. This is not the same as repeatedly saying the same thing to the child or pressuring them to respond. It's more a question of keeping the issue alive in your house.

Later, Jade said it again. 'It is hard to leave the house at the moment.' Elijah huffed and puffed. Jade left it.

The next day, she tried to empathise. 'It feels hard to think about leaving the house.' Elijah looked at her and didn't shout, but said nothing.

Later that day when they were playing *Minecraft* together Elijah said, 'Why do you keep on mentioning leaving the house? You know I don't like it.' That was Jade's cue to move onto the next stage.

Step 4: Add another perspective (Drip again)

Here, you expand the problem to bring in another perspective. For more flexible children, you may be able to start at this point by naming both parts of the problem. Others need to get used to the idea of the problem first. Sometimes I actually hold both hands out in front of me when I do this – on one hand, you don't want to leave the house, but on the other hand, your mum needs to get out sometimes. In this way, the two parts to the problem are obvious. For a younger child, you could draw both parts of the problem.

Jade said, 'It is hard to leave the house, but I would like to sometimes.'
Elijah shouted at her, 'Well, that's tough luck because you can't.'
Jade backed off for the rest of the day. She didn't mention it, didn't tell Elijah off, didn't tell him that this made her sad or tell him not to shout at her. She didn't insist. She just left it.

Step 5: Percolate

Again, the aim here is to keep the issue live in your home, without being put off by negative reactions and without resorting to pressure.

The next day, when Elijah was fed and they were playing, she said it again, 'It is hard to leave the house but I really would like to sometimes.' Elijah said, 'No. Stop saying that', but this time with less fervour than before.
She left it a couple more days before bringing it up again. 'I would really like to leave the house sometimes, but I know you find it hard.' Elijah looked at her, 'I don't like it when you talk about that,' he said. Jade said, 'I know, it's hard for you' and left it there.

Step 6: Listing solutions (Pour it out)

At this stage, you and your child look for solutions to the problem. At first, most of these solutions will probably come from you, but don't be put off. Try the process anyway. You may learn more about the problem from your child's perspective. This stage may look like generating solutions, but it also might look like a discussion.

Elijah moved them on to step 6 himself. 'I don't like it when we go out and then you say, "Just ten more minutes",' he said, right in the middle of a *Roblox* game.

Jade had guessed right. Elijah disliked the way that she kept adding on extra time out of the house when they were out. She made a suggestion. 'Maybe it would help if we made a very firm plan when we go out and you know exactly when we will come back?'

Elijah was doubtful, 'I'm not sure you can do that,' he said. 'You always want to add one more thing and it's like you can't walk past the local shop without going in.'

Jade agreed that this was something she found hard, particularly when they needed milk. She asked Elijah if he had any ideas which might help her.

'I know,' he said. 'What if you get punished if you go into that shop?' Jade wasn't thrilled at this suggestion and asked Elijah what punishment he had in mind.

'I get to buy anything I want no matter how expensive,' he said.

Jade didn't think her budget could manage this, but she wrote it down.

Then he came up with another one, 'How about we go out with no money? Then you can't buy anything.'

Jade added that to the list and made a suggestion of her own based on their discussion. 'How about if we agree we will go to the local park for 20 minutes and I will absolutely not say 'five minutes more' at the end? And I won't talk to anyone or suggest we buy milk. It could be a challenge for me.'

Elijah liked this idea. 'Okay,' he said, and got his coat.

Step 7: Trying something new (Drink the coffee!)

Jade was taken aback, she had been thinking about tomorrow or next week, not right now. She went with it. She grabbed her coat and keys, and off they went. She didn't ask Elijah if he was sure or introduce any delay. She took his shoes in her hand rather than insist he put them on before they left. They had fun at the park, she kept her word and didn't talk to other people and after 20 minutes they came straight back, no questions asked.

Elijah was pleased. 'I thought you could do it if you tried hard enough,' he said.

Jade was pleased too. 'Could we try again tomorrow, do you think?' she said.

Elijah grunted.

They didn't go out the next day but they did the day after that.

Over time, Jade and Elijah went out more often, and they were able to go out for longer. Sometimes they negotiated in advance and Elijah agreed that Jade could go into the shop, although he still didn't like it being sprung on him. Jade agreed that if Elijah said he really needed to go home urgently, she wouldn't try to persuade him to stay.

Elijah started making suggestions as to things he would like to do – often expensive ones. They made a list and started saving up and looking for vouchers. They kept the list up in the kitchen and added to it as time went on.

Six months later, they went into London to visit the dinosaur skeletons at the Natural History Museum. Dinosaurs were a particular interest of Elijah's but before, Jade couldn't even suggest the idea as Elijah would immediately refuse. This time she suggested it, waited a few days, and said it again. The second time, Elijah thought for another two days and then said he'd like to go.

They went in on the train, went straight to the museum, saw the dinosaurs, and then came straight back again. Jade bit her tongue and did not suggest a quick detour to see the blue whale. They didn't try to meet up with anyone else when they were there. They were both really pleased with themselves when they got home. They were also exhausted and took several days to recover.

What changed?

Elijah and Jade started to work on the same side. Jade saw what was hard for Elijah, and Elijah was able to suggest ways in which things could be manageable for him. They collaborated. Jade stopped seeing Elijah's strong 'No' as a reason to give up, and instead saw it as a sign he needed more time to get used to new ideas. She realised that any new suggestion would get a strong 'No' at first because that is how Elijah expressed his anxiety. And new suggestions made Elijah anxious.

Once they were going out of the house, the same principle applied. Each new experience needed time to percolate. It was fine to try something small and succeed. Over time, those small experiences would grow.

An important step in this process is naming the two perspectives. For some kids, taking the perspective of others doesn't come easily (and it's something that many adults struggle with too) and practising holding your own needs in mind at the same time as considering the needs of someone else is a challenge in itself.

Taking this approach requires patience, and not being put off by initial negative responses. It is normal for children to react strongly and nega-tively when you talk about things which they find uncomfortable, and it's equally important to keep talking about it, because over time avoidance will only make the uncomfortable feelings worse.

For more flexible kids, or those who are experienced with this approach, you may be able to go straight in with naming the two parts to the problem. You might be able to start off with something like, 'We have a problem, you said you'd like to have piano lessons but whenever it's time for your lesson you are busy doing something else and get upset. Is there a way it could work better for you?' Or, 'We have a problem, you love Forest School when you get there but beforehand you often think it's going to be boring. Any ideas?' Or even, 'We have a problem, your sister comes to the things which you want to do but then you won't come to the things that she wants to do and she feels that is unfair. Any ideas?' However, I would only do this for kids who can definitely handle this much information upfront. Don't use it as a short-cut because it won't work. For younger kids, those who have more difficulty with flexibility and those who are highly anxious, you need to spend the time dripping and percolating before they are ready to collaborate.

Parents often want to have the answers, and think that good parenting involves knowing the solution. Collaboration means being open to the children's ideas and to a different understanding of the problem when the child's perspective is heard.

This doesn't mean it will come easily. It's a new skill for all of you, and you may find it's very messy when you actually try it out. That doesn't matter. What matters is keeping going, and keeping in mind what you are trying to do – find a collaborative solution to a problem.

Collaborative solution finding involves many other skills and you'll find that you and your child will get better at it over time. You'll find your rhythm and you'll know how much percolation time they might need for a particular issue. Some problems might move in a day, others might take months. When change isn't yet happening, you just keep dripping the ideas and percolating.

I asked Heidi Steel, highly experienced unschooling mother of four, to tell me a bit about what this process looks like in her family. Heidi runs an unschooling consultancy and coaches parents who want to move to self-directed education (disclaimer, she also runs courses for parents with me). Heidi and I have known each other since her youngest child was a baby – eight years – and I wasn't aware of how delicately she approaches new shoes until she sent me this wonderful story.

THE SHOE SHOP SAGA

There is a child in my household who refuses to go to shoe shops. They also refuse to try on different shoes bought in different sizes. This causes a problem when they are unable to physically fit into their shoes and we have very little idea what shoe size they are.

So, the problem is that they need new shoes but won't have their feet measured or try on shoes. It is important to note that this is a genuine problem and not something arbitrary or contrived. I have a good understanding already of what my child thinks and feels about this situation, namely, that they aren't interested in new shoes, find decision making difficult when being pressed, and struggle with the process of in-person foot measuring.

The question is, where do I start when I know that the reaction is going to be no? My previous expectation in this scenario would have been that we would buy new shoes by going to the shoe shop and having their feet measured. For me, this is the quickest solution and most logical. Alternatively, I could buy multiple sizes online and try them on at home.

Neither of these solutions is feasible. I need to begin by putting aside my expectations and then create opportunities for my child to express their opinions, sit with the problem, and contribute solutions. This is not going to be a quick process.

I think about the way forward in microscopic steps. I might mention the idea of new shoes to them in passing, for example, 'I noticed that your shoes are getting tight.' I would say this without any expectation of a positive response, and I am totally open to being ignored or receiving a strong negative reply! This is where taking my time and giving my child all the time that they need begins. I leave the conversation and allow space for the idea to percolate. Being aware of my child and noting their response then allows me to assess when and how to raise the idea again.

This process is repeated as many times as is needed. I add further information or observations based on their response, for example, 'I noticed that your shoes are too tight, shall we think about getting you a new pair?' or, 'I know that you find getting new shoes difficult, is there something that we can do to make it easier for you?' I always remember each time to provide space for them to respond in a way that they need to, and I allow them time for the idea to percolate. This means that if they continue to vehemently oppose the idea then I back off, or if they have suggestions, that I listen to their contribution.

Creating this safe space means that I do not need to respond to their ideas with my own opinions. Simply listening to them is enough. If the conditions are right, I might respond with some of my own ideas but it is always like planting a seed, drop it into the conversation and then leave it to be thought about. This process can take days, or weeks, or months depending on the child, and the problem.

In the case of the Shoe Shop Saga, my child made several suggestions over the course of a few days (that turned into weeks.) They suggested that I bought them the same shoes that they had now but in a bigger size; they suggested that they could go barefoot. Another idea was never going anywhere where they needed to wear shoes. All these ideas were listened to and taken on board without comment. This is part of the process of holding a space – a place where they are safe to say anything that they need to without judgement. Their ideas are valid and heard without immediate comment. Everything is considered, no matter how illogical or silly the idea seems at first.

There is frequently more time for percolation – sitting with an idea and mulling it over, individually or together, before we come to a way forward that suits us all. There is rarely a time where something must have an immediate solution, and we try and pre-empt those as far in advance as we can. Even at the point where we are ready to put into practice a solution, we are always ready to acknowledge that the 'doing' of something can be very different from the 'idea' of doing it. Sometimes we go back to the drawing board and start again.

In the case of the Shoe Shop Saga, it was decided that I would draw around the child's foot and take it to the shoe shop to be measured and then they could choose a pair of shoes online and I could order the correct size for them. We have also discovered since then that you can measure your own feet online. There are usually lots of solutions to a problem when we open ourselves up to exploring the possibilities and take the time to hold space for our children to make peace with the idea.

As you can see from Heidi's story, allowing time for changes and being proactive rather than reactive are the keys to effective change. She could have insisted and her child would have resisted – but instead they found a way together which worked for them both.

FIVE-POINT SUMMARY

1. Behaviour is an integral part of children's learning and one of the ways in which they express themselves and communicate.
2. An important part of a self-directed education is working with your child to help them develop new skills and explore the world – and making sure you have an influence too.
3. An alternative to control or letting it go completely is collaboration with your child. This can be tricky when children's first response is 'no'.
4. This collaborative approach involves being proactive and taking lots of time to let the child become comfortable with new ideas and change. This can't be rushed, rather like making a good cup of coffee.
5. With some children, collaboration works best when parents introduce new ideas very gradually and over a long period of time.

FIVE-POINT SUMMARY

CHAPTER 10

ACADEMICS

Introduction

I've put this chapter towards the end of this book on purpose, but I wonder how many of you will have started here. You're worried about how your children will learn to read, or do maths, if you don't make them. You see your children playing all day and you can't imagine how this will ever lead to academic excellence, or exams. You worry that you're curtailing your children's future by not making them learn now.

If is you, please go back and read the earlier chapters. At least skim through them. My approach to self-directed education can be thought of as a pyramid, and it's vital to have the base firmly in place before you start to think about academic skills. The base of the pyramid is emotional well-being, physical comfort and strong supportive relationships, and the last three chapters explain ways to achieve that. If you try to rush in without spending the time on the lower layers of the pyramid you will end up right where you started.

Children's learning can look very different outside school. When they can choose what they do, children generally spend a lot more time playing than do schooled children, and therefore their academic skills can appear to lag behind. This doesn't, however, mean they aren't learning. Their learning is often hidden or informal, while schooled children's learning is formally presented, constantly assessed and monitored. This makes it easy for parents to make comparisons, find their children lacking, and panic.

I will talk a lot about reading in this chapter. This is because reading is typically something which causes parents a lot of anxiety. However, the principles apply to all forms of academic learning.

Throughout this chapter, bear in mind what Paul Lockhart says so well in his powerful piece 'A Mathematician's Lament' (2002): 'There is surely no more reliable way to kill enthusiasm and interest in a subject than to make it a mandatory part of the school curriculum.'

Being behind

School and self-directed education come at learning from very different standpoints. At school, learning is about being taught a curriculum. Demonstrating that you have learnt that curriculum is the outcome of a successful education.

There is a problem with this goal which many of you will have already encountered. Many children are not able to learn the curriculum at the desired pace. These children are often judged to be 'behind', something which they and their parents remember for years in the future. As education progresses, at each level children are sorted and compared against each other. Those who cannot manage mainstream school are sent to special units or schools, which vary greatly in what opportunities they offer, and those who continue in mainstream find themselves subject to increasing pressure and competition as they get older.

Education at school is inherently competitive. Children are ranked against each other – through tests, or setting them by ability – from early on and right the way through. About 30% of children fail their GCSEs (the school leaving exam taken at age 16), and it's not possible for them to pass. GCSE exams are graded by comparing the scores with previous cohorts of teenagers and making sure that grades are similarly distributed. If everyone did exceptionally well one year, for some reason, the pass mark would be set at a higher level, and 30% would still fail. These exams are about comparing young people with their peers, and they can't all be the best (or even above average).

This means that 30% of children will inevitably end their school career failing their end-of-school exams, no matter how hard they work. Passing isn't just about objectively doing well, it's about doing better than everyone else. Failure is built into the system.

This is a particular problem for children with unusual developmental pathways. As I explained in Chapter 1, when we compare young people of the same age group, we assume that they are developmentally at the same stage, but this is not necessarily the case. Neurological maturity happens at different rates. Human development is not standardised.

Rebecca told me about how her son was quickly identified as being 'behind', even though he only went to Reception.

> I was quite quickly told by the teacher that he was behind, they actually put it that way. He's behind the other children. I was like, 'How can you be behind anything? What is he behind?'
>
> They said, 'Yes, he's behind and he can't sit still. He's quite disruptive

when he's on the mat, and when they're doing phonics. He doesn't seem to listen to anything that we say.'

'What are you going to do about it?' was the way it was framed to me.

I explained that his brother has a lot of medical issues and had been in and out of hospital. I'd told them this before he started, I told them everything that was going on the whole time and said that he probably was having a tricky time, anyway. But all that aside, I didn't expect there to be this much focus on academic work. I'd worked in several schools and I'd never seen so much focus on it.

I don't know if it was just that school, or if it is something that is a trend in a lot of schools. Anyway, they basically said I didn't know what I was talking about, that he was behind and it was a problem. They said they'd started removing him from the class to take him to sit out with the teaching assistant to practise his phonics when the other children were playing. Not only did he have to sit through being on the mat with them but during their free play, he had to go and sit outside with the teaching assistant, and do more stuff that he wasn't interested in the slightest.

Self-directed education does not require everyone to learn the same curriculum. Learning is about whatever the child finds meaningful. It makes no sense for anyone to be 'behind' when every child is learning something different, and learning things in different orders is simply part of the process. There is no expectation that everyone should learn to read at age five, for example. This makes it well suited to those with development which is far from the standardised expectations.

Does this mean they will never learn to read or do any maths? No. A principle of self-directed education is that children learn skills in context, rather than in the abstract. They learn things when they need them. Reading and numbers are everywhere in our society. Understanding them is an extremely useful skill, and children see that. They learn to read because they want and need to read in order to live their lives, rather than because a teacher has told them it's time to learn to read. This can happen at very different ages.

When differences become problems

Every Reception class is full of very different children. By age four, they have different life experiences, different interests and different priorities. They will have spent their preschool years in different ways, with some already knowing how to read and count to one hundred, while others have experience of different cultures and languages. Some will be able to ride bicycles and swim, while others will be scared of the water and prefer to stick to a scooter. Some of their differences will be valued by the school system, while others won't.

The outcomes for these children will be to a large extent determined by how their individual differences interact with the school system. They will spend many days of the next 12 years in a classroom, and there they will learn things about themselves. Some will learn that they are capable and worthwhile, others will learn that they are less capable and seen as badly behaved. Children's experiences determine how they learn to think about themselves, and some children get many more negative messages about themselves than others.

Some differences are perceived as serious problems by the school system. When a difference is treated as a problem, it can become more and more of one. The example of Kai and Katie shows how different the experience of two children can be.

Kai is seven and still can't really read simple words. School is concerned and so are his parents. Kai is getting a lot of extra support with reading, and it doesn't seem to be helping. His problem with reading means he can't access the rest of the curriculum and so he is behind in almost everything. He used to be really interested in history but now it's all about reading, and so he dislikes that too. He has to read every day at home, and he hates it. He knows that he is behind, and so do the other children, who call him stupid. He is fast developing a sense of inferiority and shame, and is resisting the extra help which he is offered. His parents have found a special tutor, but Kai runs and hides when she is coming. His parents are considering a private dyslexia assessment in the hope that this might provide solutions.

Katie lives next door to Kai. She is also aged seven and can't read yet. She's a self-directed learner and doesn't go to school. Many of her friends can't read either, because self-directed children often learn to read later and at a wider range of ages. She is surrounded by books, she listens to audio books and podcasts, and her parents read to her regularly. Her lack of reading is not holding back her learning. Katie has no sense at all of herself as inferior or 'behind', because in her world, she isn't. She knows she is capable of learning and is confident that she will learn to read in the future.

Both these children are not reading yet, but for one of them it is a problem, while for the other it isn't. Even when Kai does learn to read, he may still think of himself as stupid and behind. He may still feel ashamed.

These feelings will make it harder for Kai to learn to read and also to learn other things in the future.

When Katie does want to learn to read, she won't have the barriers that are making reading harder for Kai. She won't have learnt to think of herself as stupid, and she won't be ashamed of her lack of ability. This means that however she learns to read, her belief in herself will help her rather than hinder her.

Jessica told me about what had happened to her son, whose love of reading before he started school became a complete avoidance of books after he left school in Year 2.

My son always loved books and reading time. He always wanted to be read to. We have hundreds of books. Sometimes it would be the same books over and over again. I have photos where he has piles of books out by breakfast. The demand to eat was really, really a problem for us; reading to him helped that. He had a lot of exposure to books. He was starting to read before he went to school. But, oh my god, school killed his love of reading books. And by the time he'd finished school, he wouldn't even look at a book.

The demand to read every day, to read out loud regularly, was just way too much. I've got a friend who had a child in a parallel class, but she used to come and do reading with our class. She told me after we had left school, 'I couldn't tell you at the time because I wasn't allowed to. I used to be given his group. He never wanted to sit on the chair. I never made him sit or read if he didn't want to. But the other teachers did, and it caused all kinds of issues.' But none of this ever came back to me at home and when they're in school, as a parent, you are blind to what's actually happening.

This isn't just about reading. It's about any skill which school expects children to acquire on schedule. Some children won't be able to do that, and for them, the fact they have not met the expectation causes other problems. It can cause shame, a feeling of inferiority, or a negative evaluation of themselves. It can also cause them problems with their peers, because everyone else will know that they are not considered to be doing well.

This is because of the way in which the school system deals with difference. It is not flexible enough to accommodate different trajectories, and so it tends to try and make children more similar, to bring them in line with their peers. Children are given extra help so they can 'catch up' to the level they are supposed to be at. If the extra help isn't enough, they are diverted into specialist schools or units, where they mostly do the same stuff, but more slowly or in less depth.

Many children have unusual developmental profiles, with some children acquiring skills very early and others very late. At school, this is a problem, in self-directed education, it isn't. This is partly because lacking one skill doesn't need to hold the child back in other ways. The child who can't read at school can't access a lot of the curriculum and is likely to be behind in almost everything. The child who can't read outside school can spend their time listening to audio books, playing, watching documentaries, visiting museums, doing activities and learning through conversation. Their learning isn't stalled.

How do they actually learn?

It's hard for parents to imagine what academic learning looks like when it doesn't involve teaching and textbooks. Dr Harriet Pattison and Professor Alan Thomas carried out research into how home educated children learn and their book is full of examples of how effective informal learning can be. *How Children Learn at Home* (2008) is also an entertaining read and I'd recommend it to anyone who is having trouble envisioning what actually goes on in self-directed families. Dr Pattison's book *Rethinking Learning to Read* (2016) is also useful for seeing just how variable pathways to reading can be. Both books are based on research.

Close-up observations of this type of learning are invaluable. I asked parents of self-directed neurodivergent learners to tell me about what academic learning looked like for their children. Mary told me about her son, who had been at school.

> I started trying to introduce topics and lessons, and I very quickly realised that my idea of what home education was going to look like, and my child's idea of what an education was going to be were entirely different. I realised that I should relax more. When I tried to do sit-down work, for five to ten minutes, or if I tried to introduce something, if maybe I'd gone on Twinkl and printed off reams of work, I quickly realised that actually letting him lead and following his interests was far more constructive. We let him teach himself to read as well.
>
> Reading had been such a painful experience for him at school. He decided to continue reading stories, and we still went to the library, which he enjoyed. There was no point when we sat down and said, right, read

this book with me. We just left him to it. Then one day, we came across the fairy books. They are absolute trash. He absolutely devoured them. So, we bought the books, and then he went on to Harry Potter and Enid Blyton, all this other stuff. And then suddenly, I had a reader.

Mary's story reflects that of many others. Parents start out thinking they will teach lessons, and then learning gradually becomes more informal. Alan Thomas interviewed home-educating families about their children's learning processes. He expected to find parents teaching their children, but in fact what he found was that children at home learnt informally, with a lot of conversation, a lot of activity, and living alongside each other.

This difference in learning means that a self-directed child sees themselves in a different way. A child out of school is not constantly compared to their peers and does not compare themselves to their peers in academic skills. This means that they do not see themselves as lacking if they are late in acquiring skills which schools value. They avoid seeing themselves in a negative light, and this means that when they do want to learn, the process is easier.

This isn't to say that some children won't find it harder to learn some skills. They will all learn different things at different rates. Holly, an American unschooler, told me about the differences she saw between her three children.

I didn't compare my children to each other because they were so different. My oldest was devouring full-page chapter books at five years old, re-reading the ones she enjoyed most. My son simply was not interested in reading. When asked what a letter sound was he would say, 'I know what that letter says, but I don't really care.' Then he found Pokémon cards and realized he needed to know what the card said to trade and play. He literally taught himself how to read based on his need for the skill. It still blows my mind that he could read so well because I don't remember teaching him any of it. We were very intentional though. We would walk and talk and I'd point out letters and words and made it a part of our every day.

Then my youngest was a slow emerging reader who did not achieve reading fluency until about age eight or so. She could recognize letters and put small words together but she did not have a whole lot of confidence in herself. It was also a different era for her because she had access to an iPad that she could talk to. It was very simple for her to use text to speech and tell it whatever commands she needed. To me, that was a sign that she had figured out how to work the system. She had found a way to work around the weaker areas, and build them up at her own pace. Just because she couldn't necessarily read didn't mean that she wasn't learning and figuring things out.

For some, academic skills come easily while for others they are harder. Parents sometimes ask me if it isn't better to start teaching reading earlier if you have a family history of learning disability or suspect your child might be dyslexic.

No. And the reason is that learning is always easier when the learner wants to learn. If you are someone for whom reading is going to be hard, then the last thing you need is to be trying to learn to read when you yourself don't see the point yet, and aren't very interested. This is likely to make reading much harder, and may lead to you developing fears and hang-ups about reading that will stick around for years – many of the parents in this chapter describe exactly this happening. This doesn't mean that some children won't need extra help to learn to read or do other things. They may well do. But that extra help will be more efficient when the child wants to learn and that learning has purpose for them.

Yes, yes, but what about exams?

Having said all this, I'm guessing you're still thinking, but how will they learn to read and do maths? Can I really leave them to do what they want and how will they ever do exams or get qualifications in that case? You may be thinking the same as I did when my children were young – first, that I know there are people in the world who never learn to read or write, so why would I assume that my children can do so without being taught, and second, how would they ever learn the content of an exam syllabus through self-direction?

It is, of course, possible not to learn to read. Learning cannot happen in a vacuum. A child can only learn the things that are available to them in their environment, and they need available adults or older children to help them. If they live in a society where no one else can read, and where there are no books, they will not learn to read. In this case, school may be only the place that provides this opportunity, just as it was for the English Victorian children who attended poor schools.

However, this should not the case for self-directed young people. It is the responsibility of parents to make sure that their children have access to opportunities in their environment. If parents can't read, then they need to find people who can and who will spend time with their child. If parents can't speak the language spoken around them, then they will need to find ways for their children to hear and use that language because otherwise, they too will not learn to speak it. Planning that learning environment is part of the work of self-directed educators.

It's also the case that school does not guarantee academic success. Many young people go through the entire school system and do not learn to read to a level which means they are functionally literate.

The worry about not learning exam syllabi is based on a misconception of what a self-directed education really is. Whereas for younger children it often does mean informal or play-based learning pretty much all time, for older children it can involve classes, textbooks and tutors, if that is what they choose to do. The element which makes it self directed is that the learner is in the driving seat of what they do. Self-directed young people are not forced to do GCSEs, but that does not mean that they don't do them. They aren't forced to learn anything, but that doesn't mean they don't learn. In fact, the self-directed teenagers that I know are learning the most incredible range of things. Right now, I know self-directed teenagers who are learning Spanish, Russian, coding, the oboe, music composition, calculus, touch-typing, physics, biology, novel-writing, art, climbing and Japanese, all because they want to.

I talked to Sallie and her 17-year-old daughter Madeleine together. Madeleine has been home educated for her whole life, has done GCSEs and is now studying for A-levels. She has severe dyslexia and ADHD. Sallie described how they worked with this.

I was reading to Madeleine till she was 14. I still do read all her textbooks to her. Because I was able to read to her, she realised that reading was an interesting and enjoyable experience. And we were able to read good books, so it kept her English going, because she learnt things like how to start your sentences. She knew all that through me reading the books, which meant that when she wanted to read, she could. I see so many kids being sort of bashed over the head with books every day because they've got to read. We didn't do that.

Madeleine told me that she didn't learn to read until she was 11, and that while she has learnt to read now, she still gets things jumbled up and uses overlays. She talked about the time before she could read.

I used to just sit there and play with bits of fluff and sometimes I would listen to audio books. I have a wonderful imagination. Before I could read, it was like, I've got stories in my head. And I've got stories being read to me. I've got stories all around me. I didn't really register that other people were reading and I wasn't.

I think the first series I ever finished was the Tom Gates one. I read one of the short ones first and it's slightly cartoony, but it's got writing and cartoons. I got the book series. I ended up reading the third book in something like two days. And I thought, 'Oh, now I can read things like Percy Jackson.' Percy Jackson has ADHD and dyslexia.

When children are allowed to choose what they do and to retain control of their education, they go through distinct phases. Young children learn naturally through play and discovery learning, and then as they get older they move on to more intentional, goal-focused mastery learning. This means that when parents are looking at their children aged under-ten and trying to imagine what their learning will be like as a teenager, it's very hard to visualise. It's also worth bearing in mind that the latest neuroscientific research shows that adolescent brain development continues until at least age 25, and important parts of the brain may still be maturing up to that point. Not doing GCSEs at age 16 does not mean a young person won't want to do them a bit later, and keeping options open is an important part of self-directed education.

Most of us only know schooled teenagers, or remember our own experience of being schooled teenagers, and so we assume that teenagers naturally behave in the way in which many of them do at school – that is, that they will avoid challenge and will seek to find the easiest way to get through whatever is required of them. This approach makes perfect sense in the school system. There, the aim is exam results rather than learning, and so finding the easiest way to do that is logical.

This is not the same for self-directed teenagers, who are learning because they want to. Young people who are allowed to choose what they do set themselves challenging goals, including taking exams, and then apply themselves to succeeding in those goals. It's always seemed a bit odd to me that we don't think young people would do this, since adults make challenging choices for themselves all the time. I am surrounded by adults learning complicated skills because they want to, and I really can't see why young people wouldn't do the same, unless their relationship with learning has been damaged by years of coercion.

Alice told me about her autistic 15-year-old, who spent several years gaming as younger teen.

He thinks he'd like to go to further education and university, but I see that he is not ready to engage in a formal GCSE. At the moment, he is wanting to really improve his handwriting and his maths. So pretty much every day we do half an hour of maths together. He's always looking for new ways to study maths. Looking at the GCSE maths book is nuts, because I can't remember any of it and I've never used most of it. I think because there's been such progress in the last year since he is intentionally studying, I can only see that next year will be even speedier.

What about the essentials?

Okay, you're saying, but what about all the different things covered at school? What about history and geography and the Periodic Table, or what about racism, climate change and oppression? Shouldn't we ensure that young people are taught about these things, and isn't it neglect if we just leave it up to chance? Won't they have gaps?

Let's turn that around. How do you learn new things? How do you even know what you want to learn? Did you stop learning when you left school? Do you think of your school years as a time of exceptional learning and opportunity, when you were exposed to an unparalleled range of useful and interesting information?

If so, you're unusual. Most people I speak to tell me that it was when they had left school that they really started to see how to learn, rather than going through the motions. I know no one who ended school confident that there were no gaps in their knowledge – in fact, if they had, I'd be worried, since schools teach such a small percentage of all that there is to know.

So how do self-directed learners acquire academic skills and knowledge? I can't tell you the answer, because there are as many answers as there are children. I can tell you what I do. When I want to learn something new, I typically first talk to people I know who might be able to help. I might google prominent authors in the field and search for academic journal articles. I look up YouTube videos or podcasts. I may order a book. I might sign up for an online course, or I might look for a tutor. I rarely find a curriculum to follow because my learning is driven by interest, and the curricula often don't quite fit.

I see self-directed teenagers doing something similar. Some will learn informally, others will choose more formal approaches. Some will learn by themselves, others may choose to go to classes or to work with a parent. Self-directed education doesn't rule any methodology out, but the child will be an active agent in the process. When a child wants to learn, their learning is much more efficient than when a teacher is trying to persuade them to learn. There's no problem with motivation, and so they tend to learn quickly.

How will they discover new things?

Okay, you're probably thinking. It's fine for you to say they'll learn, but how will they ever find out about new things? All they do is watch YouTube and play video games! Surely a curriculum is essential, or how will they know they might be interested in Ancient Egypt, or Spanish, or Wilfrid Owen's poetry?

The first thing to get out the way is the idea that the best way to spark interest is by making children follow a curriculum. Compulsion generally has the opposite effect. It makes things less interesting. When I worked for the NHS, we had to do several hours of mandatory training every year. It involved things like fire safety, how to safely move filing cabinets and use hoists to move people to and from their beds (even though, as a psychologist in an outpatient clinic, I never saw a patient in bed). I remember those hours as some of the most boring of my life. I deeply resented being forced to attend rather than being able to study it in my own time or just take the quiz and I found myself behaving as if I was back at school. I would whisper to the person sitting next to me, crack jokes and ask irrelevant questions to keep myself awake. Most of the other attendees looked as if they were hardly there, just putting in the hours to get their certificate. I did not learn very much and I can't remember any of it now. But I got through it and I passed the test at the end.

Make a person do something, and most of us will immediately like that thing less. For many, including myself, knowing they have to do something is enough to make an interesting thing boring. It's tragically commonplace that school kills off interest in something which a person might have found fascinating had they come across it themselves. This seems to happen disturbingly often with reading. I have been told by many parents that their children refused to look at a book for years after leaving school. This is particularly likely to happen with children with a PDA profile, but I've heard of it happening to many.

Outside school, exposure comes through connections, much as it does in adult life. A passing remark, a reference in book, or a comment heard on the radio can all lead to new interests. These unexpected sparks can happen all the time. My daughter developed an interest in glass blowing after a visit to a tourist attraction where they had a glass-blowing demonstration.

She found a documentary on Netflix about glass blowing, and learnt how all the different parts of the workshop functioned. We took her to another glass-blowing demonstration and she was able to explain the process to us, chemistry and all. She was interested in the heating and cooling process, the properties of glass and how it changed, and the artistic process. Next, she told us, she'd like to try it herself. Unfortunately glass-blowers don't run workshops for children due to health and safety issues with hot glass, and so we're going to have to wait until she's older for that.

Follow the trails

Parents told me again and again of how for their family, self-directed education meant helping the learner to follow the trails of what interested them. They moved from question to question, or experience to experience. Some trails lasted an afternoon, others lasted for weeks or months. Some trails would lie dormant for ages, and then would re-emerge, when suddenly a child would rediscover an interest in fossils, or World War 2, or mystery stories. These trails were often very detailed and highly specific, but they all started from a spark of interest and then continued as the child asked questions or made discoveries. The amount of support children will need with this and what form this might take will depend on their age and ability. A teenager, after several years of self-direction, will be able to follow their own trails and find their own resources. A younger child will need more help and collaboration, in a dynamic learning process in which both child and adult can contribute new information or ideas.

Let's take an example from my own experience. Shortly after we moved to Hove, we were walking along the beach. Hove beach has concrete groynes stretching into the sea, and my daughter saw that one of them was covered with barnacles. She was intrigued and asked several questions. I know very little about barnacles, so we went home to look it up. We found a YouTube video of barnacles, which has shots of how barnacles feed under water, and their life cycle. This led to discussion of food chains, evolution and then the make-up of the extraordinarily strong glue which barnacles use to attach themselves to rock. Here we moved off biology on to a desire to understand how glue works, which took us to molecular structure and atoms – we'd covered a lot of ground from that encounter with a barnacle. We found an app about molecular structure. If the discussion had gone another way I might have suggested a visit to a natural history museum, where there's more about lifecycles and other shellfish. Or an aquarium. As it was, it led us to our hot glue gun and she went off to make a glue and cardboard cave.

Before you get excited, sometimes the trail ends abruptly after the first question, when the child moves on to something else, leaving the adult feeling that they were just getting going. It's very easy to kill an interest by being too enthusiastic. Watch the child. If they are moving on, the adult needs to back off. You can go and research barnacles for yourself if you want, but don't foist it on an uninterested child. Follow your own trails of learning. Mine have led me down many rabbit holes.

Making space for that trail of connections to happen is an essential part of self-directed education. Unfortunately, deliberately stopping the connections so that the learner focuses on the curriculum is often what happens in conventional schooling. If you've gone to the beach to learn about limestone rock formation, you can't follow an interest in barnacle glue.

Self-directed education doesn't leave learning up to chance. Providing opportunities and facilitating connections are not chance. It doesn't define content in advance, but it priorities learning. It makes learning more likely by preserving intrinsic motivation. It removes compulsion from learning, because learning works best when it is not forced. Adults provide the opportunities and support, and then trust in children's drive to learn. We have to enable them to follow the connections, with discussion, resources and an attitude of enquiry.

Jessica told me about watching that happen for her younger son, who did not go to school.

He's never been interested in books. He's consented to/tolerated having a few bedtime stories, but he's never loved it. We've had full reading schemes of all manner of types here. He's never been as interested in books, not really inspired by phonics apps, games and so on. However, I had been learning about natural reading and I did trust that this will work. I was supporting him doing the usual kind of reading: *Fortnite* challenges or *Minecraft*. I was reading for him, and we had subtitles on.

A few years ago, he got a new water bottle and he said, 'Oh, this stays hot for up to six hours.' I asked how he knew that. 'I read it from the box,' he replied. Those little nuggets happened once in a while, then they started coming every week, or more. Confident that this would happen naturally I gave away all our reading scheme books.

When we reasonably recently started reading Harry Potter together, out of the blue he asked me to use the bookmark to move with my reading so 'he could follow along'. I thought at the time that if he does this all the way through the eight books like this he'll be reading by the end. We were midway through the *Half Blood Prince* (#6) and after I was coughing he said, 'I'll take over' and he literally just took over from me and read the whole page. It was one of the most amazing things I have ever witnessed and totally and utterly validated the trust I had in self-directed education and the power it has.

FIVE-POINT SUMMARY

1. Parents are often very concerned about academic achievement, and the school system typically values this over all the other aspects of an education.
2. Parents of self-directed learners describe a change in how children learn as they grow up, from the more play-based discovery phase to the more intentional, goal-focused mastery phase.
3. Young people learn to read at different times and in different ways. Some ask for help while others work it out independently.
4. Self-directed young people can and do choose to take exams, learn challenging skills and go into formal education as they get older.
5. A very high degree of variability in learning is to be expected in self-directed education, and this is particularly good for unusual children. Inconsistent 'spiky' cognitive profiles are less of a problem when no one expects consistency.

CHAPTER 11

NON-ACADEMIC SKILLS

Krista's story

Krista is eight, and she finds school really difficult. Not the academic work, as she is ahead of her age group in maths and English. But she finds it very hard to stay in her classroom all day. She feels out of place there. She doesn't make friends easily and she hasn't made friends with anyone else in her class. She just doesn't seem to 'get' them and they don't 'get' her. She wanders alone at playtime. She doesn't know what to do, and she is getting picked on by the older children. They call her 'weirdo' and some of them trip her up as she walks past. They ask her why she hasn't got any friends and if it's because she smells bad. She doesn't know what to say.

At home, Krista plays happily with the neighbour's daughter who is five. They get along really well and have lots of shared interests. But Krista is teased at school for having a five-year-old friend, and so she won't play with her friend at school. She ignores her.

Krista cries every night and asks to stay at home. Her mother Kendra has spent the last four years organising play dates to try and help Krista make friends in her class, but to no avail. Every time she is hopeful, something seems to go wrong.

When Kendra contacts the school with her concerns, she mentions the possibility of home education. Krista's teacher tells her that Krista must definitely stay in school as otherwise she will miss out on acquiring vital social skills, and that she doesn't think there's any reason why Krista won't make friends soon. She says that academically she is fine, she looks fine at school and there's no reason to try an alternative. Kendra isn't so sure. She's not sure what social skills Krista is actually learning at school, since most of her interactions with other children are negative. She's worried that Krista is learning to feel terrible about herself and that this will get worse at secondary school

Invisible expectations

The school system has many expectations which are invisible until children fail to meet them. It expects children to be able to manage themselves in a large group of same-aged peers, making friends with some of them and at least tolerating the others. It expects them (from the age of about five) to be able to control their impulses, sit down when they are told to sit down, pay attention on demand and listen to what the teacher is saying, rather than attending to anything else interesting that is going on. It expects them to be able to take on board what a teacher asks them, and to focus on that rather than on things which might interest them more. From the age of 11, it expects them to make multiple transitions every day, from room to room, from subject to subject and sometimes from teacher to teacher. It expects them to keep track of what they need each day, and to remember their PE kit and homework on the right days.

And hardest of all for some children, school expects them to manage all day surrounded by others, with no privacy or time to decompress. School is a place where children are always in public, always on view. They can never let their guard down. Showing your emotions is not okay, and might well get you mocked, so you must keep up the pretence that you are okay. Putting on a front is part of being at school.

It always surprises me how many adults have forgotten this. When I was 13, I was very unhappy at school. I disliked almost every aspect of it, and particularly did not get along with the other teenagers. I told my parents. They told the school. The deputy headteacher said, 'I saw you with a group of girls just yesterday. You looked fine to me.'

I said nothing. I felt as if she was saying that I was lying. Inside I thought, 'Of course I looked fine. What other choice did I have? Did you think I'd draw attention to myself, when one of the problems is that the others make fun of me for being different?' It seemed to me then, and it still seems to me now, that there are very few other options besides 'looking fine' at school. Certainly, there are no other options which don't draw attention to yourself. And if one of your problems is that you don't want to stand out, then you aren't going to draw attention to yourself. It's safer to 'look fine'.

Of course, not everyone does 'look fine'. Some children clearly show that they aren't fine. They either become very unhappy, they refuse to go or they are continually disruptive when there. They don't do what they are told and their interactions with the other young people are difficult, resulting in aggression or physical violence. This is usually seen as a behavioural problem, and so systems of punishments and incentives are put in place.

In line with how our society tends to respond to difference, the problem is located in the children rather than in the expectations. They are said to be 'not school-ready', to have an 'attitude problem' or their parents are blamed for not having taught them 'how to behave'. Or it's assumed that because they are 'bright' and not struggling with academic work, they shouldn't really be struggling with anything else and the problem is lack of effort. A particularly perverse aspect of the school system is that parents whose children are really struggling with non-academic school requirements are often told that the only way for them to learn the skills they need is to keep going to school.

Basic principles

Many parents ask me how they can help their children to learn the non-academic skills. They sometimes ask about social skills training, or programmes for emotional regulation, which encourage young people to put themselves in the green, orange or red zone, depending on how distressed they feel. There's nothing to stop a self-directed young person from using these programmes if they want, but they aren't something I think is necessary. These are like the school-based approach to anything else – take it out of context, create a curriculum and then try to teach it to children in the hope that they will be able to use them when necessary.

The self-directed approach to non-academic skills is the same as any other part of self-directed education. Start where the child is, help them do more of what has value to them, and provide opportunities for them to expand into. Appreciate that children learn these skills at different rates, and that the process of learning can be a messy and unpredictable one. Abandon your preconceptions about what a child should be able to do at any particular age, and instead meet them where they are.

With these, non-academic, skills, there are two elements to self-directed learning. One part is providing the space for children to develop these skills. The other part is providing the space for them to get to know themselves and how they work best, so that they can plan their environment to make it work for them. Not everyone is going to acquire every skill, and part of self-directed education is allowing that to be fine. I am terrible at paying attention to things I find boring, and useless at following instructions when I don't see the point – in my adult life, these things rarely cause me problems and I can work around them if I need to.

Social skills at school

We're used to thinking that school is the natural environment for children and young people. Even many home educators will talk about how when they first started home education, they assumed that at some stage – perhaps around the age of seven or eight – their children would gravitate towards exercise books and lessons, and that their environment would start to look more like school. It's a surprise to them when this doesn't happen, and when young people continue to learn in a more informal way.

This goes for social development too. We tend to think that being a with a large group of same-aged peers must be the right environment for social development, simply because that is what schools do. We judge a child's social skills by how well they manage in that type of setting.

This is odd, because the social setting of school is very different from the social world most of us inhabit as adults. For a start, it's rare to spend your time with a large group of age-matched peers. It's vanishingly rare as an adult to all be expected to do the same thing, and then to be compared on that thing. And it's unusual not to be given any chances to get away from other people, or to do things in your own way. Schools puts children in a large group of others of their age and expects them to learn how to manage socially. This is very hard for some children, who end up being bullied, being bullies themselves, or being socially excluded.

Nicole and James told me about their son Sam's experience of socialising at school.

Sam was scared of playtime at school. All the peers in his class were always very kind. The parents were lovely, always invited us to birthday parties and everything else. He always struggled, he'd have his ear defenders on and find it difficult. Just before we took him out of school, we went to the playground with two of his friends from school. It was the most relaxed I'd seen him around other children up to that point. He was really chatty and having a great time.

Afterwards he said to me, 'I find it so much easier when it's just one or two other children. It's too much when there are more.' That was coming from him. He was obviously finding it too hard to socialise. Take him out of that environment, reduce the number of children and with a more conducive environment, he was more able.

Their daughter, Eva, found other things about the social aspects of school difficult.

It's been much more difficult for Eva with other children in general. Being in school was just really difficult for her, around other children. Since coming out of school it has been difficult for her to find people. With her facial blindness, she didn't really engage with the other kids well.

She'd come home and say she'd been playing with so and so. She just didn't know who was who. She needs quite solid features to identify them. I think she also struggles with subtle emotions and that made it quite difficult. If you've got lots of kids, she's not going to know who's who, whereas if you've got one, she knows what their name is.

If she's in a group of children, she becomes quite anxious, affected by other sensory things as well as social aspects. It means that she can't learn or be social.

If she's one to one with another child, you see a child who's very verbal, very chatty, quite flexible. You wouldn't realise she has all these other difficulties in a different context.

School may feel inevitable to those of us who were schooled, but in terms of human history it's a very recent arrival. For the vast majority of history, young people were not sent off in large groups of others their own age, supervised by adults to whom they were not related. Groupings would have been smaller and more mixed in terms of age. Learning was more informal. There's no reason at all to assume that school is necessary or ideal for social development.

Social development outside school

When children go to school, they are expected to spend five days a week away from their families in a large group of their age-matched peers, from the age of four. Many of them will have already done this at nursery or day care. There isn't a lot of space for variation in this. During that time, children are typically with others the entire time. They can never truly be alone, or even really choose who they spend time with. Social development out of school looks very different and, as is generally the case in self-directed education, it's more variable.

Self-directed children do spend time with others, but the shift from being mostly with your family to mostly being with people outside your family is usually far more gradual. Families often socialise together, so at the age when schooled children are being dropped off on play dates, families continue to meet with parents present as well. They spend more time with their parents and can spend more time with adults such as relatives or other members of their community.

Self-directed children typically spend very little time in large groups (meaning the size of a school class) unless that is for a specific purpose like a museum trip. Even when they do spend time in groups, these groups are likely to be smaller than school, and of mixed ages. This age mixing is part of what Peter Gray calls the optimising conditions for self-directed education, and it gives a very different flavour to social development.

Nicole and James told me about the difference they saw in their son who is now home educated.

> He is quite social. He's happy to play with his friends daily. They play games together. They also watch series together online and chat about them. They come to visit; some of his friends live a long way away. He does still see one of his friends from school who is also autistic, and has since been taken out. He sees him, the neighbours, cousins, he's got friends. He spends pretty much all of his time with people, whether they're online or within the home. He'll spend short periods of time, maybe watching YouTube or doing things on his own, but most of his time is interacting.
>
> Socially he's doing really well, and he's much more flexible than he used to be. He's able to negotiate with others. It's not all on his terms. Maybe that's maturing with time, but I think also in school he wasn't able to develop those social skills because he was overwhelmed. He couldn't actually develop and nurture those skills that he needed. Taking him out has meant that he's been able to do that.

It's often hard for adults to imagine what social development looks like outside school, and so Table 11.1 gives some of the ways in which self-directed children make social connections at different ages. These are not the only ways, just what I have observed myself and through the parents and children I talk to.

Table 11.1: Social development in and outside school

Age	Social development in self-directed education	Social development at school
Under-7	Main social life is usually in their family and the wider community within which their family lives May spend time with other families or attend groups which are typically mixed age (but also may not) May spend time with grandparents, other relatives or childminders May join groups like Rainbows, or groups for a specific purpose like gymnastics or football Parents take the initiative to organise social events and groups, depending on what they know about their child Parents find connections through online and local groups even if the children do not want to meet up Social life is actively managed by parents who will be present for much of it Child is typically not expected to manage socially alone for extended periods	Large group of same-aged peers in class at school Consistent adults for a year and then it changes After-school activities start, often without parents present
8–11	Lots of time with family Relationships with other families continue and new ones are established Many visits are parents and children together and are mixed age Friendships are usually based on shared interests Online friendships may start or be a way of maintaining other relationships Some children attend part-time learning communities. Others will attend mixed-age social groups Some children may attend drop-off groups and classes, others may not Families may attend camps and festivals where they meet others Parents are proactive about creating opportunities for children to form relationships Parents make connections through online or local groups. These may or may not involve the children	Large group of same-aged peers (usually the same as when they were younger) Adults change every year or more After-school activities are usually in large groups and run in a way which is not that different from school

cont.

Age	Social development in self-directed education	Social development at school
11–16	Responsibility for social life starts to shift Parents start to organise less as young people organise more Family and parents are still important Young people usually start to focus more on their peers Young people may start volunteering or working and form relationships there Relationships already established continue Online relationships become more important, often based around gaming Teenagers may attend social groups or youth clubs Some get involved with Scouts, drama groups, gymnastics or other sports Some have tutors or attend groups for specific things they find interesting Home educators often set up groups for teenagers to work towards exams Some attend mixed-age learning communities Some young people will go to college at age 14, 16 or older in order to access GCSEs or other qualifications	Large group of same-aged peers in the context of an ever larger group Adults change every hour through the day, as well as every year After-school activities are often more specialised and may be competitive and/or pressured

You can see from the table that the social experiences for self-directed children change as they grow. There are several significant differences with school. One is that it is much more gradual, with younger children spending much of their time in their families or with a few trusted others who they get to know well. Another is that there is much more time spent in mixed-age groups, whether these are family groups, home education groups or learning communities.

Social exposure for self-directed children can be adjusted to fit their needs. They are not obliged to spend 30 hours a week with a group of others of the same age, whether they like them or not. Instead, they can meet up with one other family for a day, and then have a day at home. Or they can attend a group one day and then have two quieter days with relatives. They can connect with people on different levels at different times.

Jessica told me about how this happened for her older son, Luke, who had a very bad school experience and left school in Year 2.

His school friends dropped him like a hot potato when we left school. I remember when we first joined home education, I was really worried because the only person in the world he was interacting with was me.

I remember the first time we tried Lego club. I don't think we got out of the car. For a long time, I was extremely worried. I also knew we couldn't go back to school. I also worried about what the heck we were going to do. I can't say I had a plan. I just went with the flow.

Over time, we formed one-on-one friendships. Another friend of ours left the same class in the same school to home educate and friendships grew from that. We also met a new home educator in the local area. Her eldest was a similar age to Luke, had been in school a few years and was also autistic. They hit it off almost immediately, and the linking interest was gaming, *Mario Kart* in fact. They have been firm friends ever since.

Interestingly, the family also had a younger son who is exactly the same age as my younger son Oliver and he has never attended school either. These friendships have been absolutely pivotal. They have a beautiful friendship. Off the back of that, they have met more people, and done things that alone they wouldn't have attempted. There are events, places and activities Luke will now do because Zach is going and he will access because Zach is there. Similarly, Zach goes because Luke is there.

This gives them the space to develop and blossom. They can gradually develop socially, rather than being surrounded at all times by other people. They can do more of what works for them right now, without the pressure to do it the same way as everyone else.

Some children are not ready for any contact with other children for much longer than their parents expect. I know children who up to the age of nine or ten still hardly related to others of their age, but who were able to manage interaction with an older teenager or adult, or even with a younger child. Then as they got older, they started to connect with others closer to their age through particular interests, often gaming, be it video, board games or role-playing.

Social conflict

It can be a shock to some parents when their child behaves aggressively with others. They didn't expect this type of behaviour when they decided to take a non-coercive approach to their child's upbringing and they may feel defensive and blamed by others.

Many self-directed children spend no time at all in large groups when they are young, because it is clear to their parents that this is not a setting they feel happy in. Instead, their parents find settings where they can feel comfortable. Others are really keen to socialise in groups, and so their parents find places for them to do so.

Alex (they/their) told me about their son Daniel, who found being around other children in groups very challenging. Alex had to make an ongoing effort to keep some social options open and find places where he could cope. This required work on their part, and was not easy. Daniel never went to school.

> Socialisation is one of these words that can mean lots of things. I do think that trying to get kids to interact with other kids is something that they need to do. It's just that sometimes, not all children cope with it in the context of 29 other kids in a classroom. But playing with another kid in the playground is also social and that's what I was concerned about. That's what we kept trying to do, in terms of informal playdates or running around groups. That was pretty alright, and most of those things were things where I could be there. Once we got to the point where I was no longer worried that he was going to hit somebody it became easier. If it is kids shouting at each other and having an argument it's a different situation from hitting. That happened around the age of six or seven.
>
> We used to go to a weekly group at an adventure playground. When we first started going I think Daniel was four, rising five. And I felt I needed to be very much with him all the time there, partly because it's big. There's big, tall stuff and I was terrified that if something happened up there, a small scrap could turn into a really big, serious accident. So I did a lot of climbing up and down. Then at some point over the next year or two, I stopped, I started keeping an eye from the ground. If I saw or heard something starting to escalate, I could go and coach from the sidelines or intervene as required. I felt as if he did know that you use your words, even if it's at an extremely high volume. I guess we started doing gym, maybe when he was six and I must have thought he wasn't going to get physical there. They wouldn't have tolerated it.

Alex had tried several groups to find a place where Daniel would feel safe and could be around other children. This wasn't easy, particularly when adults weren't allowed in the room. Alex found that the conversations which group leaders would have with them were indirect and weren't clear about the problems Daniel was having, meaning that Alex was unable to intervene before it was too late.

We had this problem with a different group, a drama group, a few years ago now, pre-pandemic. They didn't want parents to be in the room. We tried doing that, and I was aware that Daniel was being quite loud and needed a bit more support in terms of calming. But as far as I knew (and I did ask), it was okay. They said he was a really valuable member of the group. But then, literally the next week, they said don't come back, because he had shouted at and scared another kid. I found it absolutely infuriating, and I'm still cross about it. There was no point at which somebody said to me that there's a problem, can we work it out? There was no scope for trying. If I had been in there with him, I could have made sure that this didn't happen. I could certainly have prevented it getting to that stage.

Afterwards I was very upset because I realised that in the conversations I was having with the person running the group, when they were saying things like, 'He's such a vocal member of the group', they were actually saying, 'You need to get him to shut up', but without saying it. It took me about ten minutes into the final conversation to realise that they were saying he definitely couldn't come back. It was all very evasive because they didn't really want to say there was a problem. I suggested that maybe if I went in and sat with him next time, and they said they weren't sure that would work. In the end, I said, 'So you're saying you don't want him to come back?' We were explicitly having a conversation about the fact that we weren't allowed to come back, and she still couldn't say that clearly. No wonder Daniel was struggling with those people's communication. Our current group isn't that bad about being subtle. That's an extreme example.

Alex describes a problem which other parents also mentioned – many groups have unspoken assumptions about how children should react and behave, and when children don't conform to these norms, they may not be able to communicate clearly what the expectations are. Requirements like adults staying outside can be important for the way in which the group runs, but they can also exclude some children who still need their parents present. Screen-time rules are another way in which some children can be excluded. If a child uses their device to calm themselves or uses gaming as their primary way to connect with others, then rules such as 'no devices' can mean that these children don't attend the group at all.

Self-management skills
There is a whole set of other skills that can make learning more difficult. These are what are sometimes called 'higher-order' thinking skills, 'meta-cognitive'

skills or 'executive functions': things like setting goals, problem solving, flexibility, controlling your impulses and organising and structuring your time, thinking about thinking. All of which children learn as they grow, and some of which some children learn much more easily than others.

Table 11.2: Skills of self-management

Self-management skills	How they show up
Setting goals/ intentionality	Deciding that you want to learn something and working on something so you can do so. For example, I want to learn Japanese so I am going to use Duolingo and find some Japanese anime to watch
Problem solving	Working out what to do when something goes wrong. For example, I missed the bus so need to find another way home – I could walk, take the train or ring my mum
Inhibitory control	Being able to stop yourself from doing something when it is inappropriate – like hitting other people, or breaking things. For example, I am really angry with my brother but I'm not going to hit him
Adaptability/ flexibility	Being able to 'change direction' or cope with a change of plans. For example, coping with the news that actually your plans for the day have been cancelled because your friend is sick, and so instead you are going to visit your relatives
Working memory	The amount you can hold in your (very) short-term memory and therefore what you have available to think about and manipulate. For example, remembering a list of five different things you need to buy at the supermarket, and being able to hold these in mind when you discover that they have no potatoes, so you will need to find an alternative
Emotional regulation	Being able to keep yourself on an even keel emotionally when something stressful or challenging happens. For example, coping with the absence of your favourite food in the supermarket without crying or becoming very angry
Planning and prioritising	Being able to organise your time by making a plan and prioritising the most important things. For example, writing a to-do list and deciding which thing needs to be done first, and then doing it
Sequencing	Working out the order in which to do things. For example, before I can put my trousers on, I need to put on my underpants; before I can go out for a walk, I need to put on my shoes

Parents of children with an ADHD diagnosis (in particular, but not exclusively) are often told by health professionals and teachers that self-directed education will not work for them because of their difficulties with executive functioning. The assumption is that they will not be able to organise themselves and so the structure of school is necessary for them to learn.

This is based on a misunderstanding of what 'self-directed education' means. Professionals tend to think it means providing a curriculum or textbook and expecting children to get on with it in their own time. When children don't do that (which most children don't), they deem self-directed education to have failed.

This makes sense if you think that the most important part of education is the curriculum. It's true that children whose self-management skills are less developed will find it harder to access a curriculum and may need a lot of support to do so. They are having difficulty with skills which aren't often explicitly being taught but which underpin their ability to learn the curriculum – things like sitting still, keeping their mind on the task at hand, planning their work and inhibiting their desire to run around instead.

However, the aim of self-directed education isn't to learn and retain a curriculum. Instead it's for children to practise directing their own learning, whereever that might take them. If their current burning interest is about giant jelly fish, or capitals of the world, then they can learn about that.

This makes a lot of difference, because many children who exhibit what are called executive functioning difficulties at school are showing us that they aren't motivated to engage in school tasks. The child who would rather gaze out the window than learn phonics, for example, might be defined as having problems with attention – but will have no problem at all in paying attention to something which really interests them, like Pokémon. We assume the problem is the child, but maybe it's the phonics.

That isn't to say that there aren't huge differences in the development of these types of skills. Some children are able to focus and concentrate at a much younger age than others, and some are better at paying attention to things they find boring. The difference is that self-directed education can accommodate that, because it doesn't expect children to follow a standardised curriculum.

Alice told me about her son, who has recently become interested in formal learning at the age of 15. He has started to set himself extremely challenging goals – learning Mandarin Chinese, for example – and to work on them.

His executive functioning isn't great. And I'm only realising now that he finds planning of tasks difficult. But he's doing incredibly well with his language learning where he's planning it all out. He's done everything. He's finding new apps that are better than the old ones. Chinese flashcards arrived today. I'm going to play that this afternoon. Here's where he's taken charge of his life, rather than being told that he doesn't do it right or that he needs to be more. No one is telling him his faults. No one's saying, 'Oh, that's no good.' He figures out where he has issues and he tries to work through them, and I think he is learning who he is. For a child who is not naturally necessarily going to follow some standard path, that self-knowledge and knowing how to manage all of this stuff is so important.

Changing expectations

As I talked to parents, I noticed a striking difference in the way in which self-directed educators talk about their children's differences compared to parents and teachers of children in school. Rather than their child's differences being seen as a deficit, or something to be compensated for, these parents saw differences as something to be made space for and leaned into. If a child wanted to move around, they arranged things so they could move around more. If a child was only interested in a few things, they found ways for that child to learn more about those things. They accepted the child as they were, and created a life around that.

Rebecca's son is now ten and needs to move a lot of the time. She has found places for him to do parkour and aerial gymnastics, because she sees how much happier and calmer he is when he has had enough time to move.

He can't sit still. If you ask him to sit down and just stay there, it's like torture for him. If he's trying to learn something, you'll always see he is moving around or doing something in the process of trying to retain that information. He struggled a lot with executive function, remembering things in order and processing information. You can see the difference if he does a lot of movement. He just seems more able to process things. After he's been active he seems calmer and more grounded, he's able to be still and do a sitting activity. For example, he wouldn't be able to play a video game if he hadn't run around a lot first. He needs to have movement before he's able to do something that requires stillness.

We've made loads of parkour equipment in the garden together. He will run in the living room or in the hallway. I feel as if both my sons are in perpetual motion. I don't really know how they do it.

> We've got quite a small garden, but we think of ways to provide as much movement activity in a small a space as possible. We've got a climbing frame and a slide and then lots of logs for jumping around. We're actually designing a steel frame at the moment for him to practise some of his parkour moves. My background is in permaculture design and garden design, so I know quite a lot about how to create spaces that work for people's lives. The garden is like a mash up of me wanting to grow food and have a nice wild space, and then a trampoline. I fit my stuff in around their stuff. It's about creating different height levels, different surfaces, different ways of climbing and different ways of jumping between things. We've got an indoor swing as well, one of those Gorilla Gyms. We have lots of different ways of moving all the time.

Parents explained how they went to great lengths to arrange their space around their children's needs. Nicole and James told me how they have organised their house. The children can exercise while they do other things, and they have also arranged their space so that the children can be near them, but also in their own space. They talked about what a difference environment makes to their children, and how being the right space means that they are free to be themselves and to learn.

> We have adapted the house for their needs. We have a kitchen diner so that it is more social. There is a comfy chair in there with sheepskin materials that the children really like. They've got their desk chairs and their therapy balls and they can switch between them and the exercise bike in the sitting room. Eva struggles with her bike, but she would like to ride a bike. We bought her a second-hand exercise bike. Now when she's watching TV, she's on her exercise bike, and we're trying to pedal to Wales. She's aware of how much she's doing and every now and again someone else will write down where she was, and where they're going and how far is it. Getting an exercise bike has turned into this other challenge that we've set ourselves, which has then incorporated, if you wanted to break it up into subjects, numeracy and geography.

Knowing yourself

Parents are often told by professionals that their children 'need structure' and that therefore school is the best place for them, even as they resist and protest. This 'structure' is usually code for 'adult-imposed structure', which is actually very different from a structure which young people find for themselves.

Many schools operate under the assumption that by consistently making young people do things like goal setting, complying with structure and paying attention, they will learn to do this for themselves. For some children, this creates anxiety and that anxiety blocks their learning. It becomes a vicious cycle, with more pressure put on and the child resisting more. The more adults try to insist, the less children are able to comply – and the more upset and angry everyone gets.

The parents I talked to who were using self-directed learning described how their children were developing these skills in context and at the same time developing an awareness of themselves. In the example below, Clara, an American unschooling mother of four, talked about how her son creates his own structure. It's important to him to stick to that, but with enough warning, she sees that he can be flexible.

> Noah creates his own structure and understanding. I don't actually know everything that's going on in his head. For example, yesterday I had to drop off my husband at the airport to go to Jersey and the kids came too. So he came with us, and this is outside his normal day, as we don't go to the airport every day. We went to the airport, and then my other twin asked if we could go to the movies. Noah just started crying.
>
> He said, 'We already went to the airport.'
>
> I said, 'How about if we go to the movies tomorrow, around this time?'
>
> He said, 'Okay.'
>
> He has his structure and if I break in, that's how I know, because he has a meltdown. Tears just start coming down his face. He has a definite 'this is what I do every day'. He has to be expecting it, I have to prepare him.
>
> That's the only way he can do it without feeling physically like he can't do it. Today when I woke up, he said, 'We're going to the movies today.' He's fine with it as long as I prepare him. He has got a structured schedule that he sticks to every single day. I can't tell you what it is, but he knows what it is.

Perhaps one of the most important things with different learning trajectories is how young people come to feel about their capabilities. At school, young people are encouraged to compare themselves with others and so they frequently find themselves lacking. Seventeen-year-old Madeleine, who has never been to school, told me about how she sees her difficulties. It struck me how, despite finding some things hard, she still enjoys them. She has never felt the pressure to compare herself to others.

> I am so slow with processing. But I'm accepting of the fact that I will enjoy

it anyway. I think there's a lack of pressure to be good at anything. I don't have to do it. It's like, 'Oh, you enjoy that, so go do it.'

I'm now terrible at science and biology. But when I was younger, I was all about animals and ecosystems and general nature. I can't remember names. But I enjoy it.

To enjoy things while knowing you are not good at them is something which is rarely taught in school. Away from that pressure, young people have time to develop skills in their own way and follow their own trajectories.

FIVE-POINT SUMMARY

1. Parents described taking a gradual approach to their children's social lives, with very few finding groups when their children were young. They usually started with one-on-one friendships and then sometimes moved on to attending groups when the children were older and motivated to do so.
2. Those parents whose children did attend groups often put a lot of effort into this, providing one-on-one support for their children.
3. Parents went to great length to arrange their houses and lives so their children could move their bodies, and meet their sensory needs. Parents adopted an attitude of accepting where their children were. They provided opportunities for them to develop skills in their own time, even when this was out of kilter with what is typically expected at a particular age.
4. As the children grew older, they became aware of their own strengths and weaknesses and organised their lives around them for themselves.
5. Young people reported continuing to enjoy the things they found hard.

CHAPTER 12

THE WIDER WORLD: COMMUNITIES AND GROUPS

Introduction

At this point you may be thinking to yourself, well that's all very well, but does this really mean home education? Or are there places where children can go and direct their own learning? You might be thinking that you need to work, and you need your children to go somewhere else for at least part of their week. Your children may be saying they want somewhere to go without you, to stretch their wings.

The answer is that for many it will mean home education, but that's not the only way to get a self-directed education. There are a variety of self-directed learning settings across the world. In the UK, these are mostly part time and run for up to three days a week, or mornings or afternoons only. There are only a couple of full-time schools. This is because of the law, which makes it very difficult to establish a school which is radically different in approach to mainstream school. In other countries such as France, Israel and the USA, there are full-time self-directed schools. They mostly have some form of democratic self-governance, although it varies in which decisions are made by young people and which by staff. In addition to more formalised settings, there are groups set up by parents which run on a more informal basis. Some of these are set up for unstructured free play, while others have a specific focus such as Lego, Fortnite or Dungeons & Dragons. Some of these are drop-off, others require parents to stay.

Self-directed learning settings share a commitment to enabling young people to make choices about what they learn, but the way they achieve this varies. Some do not offer any adult structure and wait for young people to make suggestions. Others offer a full timetable but allow young people to choose if they partake or not, while also valuing other things which young people may choose to do with their time. All of them offer considerably more autonomy than mainstream schools and share an ethos that centres the choices of the learner. This emphasis on autonomy can be hard for parents, who sometimes choose these settings because they are hoping for a more nurturing approach – and while they find that, they also find that the nurturing is about helping children to be autonomous (which includes choosing not to do things), rather than making sure that they make particular choices or access the curriculum.

Learning in groups

One of the things we all seem to learn at school is that children should be in groups. School children spend most of their time in a large group of age-matched peers with few adults, and this is often replicated in their after-school activities as well. Large groups start to feel like the natural way for children to spend their time. This means when children stop going to school, their parents often look around for a substitute group. It also means that parents often despair when their children really struggle in groups.

This is something Kate Reevell has thought about a lot. She's a clinical animal behaviourist, specialising in dog behaviour, and her daughter had a very hard time at school (and is now home educated). I didn't initially think that an animal behaviour expert would have much to offer my understanding of children's behaviour. My stereotype was that dog training would be strict and would involve rewards and punishments, or perhaps clickers. I was wrong.

Kate told me that the way that dogs are socialised has changed in recent years. There used to be an expectation that it would be good for young dogs to attend 'puppy school' where they learn to get along with other dogs. These groups would have many dogs of the same age.

There is often an expectation that it would be good for young dogs to attend 'puppy parties' or 'socialisation groups' where they learn to get along with other dogs. While some of these groups can be well run with careful matching and management, more often than not, they involve large groups of dogs where the only thing in common is their age.

What you see in those kinds of groups is that there are some dogs that start to learn to bully. They're so over-aroused by the situation, they can't read or respond to the subtle aspects of body language from other dogs. They can't read when the other dogs are saying, 'I'm not too keen'. Their arousal and exuberance just takes them over and they then get frustrated that the other dogs aren't playing with them.

With this kind of experience, sometimes weekly or daily, they can learn to become what we called 'bully dogs'. They've learnt to bully other dogs to play with them. Or the opposite, the victim dogs, will get scared as the interaction becomes too much. Both groups of dogs can develop lifelong 'behaviour problems' as a result. The bully dogs repeatedly get themselves into trouble which adds anxiety into the mix, escalating aggression problems. The victim dogs also become socially anxious and fearful of other dogs which can lead to fear aggression.

What dogs really need around the puppy and adolescent period is regular, calm contact with a variety of other dogs who are already socially experienced, usually older dogs.

I advise against putting all the young socially inexperienced dogs in groups together too regularly. It doesn't matter if they have a hectic play with another dog that's a similar age to them every now and again, but not frequently for intense bursts every single day. If the majority of their experience is over the top and not balanced out with regular, calmer and more well-regulated social experiences, then they will have difficulty and struggle socially when they're a little bit older, simply because they haven't been placed in environments that have enabled them to learn that refinement of social skills.

The parallels are obvious. Many of us assume that children need to be in groups to socialise, but perhaps for many children they are not in fact an ideal environment.

Do we need a group?

Not every child learns best or can manage in a group. Self-directed learning settings may seem like the answer to fulfilling a child's social needs while allowing them to remain self directed, and for some they are perfect. They provide a way to learn to be with other people in an age-mixed environment where rules are made consensually. However, for others they are too much to manage. Some children will need a long time before they are ready to manage any social group and cope much better with one-to-one or socialising with adults or older children. Some find large groups overwhelming and continue to do so as teenagers and adults.

Many self-directed learning setting and groups cater for a highly diverse group of young people, many of whom have come out of school because it was not working for them. To be unusual is the norm. Inevitably, many children have had bad experiences and they sometimes bring some of these with them. If children can't manage their behaviour enough to keep to the community guidelines or engage with the system of governance, they may not be ready to spend much of their time in that setting. This doesn't mean they won't ever be ready. One of the advantages of self-directed learning is that getting older doesn't have to mean you've missed the boat. At school, if you don't go into Reception when you're four, you can't ever go to Reception. You miss out on the play-based early years curriculum. In a self-directed learning community, you can come in at different ages and do what works best for you. You can usually spend time with people of different ages to yourself, if that's what you prefer.

Self-directed education isn't a universal panacea, nor is it therapy. It's a way to learn, and, as such, it is vulnerable to many of the problems that other educational approaches have. Self-directed learning settings can struggle to find a balance between the needs of the individual and the needs of the community. Many self-directed learning settings are very free, with little adult-imposed structure. This can be challenging for children who find it hard to work out the implicit rules or find it hard to initiate plans. These children may need everything to be made more explicit and they might thrive with more structure. Some children strongly prefer being offered different options for learning, rather than it being expected that they will generate their own ideas. Others love the freedom from structure and find any adult structure restrictive. Some children can only manage being with others for a few hours each day, while others would love to be in a large group the whole time.

The amount of flexibility that each setting or school can offer depends on the setting. They will all have a way of working which defines how the school works and which may mean that they are more or less suitable for your individual child. Some are boarding schools, while some meet for only a few short days a week – each of these models will suit different children.

Scaffolding and structure

It's a common misapprehension that self-directed education means an unstructured environment – or at least no structure which is designed by adults. This isn't necessarily the case. No structured activities can work well for some, but also might offer less containment for those who find it harder to regulate their own emotions and organise their time. It's whether young people are in control of their learning and can choose what they do which makes the difference, not whether there is structure or not. In some cases, structure can liberate – and it can also put safeguards in place to prevent those with the loudest voices taking over and dominating an unstructured environment.

This is something which Gina Riley has thought about deeply. She is Professor of Adolescent Special Education at Hunter College New York and a researcher of unschooling and intrinsic motivation in education, who unschooled her own son to adulthood. She's an advocate for self-directed education, but she told me about her concerns that some self-directed learning settings may not provide enough scaffolding for children with significant learning disabilities.

> We talk about scaffolding a lot in terms of students with disabilities. As someone who has homeschooled, I can tell you that the home learning environment naturally provides a pretty good scaffold. I wonder about self-directed learning communities, because they vary in philosophy and supports. Some children and teens need more structure. Structure does not need to mean coercion. Everything has structure. You get out of bed in the morning at a certain time, you eat lunch within a two-hour window. When speaking of kids with specific disabilities, that structure might need to be more intentional.
>
> My fear, and I think the fear of most involved in special education, is that within a self-directed learning environment, kids with severe learning disabilities may miss out on interventions they may specifically need. If your child needs specific services, you as a parent can give some of them in a home education environment. But if a self-directed learning environment doesn't provide needed services, kids needing these services may suffer. This includes physical therapy, occupational therapy, reading interventions and access to mental health services. Of course, even if they do get intensive intervention, some kids might not respond. We do know that some students go through the school system and still have these problems at the end. But studies on self-directed learning environments and students with disabilities haven't been done yet. I am currently working on such a study now.

Some self-directed learning settings do indeed not have an adult-imposed structure at all. Sudbury-model schools typically wait for any suggestions to come from the young people and see the process of initiation as part of what young people are learning. Others, like Summerhill in Suffolk or Sands School in Devon, provide a timetable of lessons.

The Self-Managed Learning College (SMLC) near Brighton takes a different approach. (Disclaimer, my children attend SMLC and have done for the last two years.) I talked to the founder, Dr Ian Cunningham. SMLC is unusual in that it has a structure, but the structure has no content. It is up to the young people what they choose to learn – from sewing or coding, to trigonometry or Spanish. This structure requires young people to attend a small learning group with their peers every week, to set themselves goals for their learning and then to report back to the group as to whether they are achieving their goals. If young people consistently do not comply with this structure, Ian will advise that they go elsewhere.

> We want parents to know that these are the principles we work from. These are the non-negotiables. They need to come to the meetings and to the learning groups and to sign up to the list of principles. They have to buy into the structure in some way, because that's what the college is there for. If they don't want that, that's fine. Quite a bit of my time is advising parents on other choices that they've got.

Ian told me about the trajectory of one young person, Coco.

> Coco came with a diagnosis of ADHD and dyslexia. They pretty well kicked her out of school because they said she was just doodling all the time. When she came, she doodled and drew cartoons and sat on a sofa and annoyed the boys. Actually, the community was okay about it. They had these arguments, but they weren't bothered about it. Two years later, at age 15, she published her first book, a graphic novel, and she was doing various GCSEs. You just have to be patient. She just needed the space.
>
> Some people get it very quickly, but others take time. They can't undo the damage in a week. They've been at school for six or seven years, so you can't expect them to recover immediately. They come in sometimes not trusting what we say. We say, we value what you want. They imagine there's a hidden agenda, they think we can't really mean it. The main thing is the peer group, that's what makes the change. Their friends start to say, they're for real, you can actually do anything you want. Then they start to get it. We know that the peer group is the biggest influence on teenagers. What we want to do is establish a positive peer group. (...)
>
> We had a girl who was excluded for taking a knife into their school and threatening to knife somebody. I met with that girl and said, 'Well, if you actually bring a knife in, it's against the law. We could suspend you.' She gave an explanation for what had happened. She'd been threatened by

other girls and she wanted to scare them. She came in, she was okay. We never had any issues with her. We've had students who've been excluded from school in some cases for violence like that and it's worked out fine. They realise that we're different, and that the way that they've been violent has been inappropriate.

Ian is also clear that some needs cannot be met within the community of SMLC because some young people need more support. A self-directed learning setting is an educational setting, it is not a therapeutic environment. Most of them operate on a shoe-string budget as they receive no government funding. Knowing what they can't do is as important as knowing what is possible.

> Some people need a therapeutic environment. Sometimes we might be therapeutic but we always say we are not a therapy option. We are pretty used to things but we also realise that there are special issues which some people need therapeutic support for.

Inclusivity

EQUAL CHANCES FOR ALL JUST HOP THROUGH HERE

Groups and communities bring up other issues. People do not suddenly lose their prejudices and assumptions, just because they are trying to do something very different in education. Being inclusive means different things to different people – to some, it can simply mean that they don't actively exclude anyone, without thinking about what it's like for some of the families involved.

Alex (they/their) told me about some of their experiences with their son Daniel. Alex takes Daniel to a regular group where the other children are dropped off, but has found that they have to attend with him as otherwise his behaviour might mean that he is effectively excluded from the group.

> It's a general truth in my experience that groups which say that they are inclusive rarely are. It's vanishingly rare to actually do the work about what that means.
>
> Some groups say they want to include everybody and then they don't actually put the effort in to do it. They don't say what support they offer, they don't ask questions and they don't necessarily notice.

Alex told me how they make the implicit explicit for their son, because otherwise his behaviour might cause problems, which they are not confident that others would spot.

> It's very small things [that I do]. Things like spotting when Daniel is hassling another kid, or where he wants an answer to something and the answer isn't happening. He will keep asking. We talk a lot about this, that people don't owe you answers for things, even if you really want to know. He still struggles with that, and that's the sort of thing that can very quickly escalate. It's spotting when that's happening and being quite firm, saying, 'You need to let this go' and then moving to do something else. It's noticing that he's getting a bit wound up and over excitable. I suspect what I'm doing isn't wildly obvious to anyone else.

Alex told me that they think that sometimes self-directed educators equate self-direction with the expectation that children will pick things up without being told explicitly. This can particularly go for social rules and norms.

> I think the group – and this reminds me very much of what I saw in unschooling things – has this attitude that if you just leave the children, they will magically learn stuff. I accept that that seems to work for some kids, and they need some experimentation. I spend a lot of time dithering about whether I need to let Daniel screw up.
>
> At the moment, I'm trying to find that balance between doing that [allowing him to make mistakes] and direct support… Some of it is also

about being willing to be quite blunt, because I think the genuinely lovely facilitators want to be gentle, which can mean that they are unclear.

Rebecca told me about her experience as a home educator of black boys. Rebecca's dad is black and her mum is white. She feels that her father influenced their decision to home educate, as he is dyslexic and had a really hard time in the school system. However, the problems of society are still there among home educators.

> I feel like I've had to fight for this. So many of us in the black community spend our whole time thinking that we need to do things a certain way, so that society deems us acceptable. (...)
>
> There are still things within the home education community that are really difficult to manage with black kids. I was speaking to my good friend about it and we always think about the idea of the 'white gaze'; feeling that people are watching what you're doing. Thinking, do you have to stop your kids from doing certain things, because of how they're going to be seen by other people? Going to home education meets, where so often the kids are so free and run around and play fight and stuff and feeling, do I need to keep a close eye on what my children are doing in case it is seen differently from what the white kids are doing?
>
> Then there's also the idea of having an autistic child, and especially as he gets older, the risk of someone misconstruing something that he does as being violent. The impact that could have in terms of police getting involved, and seeing what's happened in America, makes me think about how I can teach them to be themselves, but not so much that someone thinks they're a threat. That thinking has to come in all the time, which is something that most people don't have to think about. It feels heavy, it's different.

Inclusivity is a loaded word. It can sometimes be used to mean 'the same for everyone'. Each group or learning community will need to decide for themselves how flexible they can be without compromising their fundamental principles. Many parents, for example, would like their children to be actively encouraged to attend lessons or offerings. Many (but not all) self-directed learning communities will not do this, because they feel it compromises the child's ability to choose and because it changes the relationship between the child and the staff. Encouragement will be felt as pressure by some children. This can lead to a tension between parents and learning communities.

If you're a parent looking for a self-directed learning community, I'd recommend being really honest with yourself about what your child needs and can manage. Can they handle themselves for five hours without a close adult supporting them? Do they find group settings really stressful? What happens if things go wrong? Can they take themselves off to calm down, or do they rely on an adult being right there to head off a crisis? Are they carrying a legacy of distrust of adults or fear of institutions? Then I would be honest with the staff of the learning community and see if there's a way to plan for success. It might mean starting with only a couple of hours a day, or it might mean making connections with other young people before starting. It might mean waiting for another year or so to give the child more time to mature, or finding a smaller group to start with. Honesty means you are all on the same page rather than hoping for the best and then having to react when things go wrong.

A learning community is never going to be the same as home, and staff will not be like parents. They have many young people to think about, and they will always be balancing needs. You can't expect the staff to be as attuned to your child as you are, and that can be a good thing. When things go wrong, that can be a chance for young people to learn how to solve problems in a safe space before they move into the wider world. Learning communities provide more opportunities to learn about being with other people, while still knowing that they have the unconditional love of their parents at home. Groups and communities can provide a safe place where young people can practise managing themselves more independently and dealing with a range of people, before the less protected realities of adult life.

Balancing different needs

Balancing the needs of different children isn't only an issue in self-directed communities and home education groups. Within a family, children can have very different preferences and needs, and it's hard for parents to find a way so that everyone's voice is heard. I'm often asked what to do when one child has very strong preferences – to stay at home for extended periods, for example – and another child in the same family has the opposite preference. How can you manage both without one child always being frustrated?

Nandi got in touch because she was struggling to meet her three children's different needs. 'Someone is always disappointed,' she said. 'My son is a social butterfly, loves to be outside and playing with friends. My daughters prefer to be at home, gaming or reading. None of them are old enough to leave alone. I feel constantly torn in two. I thought three to one was a great ratio but I feel like I'm pulled in all directions!'

This is a really common problem, and one which requires optimum flexibility from parents. It can feel a lot like juggling multiple balls (I imagine, I can't actually juggle even two balls).

The first step to managing everyone's needs is to accept how your children really are, and plan accordingly. I meet a lot of parents who hope for the best, meaning that they plan days which past experience has shown that one of their children can't manage and won't enjoy, but they hope that maybe this time it will be different. Sometimes it is, but mostly it isn't. Planning for the world as it is means accepting that right now one of your children really doesn't enjoy being in large groups of people, for example, or that they dislike multiple transitions and therefore a day which involves going swimming, then going to a friend's house and then finally to the park is going to be hard work for them. If this is you, spend a few moments now writing down the things which each of your children (and you) find difficult. No judgement. Ignore the voice in your head which says that they should have grown out of this by now. Don't write down what you wish they didn't find difficult. Just write it down.

Once you've gathered the information, the next step is to problem solve. The question to ask yourself is this: given what you know about your children, what can you do to try to meet their different needs? Not perfectly, because it will never be perfect, but enough so that each of them feels safe and heard, and they get enough opportunities to do the things they enjoy and value. Good enough is the aim.

For this, you'll probably have to let go of your assumptions about how things should look. You may not all go to a local social group and join in, but maybe you can go and one child can join in while the other sits in the car with a book, with no pressure to do otherwise. If one child really can't be flexible at all, then you're going to need to work around that, but a guiding principle should be that other children must also have their voices heard. It's easy for the child whose needs are least flexible to always take precedence over the others, and in the longer term that will lead to more problems and resentment.

If you're the only adult with young children at home, and those children are not happy doing the same thing or at least being in the same place, think about how you could bring other adults in. Are there relatives who might come for one day a week to take a child out? Or could you pay a local home-educated teenager to come and play games with those who want to stay at home? Can you find a local family who might be prepared to do 'swaps' on a regular basis? Maximise any time when you do have two adults available by separating and meeting two sets of needs, rather than by expecting everyone to do the same thing. Families often tell me that they have a dream of harmonious 'family time' where everyone is doing the same thing and having fun but that in reality it is fractious and unenjoyable. Consider flipping your week around. You can pack in one-to-one and out-of-the-house activities (for those who have this preference) at the weekend if you have both parents available, and then see the weekdays as a time when you do less or do things closer to home. You don't have to do things just because other people are. Your family time might be playing *Mario Kart* together, or all doing your separate things in the same house. Whatever works is fine. Throw out the judgement and think outside the box.

If you can't get other adults to help, is there a way you could work with the children to make a plan which works for everyone? If one child dislikes groups, can they take a device and noise-cancelling headphones and sit somewhere else? If another would love to have more playdates but their sibling can't manage too many visitors, can you find online friends or set up a virtual *Minecraft* club? Can you find a local friend they could visit themselves? Can each person have a chance to choose, so that the activities every day aren't always decided by the same person?

It may be that there won't be many things you will do as a family, and that it will work better to divide your children up whenever you can, so that different needs can be met. I know families who spend their weekends swapping, the child who wants to go out all the time goes out with one parent in the morning and another in the evening, the other children stay at home. If a child gets enough social contact and out-of-the-house activities during the weekend, they may be happier to stay at home more during the week.

Heidi Steel is an unschooling mother of four and you've already heard from her in Chapter 9. Her children have very different needs and she is often the only adult at home. She writes here about how she managed when her older two children had needs which were diametrically opposed – one really liked to know exactly what was happening and to plan in advance, while the other became anxious if they knew what was happening too far in advance and would then refuse to participate or leave the house.

I have four children in my home. All of them are different and all of them have different needs that help them navigate the world around them from a place where they are physically and emotionally comfortable. Discovering their unique need sets, knowing my children well, listening and responding to them takes time and practice (by which I mean that there have been times, many times, when I have got it wrong).

One of my children likes order and being prepared. As a young child, they wanted to know what we were doing every day, and the order of things. We had conversations most mornings, or the previous day, or week about our plans together. These were ongoing conversations that were often repeated. As they became older, they benefitted from being able to read the calendar and then invested in their own personal one. It seems easy enough to fulfil their need to know the plan and to have all the information about the day, but they have a sibling whose needs are directly opposite!

In this case, their sibling became very anxious when they were told what was happening. It caused them to become overwhelmed and stressed. Often, they would refuse to engage in any activity, or request, from that point on, and leaving the house became impossible. Meeting the need for this child to be able to seamlessly flow from one thing to another while ensuring the other child had all the information that they needed required careful consideration and problem solving.

The conversations that I had with one child had to be kept a secret from their sibling; that's not easy when they are four, five or six years old and excited about going to the park or seeing friends. We had to carefully choose when to, excitedly and enthusiastically, pack the picnic or swimming bags. The calendars and diaries that one of them needed were kept in places where the other one couldn't readily see them.

Heidi's story reminds me of a dance, attending to one child while keeping the needs of the others in mind – or as she has described it to me, keeping the plates spinning. Her children are now teenagers and have become more flexible as they've grown up, and this is something which many parents have told me. When they are young, the parent needs to be extremely flexible, and then as they grow up, things often become easier and there are moments when you can see that they have been watching all the problem solving that you did when they were young, and now they are starting to do it for themselves. Sometimes it helps just to remember that it will not be like this for ever. Children change as they grow up and the one certainty is that in ten years' time the challenges will be very different.

A self-directed education pathway

I'd like to finish this book with a young person's story. One of the ways in which self-directed education is different from school is that it isn't uncommon for young people to spend time in different groups or learning settings, or not to go to groups at all as their needs and preferences change. There is no expectation that they will go to one place for six or seven years.

Lucas is 14. He was unschooled from the start and then attended two different learning communities, a less-structured setting for two years and then most recently a more structured setting. He told me about his experiences. He learnt to read without being taught, and he spent most of his time playing, including playing a lot of video games, until he was almost 12. He still spends a lot of time playing video games, but now he codes them as well.

Lucas's story

I never went to school, I went to preschool but never to nursery or primary school. I was home educated for about six years. I learnt to read when I was about eight because I wanted to. I read Dr Seuss books and I learnt from *Minecraft*.

When I was nine we moved house so I could go to a democratic school. I was quite anxious about being away from my mum then. At first, I went there for about half the day and after a while I got used to it and started going for the whole day. It was unstructured I'd say. It was good for getting used to different environments and being away from my parents. When I was there I mostly played. I didn't study anything. I was there for about two years.

Then it was the pandemic and the school closed so we moved away. When I was 11, I moved to a different democratic learning community, which has more structure. Here there is more stuff that is happening. Mainly you organise it yourself but there's stuff going on that you can go to.

They start each day with a meeting where the day's plans are made so you can request a particular thing – like maths for example, if you want maths to happen. Other subjects too. After the meeting, the sessions that were organised in that meeting will start. Sometimes they will have been organised the day before but mostly in that meeting.

There are two types of sessions you might have. The first is group sessions, like younger maths or middle maths. Then there will be a one-to-one where instead of it being group sessions with four or five people, it's just you and a learning advisor. You get help on what you need most help with. Say you are particularly struggling with Pythagoras' theorem, you could have a one-to-one to help you understand it properly. It's not just maths, it's art or music or anything.

At the moment, I'm learning how to play pieces on the piano, I am learning how to code in JavaScript, Html and CSS using Codeacademy. I made a game for Unity. I learnt to handwrite because that was always something I struggled with. I am progressing in maths around and above GCSE level. I'm reading *The Lord of the Rings* in a book club. I also do chemistry at a lower level. I learnt how to touch-type and now I have an above-average speed. If I try hard I can get to 70 words a minute. Outside the learning community I do French and I'm teaching myself Spanish with Duolingo.

I am interested in countries of the world and so in my spare time I use the quizzes from a website called Sporcle. It's a trivia website. I find a quiz for what I want to learn, then I do it, then I forfeit, see what I have forgotten, then I try it again. It's a decent way to learn things like all the countries of the world. I'm now learning capitals of the world. I am also interested in different alphabets and systems of writing, such as why does the Russian alphabet feel related but very different at the same time and why do we have silent letters in English? I watch YouTube videos about that and I talk to my parents about things which interest me a lot.

How do I decide what to learn? For stuff like handwriting I knew I wanted to improve it because it was always one of my weaknesses. I had one-on-one sessions with the English advisor and I'm doing regular practice myself. Then other things were just interesting like my Unity game. Some people I knew were already using Unity so I got interested and had some sessions and then did it on my own. I enjoy maths and I hadn't done that much before I went to this learning community.

Other things I just tried, like chemistry, and then I quite enjoyed it. I knew I wanted to learn JavaScript because it's such a useful programming language.

If I decide there is something new I want to learn I either attend a session [at the learning community] or ask for a session, or look for resources online. That depends on what it is. For touch-typing, I found stuff online that I could use, but for chemistry, I just do that at the learning community.

In the future, I would like to be a web programmer but I'm not completely sure. That's currently what I feel interested in. I'll keep on learning like I am right now. I'm likely to do maths GCSE and English GCSE but I'm not sure about others. I might take up a science or French GCSE. I think I'd like to go to university but I'm not quite at that stage yet.

Lucas's educational path and attitude isn't unusual for a self-directed learner. He sees himself as the person who makes decisions about his learning, no matter how he does it. If he wants to learn something, he goes about finding a way to do it. His learning really is for him, and always has been.

What about the future?

Children and young people change over time, and one of the advantages of a self-directed education is that their environment can be responsive to this. There is no need to commit to one way of doing things for ever. It is common for self-directed young people to spend a couple of years in a setting and then move, or to attend a group for a while and then decide to do something else. A group can serve a purpose and then no longer be the right thing.

I'm writing this because parents are often very concerned about the future, and getting it right for the person their child will be in five or ten years' time. This is impossible to predict, particularly for children with unusual developmental trajectories. The only time we can really focus on is now. Right now, the most important things are an environment full of opportunities, caring relationships and whatever support the child needs in order to make choices about their life. The future is unknown, and that goes for everyone. Doctors and health professionals may make predictions about your child and their capabilities, but they don't really know. In particular, they don't know what will happen to your child if they are allowed to learn through following their interests, and if they grow up thinking of themselves as a person whose choices matter.

Many parents have already been through so much by the time their children are school-age. They have already been assessed, reported on and scrutinised, and have felt blamed. Parents whose children have been to school and who have struggled there have often spent years trying to help and feeling powerless to do so. This can leave them anxious about the future and feeling like failures in the present.

Self-directed education is an opportunity to find another way for your family and your child. It enables you to put the things which matter most to your family and your child at the centre of their learning. It's not an easy option, but most parents I speak to are putting enormous amounts of energy into trying to keep their children functioning at school – self-directed education means that you can direct that energy towards helping your child learn. Parents tell me that the number one thing which stops them from finding another way for their child is fear of what life would be like without school. School might be bad, but it's familiar.

That is why I wrote this book. I wanted to show that there is another way to learn, that there are families living it right now, and children who have moved from struggling to thriving. I wanted to shine a light on what happens in those families that decide to take a different approach to education, and tell the stories of those who are often invisible.

I hope that as you read this book you've been encouraged to let some of the fears go, and instead to focus on the unique child you have right in front of you now. I hope that you'll feel empowered to make choices based on what you know they need to learn and thrive right now. Because ultimately, this day, with this child, is the only place you can start.

FIVE-POINT SUMMARY

1. We are schooled to think that our children need to be in large groups in order to be socialised.
2. Groups do not suit everyone all the time, and self-directed schools may not be able to cater for every need.
3. Self-directed schools vary in how they work and how much structure they provide. They are educational establishments rather than therapeutic communities.
4. Groups sometimes equate 'inclusivity' with 'doing the same for everyone' and many parents feel this is not adequate.
5. Self-directed young people often spend some time in groups and then time at home, depending on their needs and interests at the time.

Further Reading and Resources

Chapter 1: Neurodiversity and Self-Directed Education

Johnstone, L. (2022). *A Straight-Talking Introduction to Psychiatric Diagnosis* (second edition). Ross-on-Wye: PCCS Books.

Kapp, S. (ed.) (2020). *Autistic Community and the Neurodiversity Movement: Stories from the Frontline*. Singapore: Springer Nature.

Milton, D. (2020). *The Neurodiversity Reader: Exploring Concepts, Lived Experience and Implications for Practice*. Shoreham-by-Sea: Pavilion Publishing.

Ratcliffe, A. (ed.) (2020). *Our Autistic Lives: Personal Accounts from Autistic Adults Around the World Aged 20 to 70+*. London: Jessica Kingsley Publishers.

Russell, G. (2020). *The Rise of Autism: Risk and Resistance in the Age of Diagnosis*. London: Routledge.

Chapter 2: Neurodiversity at School

Fricker, E. (2023). *Can't Not Won't: A Story About A Child Who Couldn't Go To School*. London: Jessica Kingsley Publishers.

Poe, C.A. (2019). *How to Be Autistic*. Brighton: Myriad Editions.

Pope, D. (2003). *Doing School: How We are Creating a Generation of Stressed-Out, Materialistic and Miseducated Students*. New Haven, CT: Yale University Press.

Rowe, A. (2013). *The Girl With the Curly Hair: Asperger's and Me*. Lonely Mind Books.

Shalaby, C. (2017). *Troublemakers: Lessons in Freedom from Young Children at School*. New York, NY: The New Press.

Chapter 3: Learning at School

Fisher, N. (2021). *Changing Our Minds: How Children Can Take Control of their Own Learning*. London: Robinson.

Lovell, O. (2020). *John Sweller's Cognitive Load Theory in Action*. In Action Series. Woodbridge: Jonathan Catt.

Robinson, K. (2016). *Creative Schools: Revolutionizing Education from the Ground Up*. London: Penguin.

Willingham, D. (2021). *Why Don't Students Like School? A Cognitive Scientist Answers Questions about How the Mind Works and What it Means for the Classroom*. New York, NY: Jossey-Bass.

Chapter 4: Learning Without School

Gray, P. (2013). *Free to Learn: Why Unleashing the Instinct to Play Will Make Children Happier, More Self-Reliant and Better Students for Life*. New York, NY: Basic Books.

Pink, D. (2010). *Drive: The Surprising Truth About What Motivates Us*. Edinburgh: Canongate Books.

Ryan, R. & Deci, E. (2017). *Self-Determination Theory: Basic Psychological Needs in Motivation, Development and Wellness*. New York, NY: Guilford Press.

Thomas, A. & Pattison, H. (2008). *How Children Learn at Home*. London: Continuum Press.

Chapter 5: The Safe to Learn Pyramid: Foundations of Self-Directed Education

Holt, J. (1990). *Learning All the Time: How Small Children Begin to Read, Write, Count and Investigate the World Without Being Taught*. Boston, MA: Da Capo Lifelong Books.

Richards, A.S. (2020). *Raising Free People: Unschooling as Liberation and Healing Work*. Oakland, CA: PM Press.

Chapter 6: Recovery

Kohn, A. (2004). *What Does It Mean to Be Well-Educated? And More Essays on Standard, Grading, and Other Follies*. Boston, MA: Beacon Press.

Gatto, J.T. (2010). *Weapons of Mass Instruction. A Schoolteacher's Journey Through the Dark World of Compulsory Schooling*. Gabriola Island, BC: New Society Publishers.

Chapter 7: Trauma and Anxiety

Beardon, L. (2020). *Avoiding Anxiety in Autistic Children: A Guide for Autistic Wellbeing (Overcoming Common Problems)*. London: Sheldon Press.

Ciarrochi, J. (2020). *Your Life, Your Way: Acceptance and Commitment Therapy Skills to Help Teens Manage Emotions and Build Resilience*. Oakland, CA: New Harbinger.

Cohen, L. (2013). *The Opposite of Worry: The Playful Parenting Approach to Childhood Anxieties and Fears*. New York, NY: Ballantine Books.

Faber, A. & Mazlish, E. (2012). *How to Talk So Kids Will Listen and Listen So Kids Will Talk*. London: Piccadilly Press.

Siegel, D. & Bryson, T. (2012). *The Whole-Brain Child: 12 Proven Strategies to Nurture Your Child's Developing Mind*. London: Constable and Robinson.

Van der Kolk, B. (2014). *The Body Keeps the Score: Mind, Brain and Body in the Transformation of Trauma*. New York, NY: Penguin.

Wilson, R. & Lyons, L. (2013). *Anxious Kids, Anxious Parents: 7 Ways to Stop the Worry Cycle and Raise Courageous and Independent Children*. Boston, MA: Health Communications.

Nicola Leyland's video of her and Isaac's story. A Freak Accident: www.youtube.com/watch?v=us_nBk5z9rI.

Chapter 8: When Pressure Is Toxic

Fricker, E. (2021). *The Family Experience of PDA: An Illustrated Guide to Pathological Demand Avoidance*. London: Jessica Kingsley Publishers.

Chloe's YouTube channel: @chloemejustme

Chapter 9: Making Changes: Stop and Smell the Coffee

Greene, R. (2021). *The Explosive Child: A New Approach for Understanding and Parenting Easily Frustrated, Chronically Inflexible Children* (sixth edition). New York, NY: Harper PB.

Kohn, A. (2016). *The Myth of the Spoiled Child. Coddled Kids, Helicopter Parents, and Other Phony Crises*. Boston, MA: Beacon Press.

Kohn, A. (2018). *Punished by Rewards: The Trouble with Gold Stars, Incentive Plans, A's, Praise, and Other Bribes. Twenty-Fifth Anniversary Edition*. Boston, MA: HarperOne.

Chapter 10: Academics

McDonald, K. (2019). *Unschooled: Raising Curious, Well-Educated Children Outside the Conventional Classroom*. Chicago, IL: Chicago Review Press.

Pattison, H. (2016). *Rethinking Learning to Read*. Shrewsbury: Educational Heretics Press.

Chapter 11: Non-Academic Skills

Kranwitz, C. & Miller, L.J. (2022). *The Out-of-Sync Child: Recognising and Coping with Sensory Processing Differences*. New York, NY: Tarcherperigee.

Voss, A. (2011). *Understanding Your Child's Sensory Signals: A Practical Daily Use Handbook for Parents and Teachers*. CreateSpace Independent Publishing Platform.

Chapter 12: The Wider World: Communities and Groups

Gribble, D. (1998). *Real Education: Varieties of Freedom*. Bristol: Libertarian Education.

Neill, A.S. (1998). *Summerhill School: A New View of Childhood*. New York, NY: St Martin's Press.

Rietmulder, J. (2019). *When Kids Rule the School: The Power and Promise of Democratic Education*. Gabriola Island, BC: New Society Publishers.

References

Blakemore, S.-J. (2019). *Inventing Ourselves: The Secret Life of the Teenage Brain*. London: Doubleday.

Campbell, T. (2021). *Special Educational Needs and Disabilities within the English primary school system: What can disproportionalities by season of birth contribute to understanding processes behind attributions and (lack of) provisions?* London: LSE's Centre for Analysis of Social Exclusion.

Caspi, A., Houts, R., Ambler, A. *et al.* (2020). Longitudinal Assessment of mental health disorders and comorbidities across 4 decades among participants in the Dunedin Birth Cohort Study. *JAMA Network Open*, 3(4).

Christie, P., Duncan, M., Healy, Z. & Fidler, R. (2011). *Understanding Pathological Demand Avoidance Syndrome in Children: A Guide for Parents, Teachers and Other Professionals*. London: Jessica Kingsley Publishers.

Deci, E.L. & Ryan, R.M. (1985). *Intrinsic Motivation and Self-Determination in Human Behavior*. New York, NY: Plenum.

Department for Education (2010) *Month of Birth and Education: Schools Analysis and Research Division. Research Report*, DFE-RR017, https://assets.publishing.service. gov.uk/government/uploads/system/uploads/attachment_data/file/182664/ DFE-RR017.pdf.

Fisher, N. (2021). *Changing Our Minds: How Children Can Take Control of their Own Learning*. London: Robinson.

Fried, E. (2021). Studying Mental Disorders as Systems, Not Syndromes. https://eiko-fried.com/studying-mental-disorders-as-systems-not-syndromes.

Gopnik, A. (2017). *The Gardener and the Carpenter: What the New Science of Child Development Tells Us about the Relationship Between Parents and Children*. New York, NY: Vintage.

Gray, P. (2013). *Free to Learn: Why Unleashing the Instinct to Play Will Make Children Happier, More Self-Reliant and Better Students for Life*. New York, NY: Basic Books.

Greene, R. (2021). *The Explosive Child: A New Approach for Understanding and Parenting Easily Frustrated, Chronically Inflexible Children* (sixth edition). New York, NY: Harper PB.

Insel, T. (2013). Transforming Diagnosis. National Institute for Mental Health. http://psychrights.org/2013/130429NIMHTransformingDiagnosis.htm.

Johnstone, L. (2022). *A Straight-Talking Introduction to Psychiatric Diagnosis* (second edition). Ross-on-Wye: PCCS Books.

Kapp, S. (ed.) (2020). *Autistic Community and the Neurodiversity Movement: Stories from the Frontline*. Singapore: Springer Nature.

Lockhart, P. (2002). A Mathematician's Lament. www.maa.org/external_archive/devlin/LockhartsLament.pdf.

Maguire, E., Gadian, D., Johnsude, I., Good, C. *et al.* (2000). Navigation-related structural change in the hippocampi of taxi drivers. *Proceedings of the National Academy of Sciences of the United States of America*, 97(8), 4398–4403.

Murray, D., Lesser, M. & Lawson, W. (2005). Attention, monotropism and the diagnostic criteria for autism. *Autism*, 9(2), 139–156.

Pattison, H. (2016). *Rethinking Learning to Read*. Shrewsbury: Educational Heretics Press.

Perry, T., Lea, R. Jørgensen, C.R., Cordingley, P. *et al.* (2021). *Cognitive Science in the Classroom: Evidence and Practice Review 2021*. Education Endowment Foundation, https://educationendowmentfoundation.org.uk/education-evidence/evidence-reviews/cognitive-science-approaches-in-the-classroom.

Pink, D. (2010). *Drive: The Surprising Truth About What Motivates Us*. Edinburgh: Canongate Books.

Plomin, R., Haworth, C.M.A. & Davis, O.S.P. (2009). Common disorders are quantitative traits. *Nature Reviews Genetics*, 10, 872–878.

Robinson, K. (2015). Do Schools Kill Creativity? TED Talk. https://sonix.ai/resources/full-transcript-do-schools-kill-creativity-sir-ken-robinson-ted.

Russell, G. (2020). *The Rise of Autism: Risk and Resistance in the Age of Diagnosis*. London: Routledge.

Ryan, R.M. & Deci, E.L. (2000). Self-determination theory and the facilitation of intrinsic motivation, social development, and well-being. *American Psychologist*, 55, 68–78.

Siegel, D. (2020). *The Developing Mind: How Relationships and the Brain Interact to Shape Who We Are* (third edition). New York, NY: Guilford Press.

Singer, J. (revised edition 2017). *Neurodiversity: The Birth of an Idea*. Kindle books.

Sweller, J. (1988). Cognitive load during problem solving: Effects on learning. *Cognitive Science*, 12(2), 257–285.

Thomas, A. & Pattison, H. (2008). *How Children Learn at Home*. London: Continuum Press.

Thompson, H. (2019). *The PDA Paradox. The Highs and Lows of My Life on a Little-Known Part of the Autism Spectrum*. London: Jessica Kingsley Publishers.

Van der Kolk, B. (2014). *The Body Keeps the Score: Mind, Brain and Body in the Transformation of Trauma*. New York, NY: Penguin.

Weldon, L.G. (2012). School ADHD isn't Homeschool ADHD. https://lauragraceweldon.com/2012/01/02/school-add-isnt-homeschool-add.

Willingham, D. (2021). *Why Don't Students Like School? A Cognitive Scientist Answers Questions about How the Mind Works and What it Means for the Classroom*. New York, NY: Jossey-Bass.